Irenaeus and the Glory of God

Gnosticism, Recapitulation and
True Humanity in Christ

— PATRICK WHITWORTH —

Sacristy
Press

Sacristy Press
PO Box 612, Durham, DH1 9HT

www.sacristy.co.uk

First published in 2025 by Sacristy Press, Durham

Copyright © Patrick Whitworth 2025
The moral rights of the author have been asserted.

Map by Kevin Sheehan (Manuscript Maps)
www.manuscriptmaps.com

All rights reserved, no part of this publication may be reproduced or transmitted in any form or by any means, electronic, mechanical photocopying, documentary, film or in any other format without prior written permission of the publisher.

All Scripture quotations, unless otherwise indicated, are taken from the Holy Bible, New International Version®, NIV®. Copyright ©1973, 1978, 1984, 2011 by Biblica, Inc.™ Used by permission of Zondervan. All rights reserved worldwide. www.zondervan.com The "NIV" and "New International Version" are trademarks registered in the United States Patent and Trademark Office by Biblica, Inc.™

Every reasonable effort has been made to trace the copyright holders of material reproduced in this book, but if any have been inadvertently overlooked the publisher would be glad to hear from them.

Sacristy Limited, registered in England & Wales, number 7565667

British Library Cataloguing-in-Publication Data
A catalogue record for the book is available from the British Library

Paperback ISBN 978-1-78959-407-2
Hardback ISBN 978-1-78959-410-2

For the Christians of Lyon and Vienne

Contents

Foreword vi
Preface viii

Part 1. The making of Irenaeus 1
Chapter 1. Irenaeus and the Roman world 3
Chapter 2. The Church in the second century 30
Chapter 3. Growing up in Smyrna 56
Chapter 4. The Threat of Gnosticism 72
Chapter 5. Division in Rome 88
Chapter 6. An Asian presbyter in Gaul 103

Part 2. The glory of God 115
Chapter 7. The true nature of God 117
Chapter 8. God's troublesome and testing creature 137
Chapter 9. Salvation unfolded: The Incarnation 149
Chapter 10. Recapitulation and the glory of God 161
Chapter 11. The Spirit, the Church and the Kingdom 175
Chapter 12. A word for our times 188

Timeline 196
Dramatis Personae 197
Glossary of Gnostic terms 202
Bibliography 204
Abbreviations 208
Index 209

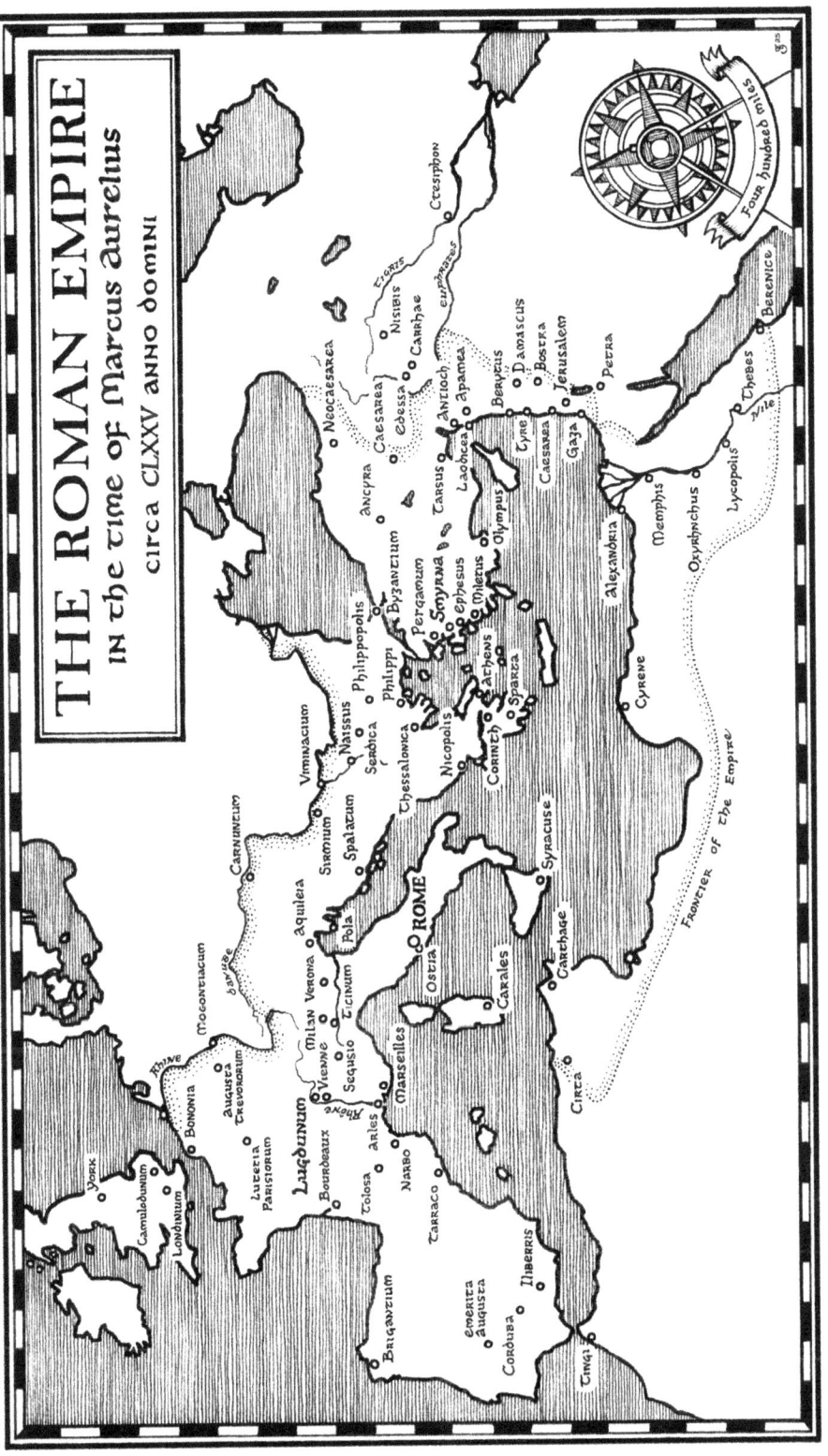

Foreword

The church was barely one hundred years old. It was still in the process of formulating its governance and creedal statements of belief and had not yet quite decided upon the New Testament scriptures it authorized for matters of faith and practice. There were still strong doubts about the use of the Old Testament canon as an equal vehicle of divine revelation. Under siege was the twofold issue of the divine status or otherwise of Jesus Christ and the consequent salvation he brought to humankind. There was a multitude of belief systems, commonly known as Gnosticism, which had competing alternatives as to how the supreme God handled the differences between the spiritual and physical realities which were considered incompatible. Despite their differences they had in common the conviction that the God of the Old Testament was not that supreme God and that Jesus had an inferior deity and needed the help of other divinely created powers to achieve the goal of salvation. The Church was being corroded by such teachings and in danger of morphing out of all recognition from its founding DNA.

Into this maelstrom of competing ideologies and theologies stepped Irenaeus. It is without question that he wrote the first serious theological treatise on the Incarnation and how it effects the process and content of salvation. His argument for orthodoxy became a template for later theologians such as Athanasius, Augustine and the Cappadocian Fathers. He was a bridge builder from the Apostolic Age to his contemporary world. He cited his education in faith under the influence of Polycarp who was Bishop of Smyrna, the town of his birth. Polycarp in turn was a disciple of the Apostle John. Irenaeus' presentation of his orthodox beliefs are found in his major work *Against Heresies: A Refutation and Overthrowal of Knowledge* falsely so-called. Not only does he display an in-depth knowledge of some particular schools of Gnosticism but he also lays down the fundamental truths of the Christian and orthodox

Gospel he believes was given to those original apostles. This was not just a battle to win a war of ideas and so preserve a corpus of beliefs about the Christian faith. This was a battle to save the Christian Church from extinction.

Against Heresies is not an easy read! This is why I am so pleased to commend Patrick Whitworth's book as he helpfully clarifies and navigates us through the Gnostic chaos of ideas and outlines the major issues of the Christian faith that are timeless and need to be relevantly owned, interpreted and shared with each passing generation.

The Revd Dr Russ Parker
July 2025

Preface

There are few more important figures in the second-century Church than Irenaeus. A Greek from Smyrna who became the bishop of a vibrant church in the capital of Gaul, Lugdunum, now Lyon, the second city of France, is an unexpected discovery in an age when leaders of the Church mostly came from Rome or the eastern part of the Empire. But Irenaeus lay in close succession to the Apostles and in particular to John the Theologian or John the Divine, the Beloved Disciple. John the Apostle lived into his late eighties or nineties and remained in Ephesus until his death in the reign of Trajan. For those years, he was the leading Christian of the region. He consecrated Polycarp. And Polycarp, the martyr and bishop, became the principal influence in Irenaeus' early life in Smyrna. Quite possibly Irenaeus witnessed his heroic martyrdom.

Irenaeus was well educated in the university of Smyrna, one of the leading universities of the East, where his teachers were part of the Second Sophist movement, once more highlighting the narratives, epics and philosophy of Greek history and thought. In Smyrna, Irenaeus was ordained Presbyter, and it is probably there that he began to come to terms with the mystery religions which had become so popular in the East, in Egypt and then in Rome. These mystery religions were to penetrate the Church deeply, re-expressing the Christian narrative within their own bizarre and overarching systems. In later years, they would be called Gnostic as they promised a secret knowledge that could bring salvation in which Christ was a much-diminished figure, inhabiting a world which was removed from an unknowable god and which was also intrinsically evil.

When Irenaeus travelled to his new appointment in Lugdunum, he almost certainly went via Rome and there discovered the extent to which both Valentinus and Marcion and their Gnostic teaching had permeated the loosely connected churches in the capital. It must have been a rude awakening. In Lugdunum, Irenaeus helped lead a Greek-speaking congregation which was diverse in background and which was under pressure from magistrates and people alike bent on stamping out the Church. Fierce persecution and many deaths followed in both Vienne and Lugdunum. But alongside that raw confrontation, Irenaeus could still find the pernicious weed of Gnosticism growing wildly in the Church and in c.175 he began his great work in Five Books of *Against Heresies*.

Against Heresies is the first work of almost systematic theology in the post-Apostolic Age. "Almost" because it was essentially a polemical work. In many ways, it is the precursor to the great Latin works of Augustine. Its aim was to re-establish biblical theology against the rag-bag theories of Gnosticism which the ancient world found so appealing. The work was both polemical and systematic. It showed that Irenaeus had very carefully tried to understand the tenets and absurdities of Gnosticism from the inside out and, in the face of its theories, had to re-establish cardinal Christian teaching. Irenaeus demonstrated from Scripture that creation was originally good, and made by God himself. Evil came as a result of fallen angelic powers leading humankind into disobedience. The fall, not so catastrophically portrayed as in Augustine's works, showed the immaturity of humanity which must go through a remaking and recapitulation by Christ. This was envisaged by an omniscient God from the beginning. Christ assumed flesh, redeemed our flesh and gave hope through a bodily resurrection. In other words, Irenaeus did not take the Gnostic view that the flesh or material could only ever be evil and corrupt. It could be redeemed and a vehicle for the glory of God.

In a word: Christ came to save us and give us back our true humanity. Hence the famous dictum of Irenaeus that, "The Glory of God is a man (or woman) fully alive and the life of man (or woman) consists in beholding God" (IV.20.7). In other words, God's greatest work, manifesting his own love and glory, is the recapitulation of human life through the Incarnate Son. This is a theme we will become familiar with. It is also a word for our times. In the Western world where we have become almost besotted with the body—its beauty, its size, its fitness, its health and its sexuality—Irenaeus is saying that true humanity is found in the glory of God permeating, irradiating, renewing and repurposing our lives. What this means in practice will be for the Church, directed by the Spirit and in accordance with the Apostles' teaching and Scripture, to work out. But Irenaeus is saying God's greatest work is making us fully alive: for it involved the recapitulation of our lives by Christ.

I have been grateful for the opportunity to reflect on Irenaeus' life and teaching and do so in the company of others. As some may know, this forms part of a project to write on both the narrative of the Church Fathers' times (three volumes) and also on the most influential of the Greek and Latin Fathers (six volumes). This is now the sixth in the set. I am grateful to Sacristy Press and my editor Dr Natalie Watson for believing in the project, also to my wife Olivia, and Michael Fowler, for visiting Lyon with me, on separate occasions, and seeing the splendid Roman remains in such a dramatic setting at the confluence of the Rhône and Soane. I would also like to thank Marian Aird for the excellent index, Kevin Sheehan for the map and the Revd Dr Russ Parker for generously writing the Foreword. Any shortcoming in properly representing the thoughts of Irenaeus are entirely mine.

Patrick Whitworth
28 June 2025, Feast of St Irenaeus

PART I

The making of Irenaeus

1
Irenaeus and the Roman world

The world into which Irenaeus was born in about AD 135 was dominated by the imprint of Rome. Six decades after the Julio-Claudian dynasty came to its fateful conclusion with Nero's death, Smyrna, where Irenaeus was most probably born, looked out onto a much more stable Roman world.

The Julio-Claudian Dynasty, of which Nero was the last representative as emperor, began with the accession of the dictator, Julius Caesar, in 44 BC, who, some weeks later, on the Ides of March, was famously assassinated for assuming untrammelled power over the state. Caesar's heir and great nephew, Octavian, pursued the assassins and their supporters across the Empire, defeating them at Philippi in 42 BC. He then turned on his former associate, Mark Antony, who had provocatively cast aside Octavian's sister, Octavia, in favour of Cleopatra, the one-time mistress of Julius Caesar and bewitcher of Roman generals. Mark Antony took up with the beguiling Cleopatra, but following their defeat by the forces of Octavian at the naval battle of Actium in 31 BC, they retreated to her city of Alexandria.

A year later, both Antony and Cleopatra lay dead; Egypt was annexed to the Roman state, and with the end of the Egyptian Ptolemies, Octavian was well on his way to becoming Augustus and ruler of probably the largest empire in the world. In 27 BC, through a settlement with the Senate, Imperator Octavian Caesar became the Augustus, eschewing the hated title of king. Yet apart from the name, in every other way he was indeed a monarch. Furthermore, from 42 BC, after the battle of Philippi, the Imperator Gaius Octavius became *Divi Filius*, a son of a god in the eyes of his citizens, a title which every subsequent emperor until Constantine would greedily take to themselves. But in a little-known province of the Empire around 4 BC, some 23 or so years later, a baby was born in Bethlehem whose kingdom, his own followers proclaimed, would never come to an end (Isaiah 9:7).

Octavian, now Augustus, Imperator and *Divi Filius*, founded a dynasty, which, from his death in AD 14 would continue for only a further 54 years until Nero. This seems an unusually short time considering the strength of the legions during most of Augustus' rule—numbering 60 with further troops besides—and considering the desire for peace after lengthy civil wars. But either the absence of natural heirs or the deteriorating abilities of those who held such a concentration of unfettered power meant that able rulers in the mould of a Cato or Cicero were hard to find, or more particularly, to breed. For the vulnerability of monarchy is that you have to rely on what you are given by birth or, in the case of Rome, by adoption, rather than elect a proven leader. A succession of increasingly intemperate Principes came to occupy the position of Pontifex Maximus, Consul and Emperor until the Julio-Claudian house ended with Nero exploding like an errant comet.

Following the death of Augustus, Tiberius succeeded, but in an unhappy state of mind. For the son of the Augusta Livia by a former marriage had been forced to marry Augustus' daughter, Julia, also from a previous marriage. By AD 14, Tiberius was an older man at 55, aristocratic in background, a proven general of great experience, austere and haughty with no common touch. After nine years of rule, he withdrew to the island of Capri where he was credited or slandered with arranging sexual orgies of which Suetonius wrote, "On retiring to Caprae he made himself a private play house, where sexual extravagances were practised for his secret pleasure", although, according to Suetonius, that was only the start of it. Disenchanted by being forced to divorce his wife Vipsania, and depressed by the early death of his dissolute son Drusus, Tiberius sank into paralyzing gloom, allowing others to rule in his stead. When his nephew and adopted heir Germanicus, the darling of the army and of the people, died while on campaign in the East, there seemed little ahead that was certain. Of Germanicus, Suetonius wrote, "He was handsome, courageous, a past master of Greek and Latin oratory and learning, conspicuously kind-hearted, and gifted with the ability of winning universal respect and affection. Of outstanding physical and moral excellence."[1] Tiberius' end could not come too soon. Yet instead of Germanicus, the fateful dial turned to Tiberius' grandson, Gaius (known to us as Caligula or "little boots", a nickname given by the army when his mother took him to the front as a child). Words cannot adequately describe the excesses and self-indulgence of his behaviour: Caligula was to terrorize his advisers, have incestuous relations with his sister, call for his favourite horse to become a senator, and order an army set to invade Britain to simply gather shells from the beach and return home.[2] He was cruel, supremely egotistical, useless and deranged. In the end, he was murdered at the age of 29 after four years of "taunting and terrorizing" his senators and family.[3] In his place a new emperor was chosen on the spur of the moment by the Praetorian Guard. Claudius was a most unlikely and un-Roman successor. He was seized by a Praetorian soldier while hiding behind a curtain and proclaimed emperor whilst clasping the guardsman's knees.[4]

Claudius was the grandson of Emperor Augustus and the son of Drusus, the campaigning son of Livia and her first husband, Tiberius Nero. Drusus had died on the Rhine in 9 BC fighting the Marcomanni and other tribes and had campaigned right up to the Elbe. Extremely popular with his troops, he had married the daughter of Mark Antony, from which union Claudius was the youngest of three. Importantly for our story, Claudius was born in Lugdunum in 10 BC and his later patronage of that city would enhance its standing as the chief city of Gaul. It was there that Irenaeus would go as bishop some 150 years later.

Claudius was an unlikely choice as emperor. He had been a sickly and most unmartial child. He walked with a limp and drooled. He preferred history to fighting, although he cleverly engineered a triumph— the ritual celebration of victory—in Rome for the conquest of Britain which his generals had achieved. He went to Britain for just 16 days at the conclusion of the campaign in AD 43, where he crossed the Thames on an elephant.[5] He was thus capable of showmanship, bribery and cruelty in equal measure. He was, at the same time, a surprisingly capable and eloquent orator. From his youth, he had been surrounded and patronized by powerful women in the imperial family, but Agrippina, his third wife, niece and the mother-in-law of his daughter Octavia, had her own plans. She came to Claudius with her own son, Nero, whom she was determined would succeed as emperor. And she probably arranged for the murder of Claudius on 13 October 54 with a poisonous mushroom, and another claimant, Britannicus, from Claudius' second marriage to the passionate Messalina, was also killed. The murder of Claudius was supposedly effected through a poisoned mushroom, of which a second dose was required, and which was delivered on a feather.[6] Such were the machinations of the imperial household.

Nero, who then succeeded Claudius, declared with acerbic wit that "mushrooms were the food of the gods", since emperors were normally declared gods on their death, and since Claudius by that means had died and become a god.[7] But in the end Agrippina, this overbearing Roman matron, was murdered by her own son Nero. It was the only way to escape her influence, he reasoned.

Nero, the last of the Julio-Claudians, succeeded the poisoned Claudius in AD 54 and the family, with all its internecine rivalries and petty hatreds, hurtled to its inevitable conclusion. Aged only 16 on his succession, Nero was initially guided by the skilful Seneca, until even he was drawn into corruption having acquired three hundred million sesterces.[8] With no military experience, Nero was far too young to become emperor of such a vast and complex empire: birth alone had qualified him, nothing else. He was at heart a showman, leaving the battles and strategy to others. And because he was supported by the palace Praetorian Guard, which he bribed with inordinate sums of gold, the Senate had no power to combat the excesses of his reign. It was, as it had also been under Nero's predecessors Caligula and Claudius, a miserable, impotent and dangerous time to be a senator who questioned imperial power. Many had been executed, and the rule of law was bent to accommodate the mercurial wishes of the emperor. Initially, the worst excesses were restrained by the more austere Seneca, until he himself succumbed to corruption. Then gradually the influence of the odious court favourite, Ofonius Tigellinus, grew dominant. Tigellinus was appointed commander of the Praetorians and "outstripped all his contemporaries in licentiousness and blood thirstiness".[9]

Nero then divorced his wife Octavia—the daughter of Claudius, his cousin and sister of the murdered Britannicus—in favour of the alluring charms and sexual fire of Poppaea Sabina, a woman who bathed in the milk of donkeys and put gilded shoes on the feet of the mules that drew her carriage.[10] He had Octavia killed on false charges concocted by Poppaea, who he then, despite his obsession for her, killed in a fit of pique while she was pregnant by jumping on her.[11] After Poppaea's cruel death, Nero sought a lookalike, and finding only a young man, Sporus, contrived to have him surgically sexually reassigned, though lacking a vagina, and made him his wife at a court wedding in AD 62, a little over halfway through his reign.[12]

While the imperial household descended from bad to worse, with the worst excesses of the family concentrated in the increasing dissipation of the court, the Empire still had to be ruled. Almost at its limits, the Empire now included the unruly province of Britain that had been conquered under Claudius, but was now subject to a rebellion led by Boudicca. Her daughters had been raped by Romans, and the Iceni tribe, based in East Anglia, had been further repressed. In consequence, Boudicca led a highly effective revolt against the Roman occupation linked to Celtic tribes further west. The rebellion was put down by the governor Gaius Paulinus with the greatest difficulty and the province returned to Roman control. Far away, at the other end of the Empire, a successful campaign had been waged by the Roman General Corbulo in Parthia and Armenia in AD 57/8, which led to the appointment of a client Armenian king, Tiridates, who then paid homage to Nero in Rome.[13] More ominous were the early signs of the Jewish revolt in AD 66. In response, Nero appointed the Roman general Vespasian to put down the rebellion. Vespasian arrived in Palestine with two legions, while his eldest son Titus brought a third from Alexandria. A long and punishing war was about to begin, which would end in the destruction of the Temple and Jerusalem, as prophesied by Jesus (Mark 13:1,2).

Midway through his reign, Nero had thrown off any restraint: his tutor Seneca was now ignored and had been suborned by the corruption of the court. His possessive and controlling mother, Agrippina, had been killed on his command. Not unlike his mother in capriciousness, he had killed his beloved but scheming second wife, Poppaea, albeit somewhat accidentally, and replaced her, as mentioned, with a surgically reconstructed male wife, Sporus.[14] There was nothing Nero delighted in more than spectacular shows, and nor was he slow in presenting himself as an artist and singer, whether in Greece, which he much admired, or in Rome.[15] But then, in AD 64, a cataclysmic fire swept unabated through Rome for seven days. Tacitus recalled that "it had its beginnings in that part of the circus which adjoins the Palatine and Caelian hills where, amid the shops containing inflammable wares, the conflagration both broke out and instantly became so fierce and so rapid from the wind that it seized in its grasp the entire length of the circus".[16] Worse was to follow for a small vulnerable group in the city called Christians. They became the scapegoat for the fire, as they would become the scapegoat for all disasters in Rome and in the Empire in the coming years.[17] So Tacitus wrote:

> All human efforts, all the lavish gifts of the emperor, and the propitiations of the gods, did not banish the sinister belief that the conflagration was the result of an order. Consequently, to get rid of the report, Nero fastened the guilt and inflicted exquisite tortures on a class hated for their abominations, called Christians by the populace. Christus, from whom the name had its origin, suffered the extreme penalty during the reign of Tiberius at the hands of one of our procurators, Pontius Pilate. A most mischievous superstition, thus checked for the moment, again broke out not only in Judaea, the first source of the evil, but even in Rome, where all things hideous and shameful from every part of the world find their centre and become popular. Accordingly, an arrest was first made of all who pleaded guilty: then, upon their information, an immense multitude was convicted not so much of the crime of firing the city, as of hatred against mankind. Mockery of every sort was added to their deaths. Covered with the skins of beasts, they were torn by dogs and perished, or were nailed to crosses, or were doomed to the flames to be burnt, to serve as a nightly illumination when daylight expired. Nero offered his gardens for the spectacle, and was exhibiting a show in the circus, while he mingled with the people in the dress of a charioteer or stood aloft on a car. Hence, even for criminals who deserved extreme and exemplary punishment, there arose a feeling of compassion: for it was not, as it seemed, for the

public good, but to glut one man's cruelty, that they were being destroyed.[18]

In place of the residential housing and the public buildings of Rome destroyed by the fire, Nero built his Golden House: a vast palace covering parts of the Palatine, Oppian (Esquiline) and Caelian hills, with a colossal 30-metre statue of himself outside. Later fires and further destruction would pave the way for the building of the Colosseum by the Flavian dynasty on part of the site. But by AD 65 Nero's days were numbered. In AD 67, a conspiracy was organized against him by Gaius Capurnius Piso. Although easily overcome, it indicated a draining away of support and a weakening of Nero's hold. A rebellion in Gaul, in and around Lugdunum, would swiftly follow. Soon Nero was almost entirely deserted, to the point where only suicide seemed a way out. Fleeing Rome for a supporter's villa four kilometres from the city, he awaited death. Asking one of his companions to kill him and muttering, "*Qualis artifex pereo*" (what an artist the world is losing!), he himself put an end to a rule that had become a byword for excess and personal indulgence. His reign was followed by civil war and the Year of the Four Emperors.

AD 69: The Year of the Four Emperors and the Flavian dynasty

One of the many omissions in statecraft of which Nero was guilty was failure to appoint a successor, either from his own family or by adoption. Instead, a succession of rivals fought for the *imperium* or right to rule as Augustus. The Empire had been spared civil war since the days of Pompey, Caesar, Octavian, Cassius and Mark Antony. There had been relative peace at the margins of the Empire (except in Britain and Parthia), but with the degeneracy and military autocracy at the centre in Rome itself, the dynasty hurtled towards its final crash. The first to grasp the office of emperor was the old general Galba, now 73, whose looks matched his vulgar sounding name. Galba was a general of the old school: grim, severe and mean. To Suetonius he was a martinet and bully, with no charm or mercy. As Governor of Spain following the failure of Vindex's uprising against Nero, he marched on Rome to claim the *imperium* for himself and was chosen by the Praetorian Guard. Rather than seek to ingratiate himself with the people, however, he chastised wherever he could. Suetonius recounts: "He sentenced men of all ranks to death without trial on the scantiest evidence and seldom granted applications for Roman Citizenship."[19] Even a visiting client king, Mithridates, from the Black Sea, was put to death for laughing at the emperor's baldness.[20] Support drained quickly away from this forbidding character and after only seven months of rule he was assassinated by Otho's men.

Otho had been a friend of Nero before Nero stole his wife Poppaea Sabina (after commanding Otho to divorce her so that he could marry the acclaimed beauty). Otho was then banished to be governor of a far-off province in present-day Portugal and northwest Spain. In AD 68, Otho had initially supported his neighbouring governor, Galba. But now, seeing Galba's unpopularity, Otho seized the chance to become emperor himself. Feminine in style, he was both an opportunist and a successful governor. Suetonius wrote of him: "He was as fastidious about appearances as a woman. His entire body had been depilated, and a well-made *toupée* covered his practically bald head."[21] His attempt at ruling as emperor was short-lived, however, as he soon heard of a rebellion against him in Germany led by General Vitellius, now marching with legions from Germany towards Rome through Lugdunum.[22] Otho met them at Cremona.

Otho did not want to plunge the Empire into civil war, and see Roman legions from Germany, Italy and Dalmatia opposing each other in battle. The prospect of civil war had always appalled him. And so, when his troops failed to defeat those of Vitellius at Betriacum (Bedriacum), he decided to commit suicide rather than facilitate further civil war. Although in life Otho had seemed effeminate and louche, in death he was brave, patriotic and far-sighted. He took his own life to save the lives of others, although he could not have known he would be succeeded as emperor two more times in that extraordinary year.

Vitellius now stayed in Lugdunum, a city patronized by Claudius as his birthplace and the principal city of Gaul. It was from here that Vitellius set out to take hold of the Empire, but another contender was to stand in his in his way: Vespasian.

Vespasian was every inch a soldier. He had been a senior officer or legate in Claudius' invasion of Britain, after serving in Germany, where he commanded the II Augusta. It was Vespasian who subjugated the southwest of Britain—Hampshire, Wiltshire, Somerset, Dorset, Devon and Cornwall. There are even farms named after him in Somerset today. He came out of retirement to go to Africa in AD 63 and then in AD 66 was sent to quell the Jewish Rebellion, which in AD 70 resulted in the final destruction of the Temple and the city of Jerusalem at the hands of his son Titus. This was later chronicled by Josephus whom Vespasian patronized.

Hearing of Nero's death, Vespasian then went to Egypt, where he was proclaimed emperor by the legions in July, after his second-in-command, Mucianus, implored him to confront Vitellius in Italy. Mucianus was confirmed at an historic meeting at Mount Carmel, whereupon he took a task force to defeat Vitellius in North Italy. Support was now draining away from Vitellius. The general Caecina switched sides on 18 October and supported Vespasian's army (commanded by Marcus Antonius Primus), and on 24 October the two sides met outside Cremona in more or less the same spot where Otho had been defeated and died by suicide in the spring.[23]

It was here that the Vitellian forces were now defeated and surrendered to Primus. Far away in Alexandria, Vespasian received the news that his forces had been victorious. In Jerusalem, Titus continued his stranglehold siege, while in Rome, civil war led to the destruction of the Capitol and the eventual humiliation, beheading and death of Vitellius by rampant soldiers.[24] Eventually Vespasian arrived in Rome and began to rebuild it after the ravages of the civil war.[25] Vespasian himself began the rebuilding of the Temples of Jupiter, of Peace, of Divi Claudius, and others beside by symbolically carrying away the "first basketful of rubble".[26]

The Flavians

Vespasian would rule for ten years and would be followed successively by Titus and Domitian, his older and younger sons. Together they comprised the Flavian dynasty, ruling from AD 69-96, almost to the conclusion of the first century AD. Irenaeus would be born some 30 and more years after their dynasty ended.

Following the year of civil war, the destruction of cities and the embittered rivalry between parts of the Empire, Roman peace was once again restored. Indeed, for the next century until the reign of Commodus—a throwback to Caligula and Nero—who was obsessed with himself and his prowess as a gladiator, the Empire would be well governed. At the same time, it would become more dangerous for the Christian community. They could be described as "the best of times" and "the worst of times".[27]

During the reign of Claudius, the Empire consisted of almost six million citizens.[28] They were guarded by some 29 legions in AD 70 (compared with 60 in the reign of Augustus), four of which were in rebellious Britain. Furthermore, there were 440 auxiliary regiments.[29] The total force comprised about 400,000 soldiers and by now the Empire extended from Britain in the north to Mauretania in the southwest; from Galicia in the west to the Tigris in the east.

Vespasian's rule saw the rebuilding of Rome and the construction of the great Temple of Peace, in itself a symbol of his intention of replacing the rivalries of the Year of the Four Emperors with a peaceful rule. But his most lasting monument would be the great Flavian Amphitheatre built over the ruins of the Golden House, which came to be known as the Colosseum: games for the masses, rather than a golden house for one! It was called the Colosseum simply because of its epic colossal size.

Unlike Nero, Vespasian was a hard-worn, proven soldier, used to command and deploying military power in Germany, Britain, the Balkans, Palestine and North Africa. His face was like that of a weathered farmer or soldier: unsophisticated but determined. There was scarcely any part of the Empire in which he had not soldiered. Vespasian was keen to stress his continuity with Octavian Augustus and Tiberius as a true soldier-emperor, and so to break with the recent past of Caligula,

Claudius and Nero.[30] And unlike his predecessors, while Vespasian showed personal frugality linked to avaricious tendencies,[31] he balanced his extravagance with public munificence: rebuilding not only Rome and many of its temples but provincial cities also.[32] He spent some 4,000 million sesterces: a sesterce being valued at $3, which was considerably more even than Augustus or the miserly Tiberius.[33] In general, Vespasian was generous to the western provinces and especially to Spain, whilst more demanding of those in the East, including Antioch and Alexandria, which had supported his candidature for the *imperium*.[34] Under Vespasian the policy of consolidating the Empire had begun, with attention paid as much to the East between Antioch and the Euphrates as to the North in Germany and Britain.[35] As emperor, Vespasian was generally good-humoured. He would lie in bed and receive guests in the morning,[36] then take a drive and receive his mistresses, especially the favourite Caenis.[37] Being of a practical and pragmatic frame of mind, he expelled most of the Stoic philosophers from Rome,[38] and had little time for their radical preaching and particularly for Helvidius Priscus, a noted republican and no friend of imperial power.[39] After a relatively long and stable rule of ten years, he died like a soldier in AD 79, standing up with the ironic words on his lips, "Dear me, I must be turning into a god".[40] He showed his humour to the end.

Vespasian was succeeded by his elder son, the general Titus. Unlike his father who died full of years, Titus ruled for only two (79-81), dying when he was 41. An effective general who served in Germany, Britain and supremely in Palestine, he was no stranger to the horrors of war, and witnessed the final taking of Jerusalem by his legions after a protracted and terrible siege and a campaign that consumed, it is said, a million lives.[41] He and Vespasian were granted a triumph in AD 71 when treasures from the Second Temple in Jerusalem were processed through the streets of Rome and a Triumphal Arch in memory of Titus was erected (which still stands in the Forum today). Yet Titus' reign was marked by conflagration. It was preceded by the fire in Jerusalem which destroyed the city and the Temple. And in AD 79, just four months after his accession in Rome, Vesuvius erupted, destroying Pompeii, Herculaneum and Stabiae. A vast cloud of ash and pumice stone rained down on the bay and a glowing red river flowed down the side of the mountain, consuming, vaporizing and immolating all in its path and in the vicinity. The ever-reading, ever-curious Pliny the Elder died at a friend's house at Stabiae, probably from toxic poisoning and perhaps with a book in hand. He had sailed there from Misenum to get a better look. And, as if that cataclysm was not enough, a further fire burned for three days and more in Rome itself the following year.[42] Reconstruction of all kinds was needed.

As if to compensate for such disasters, the great Colosseum was opened in AD 80 after ten years of construction, with games aplenty to bury the anxiety of the age, and nearby baths in which to luxuriate. The baths of Titus were also built on and over the remains of the Golden House. And in the midst of all this, according to Suetonius, the much-loved, generous emperor who had repealed the treason laws and now surveyed, for the most part, a stable Empire, had only one more year to live. He was only 41 when he died of fever *en route* to a further campaign against the Sabines in the Apennines. Dio Cassius wrote of him in a rather backhanded way: "Titus ruled with mildness and died at the height of his glory, whereas, if he had lived a long time, it might have been shown that he owes his present fame more to good fortune than to merit."[43] Suetonius, by contrast, was more lavish in his praise.[44] At any rate, Titus was succeeded by his younger brother Domitian, who was an altogether nastier proposition.

Domitian was to be the last of the Flavian dynasty, which was restricted to a single family—Vespasian and his two sons: Titus and Domitian. They failed to produce or even adopt heirs. Domitian reigned long enough for his worst traits to be magnified, however (AD 81-96). As a young man he had grown up in the shadow of his more military father and older brother Titus, whose reputations had been cemented by the Jewish wars of AD 66-70. As a character, Domitian was prone to jealousy, suspicion, control and withdrawal. Suetonius, in particular, dissects his personality. In one vivid example, Suetonius recounts how Domitian "summoned a bookkeeper to his bedroom, invited him to share his couch, made him feel perfectly secure and happy, condescended to offer him portions of his dinner—yet he had already given orders for his crucifixion on the following day!"[45]

Indeed, Domitian would talk of mercy but would act with cruelty. There were numerous gratuitous executions on moral grounds (adultery!)

and political charges.⁴⁶ Like Henry VIII in the English Tudor dynasty, he was financially acquisitive. He weakened the Senate as Henry did the nobility, preferring to rely on administrators whom he could entirely control. He summoned senators to banquets where all the decorations were black so as to evoke fear among his haunted guests. He favoured the plebs with extravagant games and the occasional handout of money and food, thereby hoping to secure their favour and his own popularity and security. His campaigns on the fringes of the Empire were partly successful. The attempt to conquer Dacia (Romania) and defeat their bellicose and very able King Decebalus was frustrated, and final success would not come there until Trajan's rule (AD 106). And likewise in Britain, the very resourceful Governor Agricola defeated the Caledonians and established a base in Perthshire at Inchtuthil (near Blairgowrie), but this forward position in the end proved untenable. Nevertheless, whenever he could, Domitian celebrated triumphs (possibly as many as four) and a further 23 imperial salutations for victories.⁴⁷ Insecure in his military prowess compared with his father and brother, Domitian overcompensated in self-congratulation. Towards the end of his reign, he became increasingly paranoid and isolated, preferring his own company and retreating to his many villas which he had built outside Rome, the most extensive being in the Alban Hills.⁴⁸ He became obsessed by whatever was happening behind his back.⁴⁹ Revolts did come: in Germany one led by Saturninus in AD 89, and one by Helvidius Priscus and others in Rome in AD 93. Both were disarmed and prevented but the mood of rebellion did not go away. They were ominous portents. In the end, Domitian was assassinated by members of his own staff at home in his own bedroom, while his assailant, Stephanus, who had a knife concealed in his clothing, was detailing a list of those who were conspiring against the emperor.⁵⁰ His body was cremated by his nurse Phyllis,⁵¹ and for good measure Stephanus himself was executed by his co-conspirators. There were to be no imperial or "divine" obsequies for the last of the Flavians. A fine beginning for the dynasty had been brought to an ignoble end.

Domitian's religious policy was conservative, and like many others of his policies, exemplified control. He expelled philosophers such as the Stoic Epictetus from Rome, as he, like Nero, could not abide any competing ideas. He enhanced worship of the emperors and their cults, which he enforced through the courts and provincial government. And into this trap the Christians of the Empire fell. Unwilling to endorse the divinity of the emperors and burn incense to them, they faced persecution, torture and martyrdom. Indeed, the charge of atheism (not worshipping the pagan gods) was rife in Italy and the East at this time. With the Colosseum now open for public entertainment, it was here that many of the indicted and condemned Christians, like Ignatius of Antioch and many more unnamed martyrs, were brought under guard and martyred. In the East, the elderly Apostle John (or John the Elder) was exiled to Patmos from where he wrote the Book of Revelation with its blistering prophecy against Rome which he renamed Babylon, and which became its nickname amongst Christians (see Revelation 18:1-24 and 1 Peter 5:13).

The Flavian dynasty, short-lived as it was, ended with Domitian. Vespasian had saved the Empire from the uncertainty and bloodletting of the Year of the Four Emperors. His was an experienced and dependable administration. Titus reigned all too briefly as a battle-hardened soldier and attractive personality. Domitian, suspicious and paranoid, seeking to control and belittle the ruling classes, was neither mourned nor deified, as had become the custom on the death of an emperor. Instead, the Senate chose a successor in the old patrician model, Nerva, who was the first of the so-called "Five Good Emperors".

The Five Good Emperors

If Irenaeus was born around AD 135, his birth would have been in the reign of Hadrian. If he was born a little later, then it would have been in the reign of Antoninus Pius, the adopted son of Hadrian who was married to his niece, Faustina. Antoninus gave his name to the Antonine dynasty. These five so-called "Good Emperors" consisted of Nerva (whose reign was short, AD 96-98), Trajan (AD 98-117), Hadrian (AD 117-38), Antoninus Pius and Marcus Aurelius. (For a few years from AD 161-9, Marcus Aurelius shared the *imperium* or rule with Lucius Verus.)

In what sense were these emperors "good"? In the first instance, Nerva was a relief after the neuroses and cruelty of Domitian. As a member of the Senate, Nerva rehabilitated the traditional power and values of this assembly. He consulted "the foremost men",[52] he cut expenses, and he provided land for the poorest. He had few enemies, but his age and ill health counted against him. Appointed emperor when he was nearly 66, he was never going to rule for long. He had the good sense to appoint Trajan as his successor, however—a successful general drawn from the Spanish colony of Italica, not far from present-day Seville.

In broad terms, these five emperors were "good" in that they embodied Roman values at their most traditional. All of them were effective military leaders. Being able administrators, they brought style, intellect and panache to the office. They did not restore the Republic, which had gone for ever with Julius Caesar and his heir Octavian—the first Emperor Augustus—and his heirs. The aim of the "Good Emperors", broadly speaking, was to enhance traditional Roman values through the power of their role and the operation of the state, its magistracy and laws. These values meant conquest; the use of military and physical power to that end, whether by the legions or through personal charisma wedded to military effectiveness; the subjugation of peoples; the establishment of Roman culture in the arts; the education of the individual in the ideals of the philosophers; the iteration of Roman law; and the support of religion based on the divinity of the gods. This represented a nexus of culture which was in turn based on Greek ideals. The "Good Emperors" would seek to follow these ideals and would oppose anything which sought to untie or challenge them. One such competing and undermining religion or belief was Christianity, and a God who was worshipped as one crucified on a Roman gibbet and risen from a Jewish tomb; known also as *Divi Filius* (Son of God), but to the exclusion of all others.

Trajan (AD 98-117) followed the brief reign of Nerva, who had been known for his frugality and generosity,[53] his tendency to compromise,[54] and his unwillingness to prosecute those of senatorial rank. Nerva's rule was mild and inclusive. It was short-lived, but it paved the way for the soldier Trajan. For Gibbon, the rule of Trajan was one in which the condition of the human race was "most happy and prosperous".[55] It was certainly true that Trajan ushered in a period of stability and prosperity, although this was not shared by all Christians.

In short, Trajan's rule can be characterized by three features: the expansion of the Empire into four further regions following military campaigns in Dacia, Armenia, Arabia and Mesopotamia; the detailed administration of provinces, as exemplified by his close correspondence with Pliny the Younger, the Governor of Bithynia; and his considerable patronage of projects large and small throughout the Empire.[56] Trajan's first great success, and the overturning of reverses experienced by his predecessor Domitian, was his conquest of Romania. The Dacian king, Decebalus, who had resisted Rome so effectively, was captured and executed, and his severed head sent to Rome in the autumn of 106. Salutations, Trajan's fifth and sixth in the field, were to follow,[57] and in Rome spectacles were offered to the city for 123 days in which "eleven thousand animals were slain and ten thousand gladiators fought".[58] Further campaigns would lead to a new province of Arabia, including land south of Jerusalem and the Nabataean Kingdom of Petra.[59] In 114, Trajan would add Armenia and then Mesopotamia to his tally of defeated kingdoms. His great dream was to re-enact the conquests of Alexander the Great. However, conquering land was one thing, holding and turning it into part of the Empire quite another.

Perhaps inevitably after such exertions, Trajan died of illness and exhaustion while returning from the campaign in the east, leaving Hadrian with the army in the small coastal town of Selinus in Cilicia (the Turkish town of Gazipaşa) about 180 miles from Antalya.

Trajan was not only a "warlike man" but also devoted himself to civil administration.[60] Previously praised by the Senate in Rome as the *optimus* (best) emperor, he endeavoured to live up to his epithet. As a general, he always marched with his soldiers and sometimes on foot alongside them.[61] As an administrator, he was punctilious. Pliny, who had earlier offered his famous panegyric in praise of Trajan in AD 100, just two years into his *imperium*, was appointed the Governor of Bithynia in Asia, covering the important cities of Nicomedia, Nicaea and Apamea, not far north of the province of Asia and Smyrna where Irenaeus grew up.

Pliny the Younger was the nephew of the Admiral Pliny who had died in the eruption of Vesuvius. He was a lawyer and, not unlike Cicero, fastidious, conscientious and deferential. He apparently spoke alongside Cornelius Tacitus for nearly five hours (determined by water clocks—five of them!) in the prosecution of Marius Priscus in AD 100.[62] But now, as Governor of Bithynia, he consulted regularly with Trajan, writing some 60 letters to the emperor on subjects as diverse as building works and their delays, and the correct judicial treatment of Christians, to which we shall return. And Trajan, no doubt using his secretariat and imperial postal system, replied pithily to all his enquiries, which, if multiplied across the many provinces of the Empire—approximately 45—made for a vast correspondence.[63]

While Trajan was an accomplished and very energetic soldier, a fastidious and inclusive administrator, he was also a splendid patron. Indeed, his love of glory was the spur to his munificence. Kingship in the ancient world, as in the medieval period, was a combination of military conquest, careful and legal administration, and generous, if not munificent, patronage. In that sense, a second-century emperor pursued the same ideals as those of a twelfth-century English king, although they were a millennium apart. Trajan's love of glory, a besetting sin of the Roman Empire, according to Augustine of Hippo in *The City of God*, led to many schemes projecting Roman culture and power, and were financed from imperial victories as in the case of mineral-rich, gold-laden Dacia. So in Rome Trajan's Baths were built; a new aqueduct to feed the baths was established, the Aqua Traiana; a vast new forum was created: new temples of Venus and Peace were completed; the great column and statue of Trajan was erected; harbours were built at Ostia and Ancona; and a policy of "bread and circuses" was vigorously pursued.[64] In the East, following a devastating earthquake, Antioch had to be rebuilt;[65] a bridge was built over the Danube in present day Serbia; an extension of the amphitheatre in Lugdunum was completed; Trajan's cartouche appeared on columns at a temple in Khnum in Upper Egypt; and a canal was created from the Nile at Old Cairo to the Red Sea, anticipating the Suez Canal by 1,700 years.

In other words, the projection of the power of the emperor was never greater. If, on the one hand, it promoted Pax (or peace and security), on the other hand it gave greater cause to challenge and supress any who disturbed the nexus of Roman peace, Christians among them. In his lengthy rule, Trajan pursued as much as any the love of glory, which, as Augustine of Hippo would maintain, was both an interminable source of human energy and an inseparable flaw of imperial policy.[66] As if in recognition of this, Hadrian, Trajan's successor, now defined the limits of empire and the conditions of peace.

Hadrian began his rule after his adoption by Trajan in 117. He ruled until the birth of Irenaeus in about AD 138 in Smyrna. He bequeathed to Irenaeus, as to others, the context and limits of imperial power. On his accession, Hadrian was 41, and his family had been of senatorial rank for five generations.[67] Like Trajan before him, he hailed from *Italica* in the province of Baetica, near Seville in present-day Spain. From his earliest years, Hadrian was fascinated by Greece and Greek studies, and from early manhood was equally devoted to hunting and military training. These twin talents were to shape and define his life: no one was more Hellenic in taste, and no one knew more the necessity for and limits of military power. He would have a sword in one hand and the poems of Sappho in the other.

Having succeeded to the *imperium*, Hadrian's first task was to "deify" Trajan, for which he sought the support of the Senate (which he consulted sedulously during his reign).[68] He remained in Rome from 118 to the spring of 121, whereupon he began one of the many tours that were to mark his rule. No emperor travelled more, and to all corners of the Empire. On his first tour to Upper Germany, Raetia and Noricum (Austria), he began the policy of building defences where there were no natural barriers such as rivers and mountains. He set in motion many reforms in the army, whilst at the same time living as an ordinary soldier, eating the same rations and sleeping rough. His policy was to look for peace but prepare for war,[69] a policy which would resonate down the ages, even to the present. From Germany he went to Britain and once again pursued the policy of peace, whilst simultaneously preparing his legions for war, and famously, in the north of the country, he defined the limit of the Empire in this its northern extremity by commanding a wall be built from Newcastle to Cumbria, to prevent attack from the unruly Picts. The wall remains to this day, and nowhere may it be more clearly seen than at the site of Vindolanda, where "life on the wall" in its social and military aspects is laid bare in written form on tablets dug up from its preservative mud! Hadrian's second provincial tour from 128-32 was, if anything, more significant. It took him south to North Africa and then east to Egypt and Syria. He initially travelled via Greece and Sicily to North Africa and the colony of Lambaesis in Mauretania, where he addressed the III Augusta Legion, congratulating them on a stone rampart built to keep out the Berbers. Legionnaires once again had become builders, and now the southern extremity of the Empire was defined as it had been in the north. He returned again to his beloved Greece, which had for him a magnetic attraction, where he dedicated a new temple to Olympian Jupiter, and where a number of vassal kings came to meet him.[70] From there he travelled through Bithynia and Apamea before passing through Cappadocia to arrive at Antioch in Syria, which for some reason he detested.[71] Then it was onwards to the desert city of Palmyra, soon to be made great by its Queen Zenobia (c.240-74), followed by a fateful visit to Judaea after entering Arabia.

It was a fateful visit for the Jews and for Hadrian, and also for the Empire. Out of his panhellenism, Hadrian had banned the rite of circumcision, or as the *Historia Augusta* puts it, "the mutilation of the genitals" (*mutilare genitalia*).[72] But such a ban struck at the heart of Judaism and incited rebellion. This was further compounded when Hadrian ordered the construction of a temple to Jupiter Capitolina on the ruined Temple Mount—ruined during the previous Jewish rebellion in AD 70. At the same time, he changed the name of Jerusalem to *colonia Aelia Capitolina*. These successive blows to Judaism, which smacked of cultural and religious cleansing, provoked a revolt which would last three years until AD 130. It was led by a new Jewish leader, Simeon Bar Kochba, "the son of a star", who was supported by Rabbi Akiba, the great Jewish scholar and contributor to the Mishnah. This rebellion, like the earlier ones of AD 68 and that of the Maccabees, would ever define Jewish resistance and resilience in the face of oppressive opposition.

Hadrian remained with his legions for part of the war, but then called his most successful general, Severus, from the Balkans to complete the crushing of the Jews. This was eventually achieved, but only after considerable losses by the Romans. Having relieved himself of command in the field, Hadrian went on a visit to Egypt and took a voyage down the Nile where his male lover Antinous was mysteriously drowned.[73] When given the news, Hadrian, it was reported, "wept like a woman",[74] and in due course the empathetic Egyptians raised the beautiful Antinous to divine status to console the grieving emperor. Meanwhile in Palestine, all Jews were banished from the Temple Mount except at the festival of Passover, and so began their effective exile that would last until 1917.

Hadrian died in his villa in Baiae in the Bay of Naples on 10 July 138 at the age of 62. He was buried in the mausoleum which bore his name on the banks of the Tiber, which was later turned into a papal fortress, the Castel Sant'Angelo. By then, and after an initial hiccough over his succession, Hadrian had adopted Arrius Antoninus, later called Antoninus Pius, on the condition that he also adopted Annius Verus and Marcus Antoninus (later called Marcus Aurelius) as his heirs.[75] In effect, given the length of life of his adopted son, Hadrian had established a line of succession, including grandsons, for a further 40 years. By so doing, he had chosen men capable of stable government and whose joint reigns would last until AD 180 and the death of Marcus Aurelius. By far the greater part of Irenaeus' life would be spent under their government before the return to the febrile dictatorship and capricious egotism of Commodus, who was more in the mould of a Caligula or a Nero. Hadrian had proved a consolidator of Roman power *par excellence*. As an administrator, he marked out the boundaries of the Roman Empire, being prepared to relinquish that which was not tenable, such as Parthia and Scotland. As a soldier, he looked for peace but prepared for war. As an aesthete, he was most happy in reviving Greek culture. He built wherever he went. He was famed for his memory and knowledge.[76] He was a disciplinarian both of his soldiers and his civil servants.[77] He would not permit horse riding in the city.[78] He wept for his male lover, Antonius, but wreaked havoc on enemies such as the Jews. This status quo would be more or less maintained for a further 40 years, although all the while the growing sect of Christians offered a different perspective on life.

Roman culture in the second century

Most Roman cities were distinguished by a predictably similar set of buildings that defined the lives of their citizens: an amphitheatre for games and spectacles; a smaller *odeon* for theatre and addresses; baths, frequented ceaselessly by men and women at different times, or at the same time in cities like Alexandria (see Clement, *The Instructor Book* III:5); forums for shopping; libraries, as in Ephesus, for the studious or learned; temples for all kinds of human need; campuses for military exercise or athletics; hippodromes for racing; and senates for government. But no churches. And there were houses great and small: spacious villas for the senatorial classes; fine townhouses for those of the equestrian order; newly acquired apartments for freedmen; small houses for the plebs; and for slaves, a space just large enough to sleep. Everyone was distinguished by their dress, with their class signalled for all to see: a broad purple stripe on the toga for a senator; a narrow stripe for those of the equestrian order; a plain white toga for the citizen or freedman; a short tunic for a pleb or slave.[79] In other words, what Roman society aimed at was a social stratification evident in buildings, clothing and status, rolled out across ethnicities and regional climates: from the German forests to the Arabian sands, from Trier on the Moselle to Antioch on the Orontes.

Despite the imposition of a monolithic culture, not everything remained the same, however. As always, education was a means to social mobility and admittance to a more elite class. Education or learning was to be found across the Empire. Pliny the Younger was surprised and gratified, like any author, that his works could be bought in Lugdunum. He wrote to Rosianus Geminus, "I didn't think there were any booksellers in Lugdunum, so I was all the more pleased to learn from your letter that my efforts are being sold. I'm glad they retain abroad the popularity they won in Rome, and I'm beginning to think my work must be really quite good when public opinion in such widely different places is agreed about it."[80]

This was patrician patronage at its most condescending. Nevertheless, literacy across the Empire was limited. Only a small percentage could read, and most writing was to be found on funeral memorials, on advertising or election placards, in business deals, or for supplying the army. The literate had to help the illiterate by reading messages out loud.

But the better off could write, as the tablets found at Vindolanda on Hadrian's Wall demonstrate (although admittedly these are from the fourth century). There a commander's wife sends a message inviting another to celebrate her birthday. The tablet is lost, but her invitation has lived on for two millennia, preserved by Northumberland mud, just as the Dead Sea Scrolls were preserved by permanent dry heat at the other end of the Empire. But a new force for literacy and change was coming that would go beyond the Jewish texts at the centre of synagogue worship, taking the form of the Scriptures of the New Testament which by the mid-second century Irenaeus would classify and endorse. To understand them, a Christian must read.

Alongside the drive for literacy was the advent of the Second Sophist movement. This was a movement which focused on the art of declamation, springing originally from Greek culture, but taken forward by the Romans. The movement is chronicled by Philostratus in *The Lives of the Sophists* written much later in 238. Amongst many others, Philostratus mentions Lucian of Samosata, Dio Chrysostom (40-115) and Aristides of Smyrna (117-81). Many of these thinkers veered towards Stoicism and Platonism, so much so that when Dio was banished from Bithynia by Domitian—who always suspected philosophers of being subversive—he took with him into exile Plato's *Phaedo* and Demosthenes' *On the False Embassy*. Later, in the middle of the second century, when Stoicism was back in fashion, Dio was considered one of the greatest Sophists or wise men of the age. Likewise, Aristides was to make Smyrna one of the principal towns for rhetoric or philosophical teaching in the East, rivalling Ephesus and Athens.[81] Indeed, it was his appeal to Marcus Aurelius after an earthquake destroyed the city in 177 that was key to the rebuilding of Smyrna. Emperors of Marcus Aurelius' stamp paid attention to good declamation.

The range of the Sophists' writing was extensive, and included history, philosophy, local geography, such as that of Hermogenes of Smyrna, and medicine, as demonstrated by the great doctor Galen of Pergamum, who published over a hundred works.[82] Then there was Ptolemaeus, the astronomer and mathematician, and Plutarch the Stoic philosopher. It was an intellectual burgeoning in the conditions of *Pax Romana*, which had been brought about by the power and stability of the "Five Good

Emperors", who for the most part revelled in it. It would end in the Neoplatonism pursued by Plotinus in Alexandria in the middle of the third century and by Atticus in Athens a little earlier. When we combine this upsurge of thought with the epigrams of Martial, the novels of Apuleius (including *The Golden Ass*), and the letters of the Younger Pliny, we have an age not just beholden to the Stoic philosophers of the Greek cities, but one spiced with the witticisms of the Latin West. It was an intellectual flowering given booster rockets by Emperor Marcus Aurelius (who established training posts in the great cities of the Empire).[83] And over time it would lead to the growth of middle or Neoplatonism, which in turn became a handmaid to the growth of Gnosticism, its eccentric offspring, which was Irenaeus' chief target, as we shall see.

For all its promise, however, this was still a wisdom confined to the human sphere. For, as the Apostle stated, "the foolishness of God is wiser than human wisdom" (1 Corinthians 1:25). Indeed, as Paul, in this same letter in the mid-first century AD, and with his typical foresight, wrote, "Jews demand a sign and Greeks demand wisdom", but he, Paul, with "in weakness and fear, and with much trembling", preached another wisdom—Jesus Christ and him crucified, "a stumbling block to Jews and foolishness to Gentiles". But to those being called by God, "Christ the power of God and the wisdom of God" (1 Corinthians 1:22,24b; 2:1-3). In other words, an incipient confrontation was about to take place, indeed was already taking place, between the culture of power and glory and of human wisdom which lay at the heart of Greece and its successor, Rome, and Christ himself, made known in this irritating group of Christians who found strength in weakness and riches in poverty, and who could not be stamped out by violence. And furthermore, there was a confrontation between a culture of entitlement, which was at the heart of the Jewish people as the heirs of Abraham (see John 8:31-59), and the followers of a crucified Messiah who turned suffering into a badge of honour. So this seemingly Jewish sect, with its allegiance to Jesus as the Messiah, was gradually to suborn the Empire with its own weapons of the blood of martyrs, the care of the poor, and a purity which called for sexual discipline of the most demanding kind. How could such a mixture win through in this arena, and how could worship of such a crucified God overcome centuries of devotion to the gods of war?

Notes

1. Suetonius, *Gaius Caligula* §3, tr. Robert Graves (Harmondsworth: Penguin, 2007), p. 146.
2. Robin Lane Fox, *The Classical World* (London: Penguin, 2005), p. 492.
3. Lane Fox, *The Classical World*, p. 493.
4. Suetonius, *Claudius* §11, op. cit., p. 184.
5. Lane Fox, *The Classical World*, p. 494.
6. Lane Fox, *The Classical World*, p. 494.
7. Dio Cassius, *Roman History*, Bk LXI, tr. Ernest Cary, Loeb Classical Library, Vol. 176 (Cambridge, MA: Harvard University Press, 2000), pp. 29,31.
8. Dio Cassius, *Roman History*, Bk LXI, op. cit., p. 57.
9. Dio Cassius, *Roman History*, Bk LXII, op. cit., p. 105.
10. Dio Cassius, *Roman History*, Bk LXII, op. cit., p. 135.
11. Dio Cassius, *Roman History*, Bk LXII, op. cit., p. 105.
12. Dio Cassius, *Roman History*, Bk LXII, op. cit., p. 137.
13. Dio Cassius, *Roman History*, Bk LXII, op. cit., pp. 141ff.
14. Dio Cassius, *Roman History*, Bk LXII, op. cit., p. 159.
15. Dio Cassius, *Roman History*, Bk LXIII, op. cit., p. 175.
16. Tacitus, Annals, Bk XV (Perfect Library Reprint of 1876 Edition).
17. Tertullian, *Apologetica* §XL, The Ante-Nicene Fathers (TANF), Vol. III, 1885 (New York: Cosimo, 2007), p. 47.
18. Tacitus, *Annals*, Bk XV, op. cit., pp. 294-5.
19. Suetonius, *Galba* §14, op. cit., p. 250.
20. Tom Holland, *Pax: War and Peace in Rome's Golden Age* (London: Abacus, Little, Brown, 2023), p. 41.
21. Suetonius, *Otho* §12, op. cit., p. 261.
22. Holland, *Pax*, pp. 97-8.
23. Holland, *Pax*, pp. 115ff.
24. Dio Cassius, *Roman History*, Bk LXIV, p. 255.
25. Suetonius, *Divi Vespasian* §8, op. cit., p. 281.
26. Suetonius, *Divi Vespasian* §8, op. cit., p. 281.
27. Charles Dickens, *A Tale of Two Cities* (London: Mandarin, 1993), p. 3.
28. Holland, *Pax*, p. 66.
29. Mark Hassall, "The Army", Chapter 9 in Alan K. Bowman, Peter Garnsey, Dominic Rathbone (eds), *Cambridge Ancient History, second edition, Vol.*

XI: *The High Empire, AD 70–192* (Cambridge: Cambridge University Press, 2005), pp. 323ff.
30   Miriam Griffin, "The Flavians", in Alan K. Bowman, Peter Garnsey, Dominic Rathbone (eds), *Cambridge Ancient History, second edition, Vol. XI: The High Empire, AD 70–192* (Cambridge: Cambridge University Press, 2005), p. 19.
31   Suetonius, Divus Vespasian §16, op. cit., pp. 284ff.
32   Griffin, "The Flavians", p. 25.
33   Griffin, "The Flavians", p. 26.
34   Griffin, "The Flavians", p. 30.
35   Brent D. Shaw, "Rebels and outsiders", in Alan K. Bowman, Peter Garnsey, Dominic Rathbone (eds), *Cambridge Ancient History, second edition, Vol. XI: The High Empire, AD 70–192* (Cambridge: Cambridge University Press, 2005), p. 400.
36   Dio Cassius, *Roman History*, Bk LXV, op. cit., p. 281; Suetonius, *Divus Vespasian* §21, op. cit., p. 285.
37   Suetonius, *Divus Vespasian* §21, op. cit., p. 287.
38   Dio Cassius, *Roman History*, Bk LXV, op. cit., p. 285.
39   Dio Cassius, *Roman History*, Bk LXV, op. cit., p. 285.
40   Suetonius, *Divus Titus* §24, op. cit., p. 278.
41   Josephus, *The Jewish War* 6.9.3.
42   Dio Cassius, *Roman History*, Bk LXVI, op. cit., p. 308.
43   Dio Cassius, *Roman History*, Bk LXVI, op. cit., p. 299.
44   Suetonius, *Divus Titus* §35, op. cit., pp. 288ff.
45   Suetonius, *Domitian* §11, op. cit., p. 303.
46   Dio Cassius, *Roman History*, Bk LXVI, op. cit., p. 345.
47   Miriam Griffin, "Domitian", in Alan K. Bowman, Peter Garnsey, Dominic Rathbone (eds), *Cambridge Ancient History, second edition, Vol. XI: The High Empire, AD 70–192* (Cambridge: Cambridge University Press, 2005), p. 63.
48   Dio Cassius, *Roman History*, Bk LXVI, op. cit., p. 317.
49   Suetonius, *Domitian* §15, op. cit., p. 306.
50   Suetonius, *Domitian* §,16, op. cit., p. 307.
51   Dio Cassius, *Roman History*, Bk LXVII, op. cit., p. 359.
52   Dio Cassius, *Roman History*, Bk LXVIII, op. cit., p. 361.
53   Miriam Griffin, "Nerva to Hadrian", in Alan K. Bowman, Peter Garnsey, Dominic Rathbone (eds), *Cambridge Ancient History, second edition, Vol.*

XI: The High Empire, AD 70–192 (Cambridge: Cambridge University Press, 2005), pp. 92ff.
54 Griffin, "Nerva to Hadrian", p. 88.
55 Gibbon, *Decline and Fall of the Roman Empire* (London, 1909 Edition), Bk 1.93.
56 Griffin, "Nerva to Hadrian", p. 117.
57 Griffin, "Nerva to Hadrian", p. 109.
58 Dio Cassius, *Roman History*, Bk LXVIII, op. cit., p. 389.
59 Dio Cassius, *Roman History*, Bk LXVIII, op. cit., p. 389.
60 Dio Cassius, *Roman History*, Bk LXVIII, op. cit., p. 379.
61 Dio Cassius, *Roman History*, Bk LXVIII, op. cit., p. 401.
62 *Letters of The Younger Pliny*, Bk 2. "To Maturus Arrianus", tr. Betty Radice (Harmondsworth: Penguin, 1963).
63 See Pliny's correspondence with Trajan, in *Letters of the Younger Pliny*, Bk 10, pp. 261-301.
64 Griffin, "Nerva to Hadrian", pp. 113ff.
65 Dio Cassius, Roman History, Bk LXVIII, pp. 405ff.
66 Augustine, *City of God*, Bk 5 Ch.18 (London: Penguin, 2003), p. 207.
67 A. R. Birley, "The accession of Hadrian", in Alan K. Bowman, Peter Garnsey, Dominic Rathbone (eds), *Cambridge Ancient History, second edition, Vol. XI: The High Empire, AD 70–192* (Cambridge: Cambridge University Press, 2005), p. 132.
68 *Historia Augusta*, tr. David Magie, Loeb Classical Library, Vol. 139, 6.1-3 (Cambridge, MA: Harvard University Press, 2022), p. 19.
69 *Historia Augusta* 10:2-11.1, op. cit., pp. 31,33.
70 *Historia Augusta* 12.9, op. cit., p. 39.
71 *Historia Augusta* 14.1, op. cit., pp. 39,41.
72 *Historia Augusta* 14.3, op. cit., p. 41.
73 A. R. Birley, "The second provincial tour, 128–132", in Alan K. Bowman, Peter Garnsey, Dominic Rathbone (eds), *Cambridge Ancient History, second edition, Vol. XI: The High Empire, AD 70–192* (Cambridge: Cambridge University Press, 2005), p. 144.
74 *Historia Augusta* 14.5, op. cit., p. 41.
75 *Historia Augusta* 24.1,2, op. cit., p. 69.
76 *Historia Augusta* 20.7, op. cit., p. 59.
77 *Historia Augusta* 22, op. cit., p. 63.

[78] *Historia Augusta* 22.7, op. cit., p. 63.
[79] Richard Saller, "Status and patronage", in Alan K. Bowman, Peter Garnsey, Dominic Rathbone (eds), *Cambridge Ancient History, second edition, Vol. XI: The High Empire, AD 70–192* (Cambridge: Cambridge University Press, 2005), p. 821.
[80] *Letters of Pliny the Younger*, Bk 9.11, op. cit., pp. 238,239.
[81] Ewen Bowie, "Literature and sophistic", in Alan K. Bowman, Peter Garnsey, Dominic Rathbone (eds), *Cambridge Ancient History, second edition, Vol. XI: The High Empire, AD 70–192* (Cambridge: Cambridge University Press, 2005), p. 900.
[82] Bowie, "Literature and sophistic", p. 913.
[83] Bowie, "Literature and sophistic", p. 926.

2

The Church in the second century

Only a short time span separated the Apostolic Church from the birth of Irenaeus. If we take the birth of Irenaeus in Smyrna to be about 135, and the end of the Apostolic age to have occurred with the death of the Apostle John in *c.*98 at the start of the reign of Trajan (98-117), then the intervening period was less than 40 years—a short space of time indeed.[1] Eusebius even quotes Irenaeus in his own fourth-century history of the Church, saying, "The Church in Ephesus was founded by Paul, and John remained there till Trajan's time; so, she [the Ephesian church] is a true witness of what the Apostles taught."[2]

The chief marks of the Church—as it entered the second century after the initial apostolic mission headed principally by Paul and his associates—were that, after a slow beginning, it had spread rapidly to almost all the main centres of the Empire, especially in the east. It was a Church which comprised both Jew and Gentile, although admittedly sometimes with a struggle. It faced increasing persecution in the Empire after meeting with initial opposition from the Jewish authorities, particularly in Jerusalem (see Acts 4; 5:17-42; 7:1-8:3). Furthermore, the Jewish War of 66-70 seems to have scattered Christians into the Near East and the cities of Asia Minor. A discernible pattern of leadership in the churches of most communities appears to have been set from earliest times: i.e., bishops or overseers, presbyters and deacons, and later orders of deacons that included both women and men. Following the deaths of the Apostles, the teaching of the Church centred around the Scriptures, which they or their close associates had written, and which came to be recognized by church communities as self-authenticating documents bearing witness to the life and teaching of Jesus and his Apostles.

A secondary group of writings soon gained traction in these communities, including the *Shepherd of Hermas* and the *Didache*, as well as the letters of early Church leaders such as Ignatius of Antioch and Clement of Rome. The distinctive features of the Church in the Empire were the refusal to worship anyone as Lord other than Jesus Christ; the care of the poor, the sick, the widow and the prisoner; a commitment to sexual purity and chastity, including a greater care of women; and, lastly, a fellowship, which, *at its best*, overturned the social barriers between Jew and Greek, slave and free, male and female (Galatians 3:28). In expressing these characteristics vividly, the Epistle to Diognetus is important, to which we shall come. These, then, were the main characteristics of the Church by the start of the second century and such characteristics would have been well known to Irenaeus.

He faced the dual struggle of persecution from the Empire and internal dissension and false teaching from within the Church. Indeed, this pincer movement would shape and characterize Irenaeus' own ministry in the second half of the second century.[3]

The growth of the Church

The Christian message, indeed the person of Christ, the Messiah and Son of God (John 20:31), was for all the world. The truth that Irenaeus would give himself to defending was that God had come in Christ *to recapitulate humankind*, that is, to restore the image of God in his own human creation and also to demonstrate the character of God as love and holiness, thereby making known the glory of God once again. This message was variously expressed in the Gospels and in the writing of the Apostles.

Matthew makes clear in his Gospel that the coming of Christ is for all the world and does so implicitly by recording the appearance at the crib of the Magi from the East (2:1-12). By the end of his Gospel, it is clear that the message of forgiveness of sins preached in Christ's name is for all nations and peoples (28:16-20), to whom the Church must now go. Likewise, Mark, most probably writing in Rome in the company of the leading Apostle Peter, whose memories of Jesus he recorded (see 1 Peter

5:13), focuses on the worldwide kingdom Christ inaugurates, in which power is exhibited in humble service and sacrifice and demonstrated supremely in the redemptive work of the cross (see Mark 1:14,15; 10:41-5; 15:33-41). Luke, who had travelled with Paul and had witnessed the latter's detention in Rome and his trials (Acts 28:30 and 2 Timothy 4:11), writes a two-volume work about the coming of Christ, especially to the weak and despised (see Luke 1:46-55; 15:31-32; 23:43), as well as to the pagan and Jewish communities of the Empire (see, for example, Pisidian Antioch in Acts 13:13-43) and Athens (Acts 17:16-34).

Finally, in the Gospel of John we find the encapsulation of truth closest to Irenaeus' own theology. It is precisely because of the Incarnation, so unequivocally set out in the Gospel and especially in the Prologue (1:1-14), that the Christian message is and has to be universal for all people, in all places, at all times. And this universality, which is dependent on the fact that *it is God himself who takes on flesh to recapitulate humankind* (Irenaeus' preferred term), lies at the root of Irenaeus' theology. The Gospels are in themselves manifestos—to the world and for the whole human race throughout time—of a new kingdom inaugurated by Jesus. And therefore, implicit in the gospel message is the need to make known their truth to all people. To aid and indeed to propel this, the Spirit is given to the Church at Pentecost and subsequently (see Acts 1:8 and 4:31).

The Church was established first in Jerusalem and then Antioch, a principal city of the Empire numbering some 200,000 people, as well as in other areas close to Jerusalem in Judaea, Samaria and Syria. Empowered by the Spirit and under the Spirit's leading, the Church then spread into Asia, Europe and North Africa.[4] The result was a series of missions to the strategic centres of the Empire, but not initially to Carthage and Alexandria, which were evangelized by others by the end of the first century. Alexandria was first evangelized, according to tradition, by Mark the Evangelist. From Antioch, the message was first taken to cities in Cyprus, Galatia and Phrygia. Later on, in his second and third missionary journeys, Paul himself travelled to the prominent imperial cities of Philippi, Thessalonica, Berea, Athens, Corinth, Ephesus and finally Rome, where he strengthened the existing churches already begun by ordinary Christians without an Apostolic mission.

What we know of these communities is that they were gathered around the Risen Lord, Jesus Christ, in whom the community believed as Lord and Saviour. Christ was the true Son of God (*uiós tou theoù*), rather than the emperors who called themselves sons of God, and whom the early Christians could not justifiably or honestly worship. These early churches were guided by leaders appointed through the laying on of hands by the Apostles or their associates (1 Timothy 5:22; 2 Timothy 1:6). The leaders were then to teach the tradition of the faith set out by the Apostles (see 2 Timothy 1:13-14) and recorded in the Scriptures. These Scriptures, which were based around the Gospels and the Epistles, were gradually being made available to the early churches.

The Scriptures and the Spirit

The development of the Scriptures in the early Church of the first century AD was a dynamic process. We have a good idea when they were first written. The three synoptic Gospels of Mark, Matthew and Luke (called synoptic because they share common material and sources) record the life of Jesus; after all, very few church members would have had the privilege of meeting Jesus in the flesh. According to scholars, these Gospels only began circulating as manuscripts through the churches from about AD 70-80, which is about 50 years before Irenaeus. St John's Gospel was probably written later in Ephesus, around AD 90, and would therefore have been even more recent. The earliest Scriptures of the New Testament to circulate were the Epistles. We know that these were written and probably in circulation much earlier, i.e., between 48-57.[5] From what we know in outline about the production of the New Testament, we can see that it was an unfolding process: first the Gospels or letters would be written, then copied in manuscript form on vellum or parchment, then finally collected into ever more comprehensive codices. Few individuals could have afforded their own copies, but churches meeting in homes would gradually accumulate their own Scriptures to be read and expounded at meetings (2 Timothy 2:15b). Gradually, a written record replaced the oral, but both were directed by the Holy Spirit.

We also know that sometime after Irenaeus was made Bishop of Lugdunum the contours of the New Testament were taking shape (*c.*180). The availability of the Septuagint, the Hebrew Scriptures in Greek, is uncertain, but it seems clear that many of the early Church teachers from around 150, such as Justin Martyr and Athenagoras, rested their teaching principally upon the OT Scriptures that prophesied the coming of Christ.[6] Apart from sections of the Old Testament like the Psalms, which were translated into Latin in the West in the early fourth century, the Vulgate or Latin Bible was not fully translated into Latin until Jerome (*c.*347-420). However, in his own great work *Against Heresies*, Irenaeus makes use of much of the New Testament. In all he quotes more than a thousand passages from almost all the New Testament: 626 from the Gospels, 54 from Acts, 280 from the Pauline Epistles (but not from Philemon), 15 from the Catholic Epistles (but not from 2 Peter, Jude or 3 John) and 29 from the Book of Revelation.[7] In other words, Irenaeus was probably the first systematic biblical theologian, and knew and accepted these books or letters as Scripture and hence authoritative for church belief and practice (2 Timothy 3:16). Indeed, as we shall see, Irenaeus' powerful arguments against the Gnostics are based on his knowledge of Scripture.

We also know from the *Muratorian Canon* that a settled number of books of the New Testament was in existence by the middle of the second century. The Canon was discovered by an Italian scholar, Ludovico Antonio Muratori (1672-1750), in Bobbio, North Italy, the monastery of the sixth/seventh-century Irish monk Columbanus, and was later transferred to the Ambrosian library in Milan. In it are several codices from the Church Fathers, a copy of the *Shepherd of Hermas*, a popular pastoral text in the early Church, which we shall come to, and a list of New Testament books in circulation and accepted by the Church at the time of writing. A reference to Pius I, an early pope (140-155), fixes the work in the second century. The books of the New Testament referred to are the four Gospels—with a vivid account of the call to the elderly John to write the fourth Gospel in Ephesus.[8] What is clear is that the four Gospels, the 13 Pauline Epistles, Jude, two or three of the Epistles of John, the Wisdom of Solomon, and the Book of Revelation were widely accepted as Scripture. Other books, such as the Apocalypse of

Peter, were rejected, while the *Shepherd of Hermas* was recommended for private reading but was not to be read in church. Thus, a process of sifting took place over the second century, in particular. This sifting involved the mind of the Church being guided by certain scholars, as well as by a process of self-authentication of Scripture itself by the Spirit in the community of the Church. The settled canon of the New Testament did not finally emerge until the fourth century, when the complete set of New Testament books were to be found in codices such as the *Codex Sinaiticus* (*c*.325), *Codex Vaticanus* and *Codex Alexandrinus*, also fourth century.[9] *Sinaiticus* and *Alexandrinus* are both in the British Museum.

We can thus be sure that by the middle of the second century and the time of Irenaeus, the various church communities would have had access to at least the Gospels and the Pauline corpus of epistles, with John's letters and Apocalypse also gaining wide acceptance. In addition, there was a large number of other texts that required sifting, and in some cases discarding. We can imagine church gatherings in homes or rented halls accompanied by the singing of hymns or spiritual songs (Colossians 3:16; 1 Corinthians 14:26-33). The Scriptures would be read and expounded by the church leaders, be they bishops, presbyters or deacons, the Eucharist would be celebrated, and baptisms would take place outside in rivers or lakes. In this way, the Church in the second century set about its life and worship. The differences from synagogue worship were that Jesus was worshipped as the Messiah and as part of the Godhead; the New Testament fulfilled the Law and the Prophets of the Old Testament; and the Spirit moved amongst the people to give encouragement and direction. Furthermore, other texts were gaining traction in local communities: some had local significance; others were more widely circulated for the administration of the Church; still others became beloved pastoral texts, and yet others, like the Gnostic Gospels, were circulating but required evaluating for what they were.

The Apostolic Fathers

A body of Church literature circulating in the first half of the second century came to be known as *The Apostolic Fathers* once it was assembled from the seventeenth century onwards. This body of literature comprised letters of early bishops such as Ignatius, Clement and Polycarp, pastoral writings like the beloved *Shepherd of Hermas*, and the *Didache*, which provided instruction on the administration of church life. A further *Letter to Diognetus* offers a wonderful insight into the witness of the second-century Church. In short, these texts came to be highly prized writings about the nature of Christian calling and discipleship in the period of the Church's development immediately after the Apostolic period itself.

The letters of Ignatius, the second Bishop of Antioch, who was martyred in Rome (*c.*110—although some scholars have argued for a later date) are a revealing exposé of second-century church life. They are letters written by Ignatius to churches *en route* from Antioch to Rome, where Ignatius was being taken by foot and ship under an armed guard which he refers to as his "leopards". Among them are letters to the Ephesians, the Magnesians, the Trallians, Romans, Philadelphians and Smyrnaeans, and to Polycarp, the influential Bishop of Smyrna. A feature of these letters is Ignatius' sense of calling to martyrdom; such that, on several occasions, he refers to his forthcoming sacrifice. To the Ephesians he says of his chains that they "are spiritual pearls".[10] To the Romans he writes more graphically, "I am writing to all the churches and giving instruction to all, that I am willingly dying for God, unless you hinder me. I urge you, do not become an untimely kindness to me. Allow me to be bread for the wild beasts; through them I am able to attain to God. I am the wheat of God and am ground by the teeth of the wild beasts, that I may be found to be the pure bread of Christ."[11] He further writes:

> Now I am beginning to be a disciple. May nothing visible or invisible show any envy toward me, that I may attain to Jesus Christ. Fire and cross and packs of wild beasts, cuttings and being torn apart, the scattering of bones, the mangling of limbs, the grinding of the whole body, the evil torments of the Devil, let them come upon me, only that I may attain Jesus Christ.[12]

Alongside Ignatius' self-sacrificing spirit to "attain Christ" is an ardent desire for unity in the Church stemming from loyalty to its leaders, especially the bishop, who despite his age should be respected.[13] Thus he writes:

> I urge you to hasten to do all things in the harmony of God, with the bishop presiding in the place of God and the presbyters in the place of the council of the Apostles, and the deacons, who are especially dear to me, entrusted with the ministry of Jesus Christ, who was with the Father before the ages and has been made manifest at the end.[14]

The quest for unity was a frequent necessity in the early Church, as in every age, reflecting the way the divine calling is too often shipwrecked on the rocks of human frailty and pride. Alongside these letters, Ignatius also writes revealingly to the church in Smyrna and to its bishop, Polycarp; but we will reserve the content of those letters to later and their influence on Polycarp, and through him on Irenaeus.

The other principal Church leader whose letters form part of the collection known as *The Apostolic Fathers* (due to their authors' knowledge of the Apostles, both first-hand and indirect), is Clement of Rome. It is not certain who he was or when exactly he lived, but he may have been the associate of Paul's named in Philippians 4:3, and, according to Eusebius, the third Bishop of Rome.[15] He may have been bishop during the reign of Domitian around 90. Clement's first long letter is written to the church in Corinth, where a mixture of jealousy and rebelliousness by some was causing division. The letter is marked by a call to abandon such jealousy and strife: "We should leave behind empty and frivolous thoughts and come to the famous and venerable rule of our tradition. We should realize what is good and pleasing and acceptable before the one who made us."[16] And the way back which Clement outlines is the way of repentance. Repeated biblical examples are used and especially from the Old Testament: Noah, Jonah, Abraham and Rahab are all cited. But more than heeding their examples, "We should treat one another kindly according to the compassion and sweet character of the one who made us. For it is written 'Those who are kind will inherit the land, and the innocent will be left upon it; those who break the law will be destroyed from it.'"[17] It is, in all, a heartfelt appeal to pursue peace and harmony across the whole fellowship. The final plea is unmissable:

> For you will make us joyful and happy if you become obedient to what we have written through the Holy Spirit and excise the wanton anger expressed through your jealousy, in accordance with the request we have made in this letter for your peace and harmony.[18]

While Ignatius and Clement were exemplary leaders working for the unity of the Church and prepared to sacrifice themselves on the altar of their devotion and obedience, there were others who were also working for the good ordering of the Church, and in particular, the author or authors of what is known as the *Didache*. The *Didache* may have originated from the Council of Jerusalem in 48-50, as some, like Alan Garrow, have argued. But it came to be known as the Teaching of the Apostles and is listed as such by Eusebius.[19] Fragments were found in Upper Egypt among the Oxyrhynchus Papyri (No. 1782) and another manuscript was discovered by Patriarch Philotheos Bryennios in the library of the Holy Sepulchre in Jerusalem in 1873, along with writings of other Apostolic Fathers. As a text it was well known to many of the early Christian writers, including Irenaeus, and later to Clement of Alexandria and Origen who both used it.

Strongly Jewish in flavour, the *Didache* is often compared to Matthew's Gospel, the most Jewish of the Gospels. It is essentially a handbook for church life and shows the growing need for common discipline in the churches of the late first century. The text begins with an ethical calling in which two paths are set out, one to death and the other to life (see also Matthew 7:13,14). Indeed, there are many echoes of Jesus' teaching in the Sermon on the Mount. Jesus is referred to, not by name, but as the servant of the Father or simply as the Lord, perhaps underlying its Jewish use at first. In the early chapters, there is a strong incentive to give money and not to accept charity or alms unless there is a clear need.[20] There is instruction to refrain from sexual passion, and to renounce astrology, divination and robbery! Moving from the ethical, in its later chapters the *Didache* deals with the ceremonies and worship of church life. Fasting should take place on Wednesdays and Fridays and not on Mondays or Thursdays.[21] In the Eucharist, the bread is a reminder that once it was scattered seed but now is a single loaf, and so too the Church that was formerly scattered is now drawn together by the grace of God (1 Peter 2:9,10).[22] Apostles (by which is meant travelling teachers) are to be welcome only for one day and then must go on their way.[23] Those teaching in the Spirit must not be condemned but heeded,[24] although those who say in the Spirit "give me money" are to be rejected.[25] Finally, the community is to elect "gentlemen who are not fond of money" to be either deacons or bishops.[26] In these ways, the Church is to be ready so that its members "might be perfect at the final moment".[27] But this final moment, as Jesus himself teaches (see Matthew 24:1-35), will be full of deceivers, lawless people and signs in creation, and if those times had not been shortened, few would be saved. The Church is to be on tiptoe waiting for its Lord to come.[28]

The early Church was thus encouraged through Scripture, through its inspirational leaders, and through this teaching, but also through its prophetic and pastoral writings. Chief among these is the much-loved book, the *Shepherd of Hermas*. Again and again, it crops up in codices, whether in the Abbey at Bobbio or in St Catherine's Monastery at Sinai. It was, after Scripture, one of the most popular pieces of spiritual writing of the early Church. What, then, was so attractive and meaningful about it?

The *Shepherd of Hermas* was written at the end of the first century AD. It is a longish work of some 150 pages and was copied and read more widely than any other book outside the canon of Scripture. It is uncertain who Hermas was. Origen maintained he is the Hermas mentioned by Paul in Romans 16:14. Others thought him a secretary of, or correspondent with Clement, Bishop of Rome, or that he was himself the bishop. Whoever he was, Hermas must have lived between AD 60 and 140 and may well have been a member of the church in Rome, and quite possibly a prophet. The story revolves around this figure of Hermas, whose angel comes to him in the form of a shepherd to instil in him a spirit of repentance.

Hermas was a slave of his owner, Rhoda. After some time and presumably after he had been freed, he loved her "as a sister". Presumably she too was a Christian. One day he saw her bathing in the River Tiber and desired her. Later, while sleeping, he was accused by her, now in heaven, of having impure thoughts about her. Despite his protests of only loving her as a sister, she said:

> The desire for evil did rise up in your heart. Or do you not think it is evil for an evil desire to arise in the heart of an upright man? . . . Those who intend in their hearts to do evil bring death and captivity to themselves . . . but pray to God and he will heal your sins along with those of your entire household and of all the saints.[29]

She calls him to pray for and witness to his household, his wife and children, and to listen to the words that she will read.[30] Hermas is then given a number of visions about the Church, depicted in turn as an elderly lady (because age symbolized wisdom), as a tower, and as water for cleansing. Hermas is then confronted by a great beast which he overcomes through angelic power, before in a later vision an angel comes to him as a shepherd and for the rest of the work acts as his guide.[31]

What follows are two collections of commandments and then parables. The commandments are essentially pastoral and personal advice with wide-ranging application. They include the need for sexual purity with the jejune or guileless advice that if he keeps thinking about his own wife he will never sin.[32] Furthermore, he should as far as possible remain with his wife, even if she commits adultery but then repents.[33] Much time is spent commending patience and condemning "irascibility" and anger.[34] Indeed "patience is a great and mighty virtue; it has a forceful power that flourishes in a spacious arena; it is cheerful, glad, and free of anxiety, glorifying the Lord at all times, having no bitterness in itself but remaining always meek and mild".[35] Discernment too is needed and the ability to distinguish between that which is true and righteous and that which is vainglorious and excessive, and between the false and true prophet.[36] Finally, forego doublemindedness, grief and evil desire. Follow these commandments, says the Angel dressed as a shepherd, and you will live.[37]

The remaining part of the book is given over to parables. The Angel who addresses Hermas presents these parables as lessons for the Church. They speak of the need for the poor (who are like a vine) and the rich (who are like an elm) to combine together to be fruitful, with the vine climbing the elm to attain greater height and so bear more fruit in the sun.[38] Further parables recall those of the Gospels, and relate to vineyards, slaves who do good service, and trees that only reveal themselves by their leaves and fruits in the summer season (see Luke 20:9ff.; Luke 12:47ff.; Matthew 7:15-20). Parables Eight and Nine are by far the longest. The eighth compares the Church to a large willow tree with various branches, each referring to different forms of service and works. The ninth parable reverts to the image of the Church as a tower. Much of the building and guarding of the tower is entrusted to virgins, who figure strongly in the vision. They are presented as symbols of the power and virtue of God and Hermas is called to join them in building the tower.[39] There are other virgins dressed in black who seek to seduce the saints, however. Although shy at first at being left with the virgins who are eagerly building the tower,[40] Hermas is welcomed and kissed and called to stay with them as a brother and not as a husband.[41] Surrounding the tower are twelve mountains inhabited by people of various ambitions. Some of these mountain populations are searching for God, while others are hostile, and the community of the Church represented by the tower is drawn from those who seek and find God.

Overall, the *Shepherd of Hermas* has a folksy and comforting appeal. Although it was popular, it is hardly Scripture, yet it reflects the growing trends in the Church of brotherly and sisterly love, of the synergy of wealth and poverty, and of the calling to sexual purity and abstinence.

The Church in the second century

The Church of the second century had spread significantly around the Roman Empire to most of the main population centres, especially in the East. It would spread further into Gaul, to Lugdunum, Arles, Provence and Spain. The Mediterranean islands of Crete, Malta and Cyprus already had Christian communities, and North Africa was soon to follow.

In particular, by the end of the first century, Alexandria and Carthage had embryonic Christian churches.

These Christian communities had distinctive features of both belief and conduct that marked them out from the surrounding pagan cultures, religions and lifestyles. At the heart of these differences was the conviction that it was Jesus who was Lord and the Son of God, and not the emperor. More than that, Jesus was not only the long-awaited Jewish Messiah, the Christ or anointed one, but was himself part of the Godhead. For a Plato-following Greek this would mean accepting that Jesus was part of the eternal One, the creator of all. Thus John, in the opening sentences of his Gospel written in Ephesus around 90,[42] and known to Irenaeus through Polycarp, writes, "The Word was with God and *the Word was God*" (John 1:2). And this Word became flesh, "and made his dwelling among us. We have seen his glory, the glory of the One and Only, who came from the Father, full of grace and truth" (John 1:14b).

The Christian conviction was that Jesus was the divine Lord who had died and was now alive through his resurrection, and whose death had procured forgiveness of sins. And the crucifixion of Christ was the means whereby forgiveness was offered to all through faith. This is made abundantly clear in the letters of Paul which were in wide circulation by the early second century, as were the Gospels (see Romans 3:21-31; 2 Corinthians 5:16-21; Galatians 3:12-14; Ephesians 2:4-10; Mark 10:45; Matthew 1:21). These beliefs lay at the heart of these church communities now proliferating throughout the Empire. Furthermore, these truths— that they were connected to the Godhead and each other by the Spirit who indwelt them—were experienced existentially by believers in their spiritual encounters with the living Lord (see 1 Peter 1:8,9).

These fundamental beliefs of the Christian communities are highlighted in the extraordinary *Epistle to Diognetus*. This telling letter, written anonymously to Diognetus, who is enquiring about the nature of Christianity and how it differs from both Greek thought and Jewish observance, is a gem of second-century writing and highly revelatory of the nature of Christian faith of that time. The manuscript, which comes from the thirteenth or fourteenth century, was providentially found by a young cleric in 1436 "in a pile of packing paper in a fish shop in Constantinople".[43] The original codex of 260 pages (the overall manuscript), which includes 22 Christian works of an apologetic and polemical nature, spanning a thousand years, was eventually acquired by the municipal library of Strasbourg, where it was destroyed in the Franco-Prussian War of 1870. By then other copies had been made, however. Such was the journey of, and the providence surrounding this wonderful text!

The writer begins by focusing on the differences between pagan worship and Jewish worship, where there is no worship of idols or need for sacrifice.[44] Rather, God did

> not send them one of his servants or an angel or a ruler or any of those who administer earthly activities or who are entrusted with heavenly affairs, but he sent the craftsman and maker of all things himself, by whom he created the heavens, by whom he enclosed the sea within its own boundaries... [O]nly then, did he, as one might suppose, send him to rule in tyranny, fear and terror? Not at all. But with gentleness and meekness, as a king sending his own son, he sent him as king; he sent him as God; he sent him as a human to humans.[45]

Acknowledging that left to ourselves we could only expect "punishment and death as [our] ultimate reward" the writer goes on in true hope and knowledge, writing:

> The time arrived that God had planned to reveal at last his goodness and power (Oh the supreme beneficence and love of God!), he did not hate us, destroy us, or hold a grudge against us. But he was patient, he bore with us, and out of pity for us he took our sins upon himself. He gave up his own Son as a ransom for us, the holy one for the lawless, the innocent one for the wicked, the righteous one for the unrighteous, the imperishable one for the perishable, the immortal one for the mortal. For what else could hide our sins but the righteousness of that one? How could we, who were lawless and impious, be made upright except by the Son of God alone? Oh, the sweet exchange! Oh, the inexpressible creation! Oh, the unexpected acts of beneficence!

> That the lawless deeds of many should be hidden by the one who was upright, and the righteousness of one should make upright the many who are lawless![46]

Knowledge of the forgiveness which comes from the sacrifice of Christ on the cross and the hope of the resurrection were at the basis of the community. These truths that undergirded the Church resulted—as both Paul and Peter frequently explain in their writings—in a new way of life which made the Christian community distinctive in the Roman Empire. Christians are called to walk in the light (Ephesians 5:8) and to pursue what is true (Ephesians 4:25). Their speech is to be seasoned with salt (Colossians 4:6). They are to be continually prayerful (Colossians 4:2). They should be willing to suffer unjustly (1 Peter 2:19-25). They should be generous and kind to all as exemplary citizens (1 Peter 2:11-12). They should help the poor and not be given over to drunkenness, debauchery, sexual immorality and dissension (Romans 13:11-14). In other words, they are to be a living witness to the life of Jesus Christ for which purpose the Word and the Spirit are given to them.

More than this, the Church is to be a place where normal social distinctions were dissolved. Paul makes this abundantly clear in a few sentences that are profoundly revolutionary in their implications. He writes, "You are all sons of God through faith in Christ Jesus, for all of you who were baptized into Christ have clothed yourselves with Christ. There is neither Jew nor Greek, slave nor free, male nor female, for you are all one in Christ Jesus. If you belong to Christ, then you are Abraham's seed, and heirs according to the promise" (Galatians 3:26-9; cf. Colossians 3:11). The Church, therefore, is to be a community in which the normal human barriers of ethnicity, sex, slavery and freedom do not threaten, jeopardize or diminish unity in Christ. These attitudes were like a slow fuse in the Empire, leading to explosive change.

Historians and sociologists studying the rise of Christianity have also emphasized at least three features of the church in Roman society which helped its growth.

The first was the role the Church played in support of communities in time of plague, sickness and bereavement, not least during the great plague in the reign of Marcus Aurelius (161-80), which afflicted the

Empire greatly and even killed the co-emperor, Lucius Verus (161-9). The care that was given and the hope that was offered was a great comfort.[47] Tertullian famously remarks in his *Apology*, "see how these Christians love one another".[48] Justin Martyr recalls how the elements of the Communion service were taken by deacons from church meetings to those who were sick or in prison.[49] By 251, some 50 years after the death of Irenaeus, the Great Church in Rome was supporting as many as 1,500 widows.[50] Care of the poor was a significant cause of growth in the Church, especially in times of great want.

Second, the role of women significantly affected the growth of the Church. The promotion of chastity before marriage and fidelity thereafter greatly supported stable communities and households, fertility and the growth of family life. Infants were welcomed, whether boys or girls. There was no exposure of unwanted females. There is some evidence that in the Christian community the age of marriage was slightly later, but with life expectancy being so much shorter (30 to 40 years), brides tended to be married as teenagers aged between 14 and 18.[51] The greater stability of family life and the large numbers of elite women in the Christian community, such as Marcia the concubine of Commodus (180-92),[52] gave the Church greater social prominence and, arguably, more security.

The third reason for growth was the network of Roman roads between towns of significant size. The *Pax Romana* offered security of travel and greater protection from robbers. There were at least 20 cities with over 50,000 people in the Empire, connected by roads or well-worked sea passages. Churches could be planted in these cities, and the surrounding countryside or villages evangelized (Acts 19:10). This extensive network provided safe routes for trade and for the transmission of the gospel.[53]

The writer of the letter to Diognetus also recognizes the revolutionary nature of the Church with its liminal or boundary-pushing characteristics: on the one hand Christians are easy to disparage or worse, but on the other they offer a truly countercultural community, something quite different from the pagan traditions which had by this time worn thin. He writes:

> For Christians are no different from other people in terms of their country, language, or customs. Nowhere do they inhabit cities of

their own, use a strange dialect, or live life out of the ordinary. They have not discovered this teaching of theirs through reflection or through the thought of meddlesome people, nor do they set forth any human doctrine, as do some. They inhabit both Greek and barbarian cities, according to the lot assigned to each. And they show forth the character of their own citizenship in marvellous and admittedly paradoxical ways following local customs in what they wear and in what they eat and in the rest of their lives. They live in their respective countries, but only as resident aliens; they participate in all things as citizens, but they endure all things as foreigners. Every foreign territory is a homeland for them, every homeland foreign territory. They marry like everyone else and have children, but they do not expose them once they are born. They share their meals but not their sexual partners. They love everyone and are persecuted by all. They are not understood and they are condemned. They are put to death and made alive. They are impoverished and make many rich. They lack all things and abound in everything. They are dishonoured and they are exalted in their dishonours... When they are punished, they rejoice as those who have been made alive.[54]

The writer to Diognetus puts his finger on a central feature of the lives of Christians: they are admired but they are also hated; they are in the world but not of it; they are indistinguishable in some ways but distinctive as a whole; they find strength through grace, and fortitude in weakness (2 Corinthians 6:3-10; 11:16-12:10). And this, together with the challenge they represented to the norms of the Empire, meant that they would be persecuted.

The persecution of the Church

From its earliest days both in Jerusalem and elsewhere, the Church experienced persecution. Jesus himself suffered immeasurably to fulfil his calling, and he put his disciples on notice that to follow him would also entail suffering. As early as the Sermon on the Mount, Jesus indicates this with the words, "Blessed are those who are persecuted because of righteousness, for theirs is the Kingdom of heaven" (Matthew 5:10). And then, nearer to his own passion, he forewarns his disciples of future suffering. Shortly before his arrest, he tells them, "You must be on your guard. You will be handed over to the local councils and flogged in the synagogues. On account of me you will stand before governors and kings as witnesses [martyrs] to them. And the gospel must first be preached to all nations. Whenever you are arrested and brought to trial, do not worry beforehand about what to say. Just say whatever is given you at the time, for it is not you speaking, but the Holy Spirit" (Mark 13:9-11). This teaching is also made abundantly clear in the Upper Room discourse in John's Gospel, when Jesus tells the Apostles, "If the world hates you, keep in mind that it hated me first. If you belonged to the world, it would love you as its own. As it is, you do not belong to the world, but I have chosen you out of the world. That is why the world hates you. Remember the words I spoke to you: 'No servant is greater than his master'. If they persecuted me, they will persecute you also. If they obeyed my teaching, they will obey yours also." All this, according to Jesus, fulfilled the words of the Psalmist that, "They hate me without reason" (John 15:18-20,25; Psalm 35:19, 69:4).

Initially, the persecution the disciples faced was from those Jews who had rejected Jesus as the long-expected Messiah. The identity of Jesus as the Messiah is central to the Gospels and no more so than in John's Gospel, where heated arguments occur between Jesus and the Jewish leaders which end with their attempt to stone him for blasphemy (see the important and revealing long discourse of John 8:12-59). From the outset, and following the resurrection, the Jewish authorities sought to stamp out the memory of Jesus and the infant Church. The High Priests denied the resurrection and the Sanhedrin sought to suppress the preaching of the Apostles (Matthew 27:62-6; Acts 4:18-22). In Jerusalem, persecution reached a new height with the martyrdom of Stephen, the arrest of Peter, and the execution of the Apostle James (Acts 7; 8:1-3, 12:1-4). Later the leader of the church in Jerusalem was James, the brother of Jesus, and he too was most likely martyred.[55]

With the conversion of the Apostle Paul, or Saul as he was first known, and the founding of the missionary-minded church at Antioch, the dynamics of the persecution began to alter. Now accompanied by Barnabas and John Mark, Paul went on a missionary tour of Cyprus and then the towns of Galatia, and a pattern began to evolve. They would go the synagogues where a combination of Jews and God-fearers or enquirers were to be found who would listen to them speak. Paul especially demonstrated that Jesus is the Messiah who fulfils all the promises of the Old Testament Law and Prophets. As he said to them, "Therefore, my brothers, I want you to know that through Jesus the forgiveness of sins is proclaimed to you. Through him everyone who believes is justified from everything you could not be justified from by the law of Moses" (Acts 13:38-9). Some believed, but others, both Jews and Gentiles, were incensed and whipped up hostility against them. In Iconium, after an initial welcome and fruitful ministry, they were stoned (Acts 14:5). In Lystra, Paul was stoned and dragged from the city (Acts 14:19). Thus, Paul explains to new disciples that "we must go through many hardships to enter the Kingdom of God" (Acts 14:22).

The pattern was more or less set. The opposition mostly came from other Jews incensed by the teaching that Jesus was the promised Messiah, something Paul himself had come to understand on the Damascus Road (Acts 9:5). The disturbances and rioting created by this antipathy led to a major turning point during the reign of Claudius, when in *c.*49 all Christians, thought to be a troublesome sect of Judaism, and Jews, were expelled from Rome.[56] Gradually this type of persecution changed as the Roman authorities increasingly intervened to keep the peace. In Corinth, the pro-consul Gallio refused to be drawn into adjudicating on what he saw as a purely Jewish dispute, telling them to "settle the matter yourselves" (Acts 18:15). But such *sang froid* did not last. Earlier in Philippi the magistrates had Paul and Silas beaten with rods and thrown into gaol (Acts 16:23-4). In Ephesus, the city clerk had to dismiss a rioting crowd provoked by Paul's preaching and the consequent denigration of the local shrine of Diana or Artemis of the Ephesians (Acts 19:23ff.). And finally, in Jerusalem, the military commander intervened to end a riot near the Temple when, having completed his Gentile missions, Paul was falsely accused of taking Gentiles into the Temple area reserved exclusively for Jews (Acts 21:27ff.). Paul was arrested, given a hearing before the Sanhedrin in *c.*58, and taken to Caesarea where he appealed to be tried by Caesar (Acts 25:11c). By now Roman law was becoming more directly involved in keeping the peace, but more especially, it was used to establish whether Christians were loyal members of the Empire. At the same time as emperor worship became more common, with citizens having to acknowledge the genius of the emperor and burn incense to him out of reverence, Christians became more vulnerable to the charge of disloyalty, or even treason towards the emperor. Thus, in the reign of Nero (54-68), they became targets and scapegoats for any mishap in the city of Rome or elsewhere.

By the time Paul arrived in Rome in about 60, Nero had been emperor for six years. His reign was becoming increasingly bizarre and unpredictable, as he was susceptible to extreme moods with violent consequences. Initially, it appears that Paul was kept under house arrest (Acts 28:11ff.) for two years. He then had a preliminary trial or hearing but was imprisoned and chained to a Praetorian soldier (Philippians 1:13). Paul also speaks of becoming isolated at the time of the second trial.[57] Then the great fire of Rome in 64 seems to have brought yet greater persecution. Eusebius tells us that Paul was beheaded and Peter was crucified.[58] One witness by the name of Gaius, alive during the episcopacy of Zephyrinus (199-217), knew the burial places of the Apostles along the Ostian Way.[59] But from 64 this obscure Jewish sect, known as Christians, was being increasingly blamed for any and every calamity. Tacitus records in his *Annals* that "Nero fastened the guilt (for the fire) and inflicted the most exquisite tortures on a class hated for their abominations, called Christians by the populace".[60] Some were even turned into human torches at the opening of Nero's palace, the Golden House. And in *c.*200 Tertullian famously wrote in his *Apology*, "If the Tiber rises as high as the city walls, if the Nile does not send its waters up over the fields, if heavens give no rain, if there is an earthquake, if there is a famine or pestilence, straightway the cry is, 'Away with the

Christians to the lion!'"[61] The branding of Christians both as "atheists" and as the cause of trouble would stick, until the arrival of Constantine some 200 years later.

Nero's death brought the end of the Julio-Claudian dynasty, and after the year of the Five Emperors, the Flavians succeeded. During their rule, which included Vespasian, Titus and Domitian, Christians were used for entertainment and punishment in the newly opened Colosseum in Rome, or they were harassed, tortured or martyred for not honouring the genius of the emperor in trials. It was during Domitian's reign (81-96) that the persecution increased. This was in keeping with the emperor's general antipathy towards any competition to his "divinity", whether from philosopher or sect, and his general fastidiousness about any rule-breaking.[62] And it was during these years that more general persecution of Christians became rife, not least in Asia along the Aegean coast in cities like Pergamum, Smyrna, Ephesus and Sardis. Indeed, the writer of the book of Revelation says of Christians in Smyrna, "Do not be afraid of what you are about to suffer. I tell you, the devil will put some of you in prison to test you, and you will suffer persecution for ten days. Be faithful, even to the point of death, and I will give you a crown of life" (Revelation 2:10). The writer of Revelation, whether John the Apostle (the view of the Orthodox Church) or John the Elder (the view of some scholars, and possibly Eusebius),[63] was himself in exile and servitude on the island of Patmos, working in a quarry (Revelation 1:9-11). Martyrs figure largely in his visionary narrative (Revelation 7:9ff.) and in many ways the book (written around 90) functions as a reassurance of Christ's sovereignty as both Lord and exalted Lamb in the context of this assault upon the Church that is orchestrated by Satan and directed by imperial power, but used by divine providence to evangelize the nations.

What is clear is that by the turn of the second century, persecution of Christians had moved from being a policy of simply keeping the peace and punishing Christians for being the cause of civic disturbances, whether in Philippi, Corinth, Ephesus or Rome, to a settled policy of punishing them for not "worshipping" the emperor as a divinity by burning incense or by saying simply "Caesar is Lord" and swearing by his Fortune. For refusing to do this, countless Christians would be martyred or imprisoned over the next two centuries until the Edict of Milan in

313, and the permission of the Emperors Constantine and Licinius to worship freely in the Empire. However, the application of this policy of persecution would vary, depending on the hostility of the emperor to Christianity and the attitudes of local magistrates or provincial governors and their response to rioting crowds or suspicions. An example of this is found in the correspondence between Emperor Trajan and the Provincial Governor of Bithynia, Pliny the Younger.

Pliny the Younger (61-113) was the nephew of Admiral Pliny the Elder (23-79), the naturalist, writer, polymath and sailor who perished in the lava of Pompeii. Pliny the Younger was a fine example of a lawyer rising through *Cursus Honorum* from Military Tribune to Senator, Praetor, Prefect and Consul, before being appointed Governor of Bithynia in the time of Trajan. Bithynia was a province along the Black Sea, west of Pontus. It was from here in the later stages of his life that Pliny wrote to Emperor Trajan about many matters. A great letter-writer by inclination, Pliny left us a correspondence of 247 personal letters and a further 121 business letters written to Trajan.[64] Of the business letters, many were about civic debts, water supplies, a failed aqueduct and the building of a gymnasium for Claudiopolis, but only 40 were directly addressed to Trajan. The emperor's office must have echoed with the comment, "Another letter from Pliny!"[65] However, Pliny's assiduity is our gain, because he also wrote about the treatment of Christians in Bithynia at the start of the second century.

In Letters 96 and 97 of Book Ten, Pliny raises the question of how to treat and try Christians. He asks whether Christians are to be equally punished whatever their age, and whether they are to be apprehended for simply being Christians or only if they have committed a crime. Hitherto, Pliny says that his practice has been to ask if they are Christians. "If they admit it, I repeat the question a second and third time, with a warning of the punishment awaiting them. If they persist, I order them to be led away for punishment; for whatever the nature of their admission, I am convinced that their stubbornness and unshakeable obstinacy ought not to go unpunished."[66] Pliny goes on to say that he is now applying a clear test to all Christians brought before him and that he will dismiss the cases of any if they repeat "a formula of invocation to the gods and [make] offerings of wine and incense to your statue (which I have ordered to be brought into the court for this purpose along with images of other gods), and furthermore [revile] the name of Christ. None of which things, I understand, any genuine Christian can be induced to do."[67]

Others, however, said that the only crime was that Christians "met regularly before dawn on a fixed day to chant verses alternately amongst themselves in honour of Christ as if to a god, and also to bind themselves by an oath, not for any criminal purpose, but to abstain from theft, robbery and adultery, to commit no breach of trust and not to deny a deposit when called upon to restore it".[68] But now, since an edict had been passed banning any political gatherings, these meetings had ceased.

Finally, Pliny sought Trajan's advice, since there could be scores of Christians brought before the courts as the religion was rapidly growing in the area: "Indeed many individuals of every age and class, both men and women are being brought to trial, and this is likely to continue."[69] Pliny goes on, "It is not only the towns and villages and rural districts too which are infected through this wretched cult. I think though it is still possible for it to be checked and directed to better ends." This, Pliny suggests, is because he sees an upsurge in temple worship and sacrifice. When Trajan replies, he commends Pliny's actions.[70] Christians are not to be hunted down, nor should he encourage the population to report them to the courts or denounce them by the use of pamphlets. And if Christians retract and burn incense to the gods or the emperor, they should be pardoned whatever their previous history. This would indeed become the method of magistrates throughout the Empire. What is clear from these observations and from this exchange between governor and emperor is that by the early second century Christianity was growing quickly, drawing all classes and all ages and both sexes from all places, whether town or country. And what was true for Bithynia was also true for the great city of Smyrna, only a hundred miles or so further south.

Notes

1. Eusebius, *Historia ecclesiastica* (*HE*) III.23, tr. G. A. Williamson (Harmondsworth: Penguin, 1989), p. 83.
2. Irenaeus, *Adversus Haereses* (*AH*) II.33.2, quoted in HE III.23, op. cit., p. 83.
3. See Paul's own warning to the Ephesian elders in Acts 20:13-38, especially vv. 29-31.
4. See Acts 13:1-3; Acts 16:6-10; see also the list of those at Pentecost from the Diaspora in Acts 2:8-11.
5. Tom Wright, *Paul: A Biography* (London: SPCK, 2020), pp. 433-4.
6. Bruce M. Metzger, *The Canon of the New Testament: Its Origin, Development and Significance* (Oxford: Clarendon Paperbacks, 1997), p. 154.
7. Metzger, *The Canon of the New Testament*, p. 154.
8. Lines 9-16 of the fragment: Metzger, *The Canon of the New Testament*, p. 195.
9. Metzger, *The Canon of the New Testament*, pp. 192-201.
10. Ignatius, "Letter to the Ephesians" 11, in *Apostolic Fathers I*, Loeb Classical Library, Vol. 24 (Cambridge, MA: Harvard University Press, 2003), p. 231.
11. Ignatius, *Letter to the Romans* 4, in *Apostolic Fathers I*, Loeb Classical Library, Vol. 24 (Cambridge, MA: Harvard University Press, 2003), p. 275.
12. Ignatius, *Letter to the Romans* 5, op. cit., p. 277.
13. Ignatius, *Letter to the Magnesians* 3.1, in *Apostolic Fathers I*, Loeb Classical Library, Vol. 24 (Cambridge, MA: Harvard University Press, 2003), p. 245.
14. Ignatius, *Letter to the Magnesians* 6.1, op. cit., p. 247.
15. Eusebius, *HE* III.4.15, op. cit., p. 67.
16. Clement, *First Epistle to the Corinthians* 7.2,3, in *Apostolic Fathers I*, Loeb Classical Library, Vol. 24 (Cambridge, MA: Harvard University Press, 2003), p. 47.
17. Clement, *First Epistle to the Corinthians* 14.3,4, op. cit., p. 59.
18. Clement, *First Letter to the Corinthians* 63.2, op. cit., p. 149.
19. Eusebius, *HE* III.25, op. cit., p. 89.
20. *Didache* 1.5-10, in *Apostolic Fathers I*, Loeb Classical Library, Vol. 24 (Cambridge, MA: Harvard University Press, 2003), p. 419.
21. *Didache* 8.1, op. cit., p. 429.
22. *Didache* 9.4, op. cit., p. 431.
23. *Didache* 11.5, op. cit., p. 435.

24. *Didache* 11.5, op. cit., p. 435.
25. *Didache* 11.12, op. cit., p.437.
26. *Didache* 15.1, op. cit., p. 441.
27. *Didache* 16.2, p. 441.
28. *Didache* 16.7, p. 443.
29. *Shepherd of Hermas*, in *Apostolic Fathers II*, tr. Bart E. Ehrman, Loeb Classical Library, Vol. 25 (Cambridge, MA: Harvard University Press, 2005), p. 177.
30. *Shepherd of Hermas*, op. cit., pp. 187-91.
31. *Shepherd of Hermas*, Vision 5, op. cit., p. 235.
32. *Shepherd of Hermas*, Fourth Commandment, op. cit., p. 245.
33. *Shepherd of Hermas*, op. cit., p. 247.
34. *Shepherd of Hermas*, op. cit., p. 257.
35. *Shepherd of Hermas*, op. cit., p. 259.
36. *Shepherd of Hermas*, op. cit., pp. 285-91.
37. *Shepherd of Hermas*, op. cit., p. 305.
38. *Shepherd of Hermas*, Parable II, op. cit., p. 309.
39. *Shepherd of Hermas* IX.13, op. cit., p. 423.
40. *Shepherd of Hermas* IX.3, op. cit., p. 393.
41. *Shepherd of Hermas*, IX.11; IX.15, op. cit., pp. 415,427.
42. See Patrick Whitworth, *The Gospel of the Trinity: Exploring the Gospel of John* (Durham: Sacristy Press, 2023).
43. Epistle to Diognetus (ED), in *Apostolic Fathers II*, ed. Bart D. Ehrman, Loeb Classical Library, Vol. 25 (Cambridge, MA: Harvard University Press, 2003), pp. 127,128.
44. *ED* §2 and §3, op. cit., pp. 131-7.
45. *ED* §7.2-4, op. cit., pp. 145-7.
46. *ED* §9.2-5, op. cit., p. 151.
47. Rodney Stark, *The Rise of Christianity* (London: HarperOne, 1997), pp. 73ff.
48. Tertullian, *Apology* §39.
49. Henry Chadwick, *The Early Church* (Harmondsworth: Penguin, 1993), p. 48; Justin Martyr, *The First Apology*, Ch. LXV, TANF, Vol. 1 (Grand Rapids, MI: Eerdmans, [1885] 1975), p. 185.
50. Chadwick, *The Early Church*, p. 58.
51. Stark, *The Rise of Christianity,* p. 107.
52. Chadwick, *The Early Church*, p. 29.
53. Stark, *The Rise of Christianity,* pp. 131ff.

54 *ED* §5.1-16, op. cit., pp.140,141.
55 Parts of the Church tradition suggest that James was a stepbrother of Jesus from a previous marriage by Joseph, from the view that Mary had only Jesus and no genetic half-brothers. James was known as James-the-Less or the Righteous as distinct from James the Apostle and was also martyred. See *HE* II.1, op. cit., p. 35, and II.23, op. cit., pp. 58ff. There are two accounts of his martyrdom, by Hegesippus and Josephus (Bk XX).
56 Suetonius, *Claudius* 25, in *The Twelve Caesars*, p. 195.
57 2 Timothy 4:16; *HE* II.22, p. 57.
58 Eusebius, *HE* II.25, p. 62.
59 *HE* II.25, op. cit., p. 62.
60 Tacitus, *Annals*, Bk XV (Perfect Library Reprint Amazon), p. 295.
61 Tertullian, *Apology*, TANF, Vol. III (Cosimo Reprint of Eerdmans' 1885 ed., 2007), p. 47.
62 Suetonius, *Domitian* § 8, op. cit., p. 300.
63 See *HE* III.18-21, op. cit., pp. 81,82 and *AH* V.30.3.
64 *Letters of the Younger Pliny*, p. 12.
65 *Letters of the Younger Pliny*, pp. 19ff.
66 *Letters of the Younger Pliny*, p. 293.
67 *Letters of the Younger Pliny*, p. 294.
68 *Letters of the Younger Pliny*, p. 294.
69 *Letters of the Younger Pliny* (Letter 96), p. 294.
70 *Letters of the Younger Pliny* (Letter 97), p. 295.

3

Growing up in Smyrna

Irenaeus was born in Smyrna (Izmir) around AD 135, although the date is uncertain. Smyrna was wonderfully situated on the Aegean with a secluded port and a thriving commercial hub. Although smaller in population than Ephesus to the south, which numbered around 200,000, it was similar in size to Pergamum to the north. What it lacked in size it made up for in quality, and it was a jewel on the Aegean. As a citizen of this city, Irenaeus was heir to a rich Greek culture. Although originally founded by the Ionians in the eleventh century BC, like so many of the great cities of the Levant, Smyrna was refounded by Alexander the Great (356-323 BC). Smyrna was also reputed to be the birthplace of Homer and a nursery of mathematics.[1] It is likely that Irenaeus received his education there, and this being the case, it would have been a very good one.

We know next to nothing of the background of Irenaeus, but if he is anything like any of the other early Church Fathers, whether of the East or the Latin West, he would have received the best education available. The precocious Origen (185-c.253) had a patron, Leonides of Alexandria, who helped with his education in the late second century, and a Christian father who was a professor of literature and a martyr. Basil of Caesarea and Gregory Nazianzus were both educated at Athens University in the mid-fourth century. Although starting life in a small African town, Augustine of Hippo taught rhetoric and philosophy in Carthage, Rome and Milan, while John Chrysostom was taught by Libanius (314-91), the premier teacher of rhetoric in Antioch. The so-called Sophist School, a group of philosophers, historians and writers which formed in the reign of Nero and continued in full spate until the mid-third century AD with such figures as Aristides, Dio Chrysostom, Philostratus, Plutarch and Nicetes of Smyrna, revived Greek thought and literature in that period.

Although the Church Fathers were always ambivalent about their pagan teachers and the Classics, there is no doubt that they benefited from their academic disciplines in their work as Christian teachers, and none more so than Irenaeus.

Smyrna in particular was a centre of Sophist and rhetorical studies, giving an advanced education beyond the initial grammar school which formed the basis of classical studies and which would give its name to medieval European schools. Previous to universities grammarians taught the right use of words and grammar to facilitate proper expression and communication. They also familiarized pupils with the works of a number of authors—Homer, Euripides, Aeschylus, Sophocles, Herodotus, Thucydides, Plato, Aristotle, Demosthenes and Menander from the East; and Cicero, Seneca, Horace, Virgil, Horace and Apuleius from the West.[2] These works were no doubt learnt by rote.[3] Sophist teaching was in essence university instruction aimed at teaching a student how to explain and persuade people through well-constructed speech, with rhetoric considered *the most valuable skill*. The schools might also have had courses on arithmetic, geometry, astronomy, medicine or pharmacy; the arts, such as painting, sculpture in bronze or marble; or even more practical subjects like farming.[4] And the best universities in the second-century ancient world in the East were at Athens, Ephesus, Smyrna and Alexandria. This being the case, the very able young Irenaeus surely would have attended the schools in Smyrna, where the likes of Albinus (*c.*150), a Platonic Sophist and teacher of the great doctor Galen, the foremost medical doctor of his age, was studying.

The reason for stressing this is that, like other Church Fathers, Irenaeus learnt methods of criticism which he later applied to his understanding of the Bible in its embryonic form, and to the refutation of Gnosticism which was to be so central to his life and teaching. When we come to his great work *Against Heresies* or to give it its full title, *Detection and Refutation of the Knowledge Falsely So Called*, we find methods of analysis and elucidation that reflect the criticism associated with the philosophic schools. In his writing, Irenaeus shows signs of being acquainted with Xenophanes (*c.*570–*c.*478 BC), a philosopher from Colophon near Ephesus who supported the Christian and Jewish view of a single Creator God. Xenophanes is quoted by Pliny the Elder as saying that God is "all seeing, all hearing, he is all Mind, and Thought and eternal".[5] Irenaeus would make use of this Pre-Socratic philosopher in his own rebuttal of Gnosticism, and would quote from him five times.[6] In this, Irenaeus was to set a trend in quoting this Greek philosopher anonymously, and after him others, like Clement of Alexandria, Novatian of Rome and Cyril of Jerusalem, would do the same. Other classical writers would be brought in to bolster Irenaeus' case against the Gnostics, such as the dramatist Menander and Zeno, who also believed in a single source of creation. All this demonstrates that Irenaeus was well educated, most probably in the Sophist schools of Smyrna, and, like others who followed him, made use of the wisdom of the Greeks in his defence of biblical Christianity. It was not that he thought this approach was conclusive, but that it provided a bridgehead into right thinking distinct from the bizarre theories of the Gnostics, which we shall come to. And it was also a form of thought widely respected in more educated circles and therefore not so easily dismissed.

While the schools gave Irenaeus a familiarity with Greek thought, some of which he would use in his campaign against the Gnostics, he was not so well served in Jewish studies. It was important for him to have a firm grasp of the Old Testament, since one of the most influential of the Gnostics (if we may call him one), Marcion, would take the view that the Old Testament was the work of a separate divinity from that of the New Testament. Irenaeus would need to refute this and do so on doctrinal and linguistic grounds. Yet his knowledge of Hebrew was limited. For instance, his translation of the opening verses of Genesis is wide of the mark.[7] Furthermore, he shared some of the misapprehensions of other Church Fathers about Judaism. He believed, for example, that the Jews had lost eternal life by killing the Lord,[8] and that the Law was like a myth that could be used symbolically.[9]

As a native Greek speaker, Irenaeus was understandably at home in the Christian Scriptures. He may well have had a copy of the Greek translation of the Old Testament known as the Septuagint. He also appears to have had access to the translation of the Old Testament by Theodotion and Aquila, also in Greek.[10] In addition, he might well have owned copies of all four Gospels as well as the Pauline Epistles, which were by then (150) in wide circulation.

Putting these influences together, what we have is a man well educated through the Greek schools of grammar and rhetoric, with a limited understanding of Judaism and a deep appreciation of the New Testament. By the middle of the second century, there was a need for a comprehensive riposte to the growing challenge of Gnosticism. In view of this, Irenaeus created a systematic response using the literary devices of *hypothesis*, *oikonomia* (arrangement) and *anakephalaiôsis* (recapitulation) and applied these to his analysis of Scripture, which we shall come to later. Furthermore, Irenaeus received immense encouragement from the oral tradition of leading Christians of the area, including Polycarp and Papias, who in turn had heard John the Apostle teach.

Polycarp, John the Apostle and the Church in Smyrna

Undoubtedly, the most influential Christian voice in Asia Minor and its churches was that of John the Apostle, the Beloved Disciple. Although it is true that the church in Ephesus and the surrounding region was founded by the Apostle Paul (see Acts 19:8-10), the fact that John came to live there permanently from the time of the Jewish rebellion (66-70) until the end of his life in the reign of Trajan (98-117), meant that he had a lasting and profound influence in the region. Indeed, there was a tradition that different Apostles were sent to different regions: Thomas to Parthia and the East, Andrew to Scythia and John to Asia.[11]

It is Eusebius who tells us that John was exiled to Patmos during the reign of Domitian, and Irenaeus records this in *Against Heresies*, although there is some debate in Eusebius and among other scholars as to whether it was John the Apostle or John the Elder who was in fact exiled to Patmos, which is a little way off the coast from Ephesus. It is Irenaeus who gives further witness, also recorded by Eusebius,[12] both that John "taught the truth to the clergy of Asia"[13] and that having John reside and teach there, the church in Ephesus was "a true witness of what the Apostles taught".[14] Furthermore, we are told by Eusebius that it was while living in Ephesus that John was urged to write his Gospel,[15] although for some reason Eusebius says John wrote more on the early ministry of Jesus than the other Evangelists. It seems, in fact, that John's

Gospel has far more on the final week of Jesus' earthly life and less on his earlier Galilean ministry.

The main point to grasp is that Polycarp, who was to be a great influence on Irenaeus' life and teaching, had sat at the feet of the Beloved Disciple and received his teaching about the Lord,[16] and had then become a leading voice and martyr in the Church of the second century. In Irenaeus' struggle with Gnosticism, one of his chief arguments in establishing the truth of the gospel against the "false knowledge of the Gnostics" was that he had received that which Polycarp passed on. And Polycarp had handed on what first came to him from the Apostles, and especially from John and *his* Gospel and *his* oral instruction. This handing on of Apostolic truth was an essential part of Irenaeus' refutation of false knowledge.

Of late, scholars have been at pains to show the connection between Polycarp and Irenaeus as one of the main sources for his thinking alongside the methodologies of criticism, evaluation and articulation learnt from the school of rhetoric in Smyrna and the Scriptures of the embryonic Christian Bible (albeit in several manuscripts rather than a codex). There is, in many ways, the threefold chord of Scripture, tradition and reason which persisted beyond Irenaeus. The connection between Polycarp and Irenaeus was an essential thread in the strands of tradition and Scripture. It was this connection and source that the German scholar F. Loofs explored in the 1930s, and more recently Charles Hill, who has made a forensic connection between Irenaeus and Polycarp, arguing that the Presbyter referred to anonymously by Irenaeus in IV.27-32 was indeed Polycarp.[17] If Polycarp was such an important influence on Irenaeus, who was he, and what was his role?

Acknowledgement of the significance of Polycarp has been growing over recent years. He has always been considered a godly bishop of Smyrna and a martyr, but the full extent of his influence both regionally and further afield in Rome is not so well known. The identification of the Presbyter in *AH* IV.27-32 with Polycarp raises the significance of Polycarp in Irenaeus' formation as a young man, Christian, and future theologian and church leader. What Hill argues is that far from being a mere child when he listened to Polycarp, Irenaeus was a student or young reader, eager to learn and understand. Others, like Sebastian Moll, have argued that Irenaeus was too young to be formatively influenced by Polycarp.[18] However, significantly, Irenaeus is able to quote Polycarp's teaching in his attempt to prevent Florinus going over to the Gnostics, a correspondence we shall come to later. Such knowledge suggests an adult understanding and appreciation of Polycarp by Irenaeus.

Polycarp was probably born during the Apostolic age in c.69, in which case shortly after the execution of Peter and Paul following the great fire of Rome. We know that he was martyred in c.155 in Smyrna during the proconsulship of Lucius Quadratus, and from the account in *The Apostolic Fathers*, we know that he famously said in his testimony at the time of his death by burning that he would not deny Christ: "For eighty-six years I have served him [Christ], and he has done me no wrong. How can I blaspheme my king who has saved me?"[19] Whether Polycarp meant 86 years since his birth or 86 years since his conversion, we cannot be sure. In any event, his birth was still very much in the Apostolic era. Growing up in Smyrna, he would have witnessed the early persecution of the Church in the reign of Domitian (81-96). And in a letter to the church in the Book of Revelation, Smyrna is warned of impending persecution: "Do not be afraid of what you about to suffer. I tell you, the devil will put some of you in prison to test you, and you will suffer persecution for ten days. Be faithful, even to the point of death, and I will give you the crown of life" (Revelation 2:10). Polycarp became presbyter in Smyrna in c.100, quite possibly ordained by the Apostle John himself during the final years of John's life. If this is correct, Polycarp was to remain in Smyrna thereafter for over 50 years, first as presbyter and then later as bishop, and was to guide and lead the church there, man and boy, for a lifetime's ministry.

It seems that Polycarp was Bishop of Smyrna before Ignatius' martyrdom in Rome, which Eusebius dates at c.108,[20] although some, like Barnes, have dated it much later. We know that on his journey from Antioch, escorted by Roman soldiers whom he calls "leopards" (anticipating his approaching death by wild beasts in the recently completed Colosseum), Ignatius rested in Smyrna. From there he wrote to the Smyrna church and to Polycarp himself, already its bishop, which means Polycarp would remain bishop for a further 40 and more years. Ignatius wrote to the Smyrneans to encourage them to maintain unity in their fellowship and obedience to their bishop, saying, "The one who honours the bishop is honoured by God: the one who does anything behind the bishop's back serves the Devil."[21] The church had experienced some division over observing the Eucharist,[22] but did believe that Jesus had truly come in the flesh,[23] and that he had been "truly nailed for us in the flesh".[24] The fact that Ignatius makes a point that the Smyrnean Christians believed in the *fleshly Incarnation and crucifixion* indicates that some Gnostics lived and worshipped there who thought that Jesus, being impassible, had not truly suffered in the flesh.

Ignatius not only wrote to the church at Smyrna but also to Polycarp, who must have been one of the rising episcopal stars in the Near East, along with Papias at Hierapolis, a contemporary and also an important voice in the region. Hierapolis (Pamukkale) was close to Laodicea and Smyrna, the former being a place of hot springs and an important Christian centre where the evangelist Philip and two of his daughters lay buried (Acts 8:4-40; 21:8,9). In his letter to Polycarp, Ignatius encourages him to "forge ahead" in his race and "urge all to be saved".[25] What then follows is advice on being a good pastor and leader, replete with many quotations from or allusions to teaching from the Gospels and the Epistles. Thus, he is told to be assiduous in prayer, and to speak to each effectively, according to God's own character.[26] With difficulty, Polycarp is "to bring those who are more pestiferous into subjection. For not every wound is cured with the same plaster. Soothe paroxysms of fever with old compresses" (these are presumably spiritual metaphors).[27] With regard to slavery, he advises, "Do not be arrogant towards male and female slaves, but neither let them become haughty; rather, let them serve even more as slaves for the glory of God, that they may receive a greater freedom from God."[28] And he hints at a way of finding freedom for slaves with the statement, "And they should not long to be set free through the common fund, lest they be found slaves of passion."[29] Indeed, the whole community should work together as he expresses in these stirring phrases:

> I am giving my life in exchange for those who are subject to the bishop, the presbyters, and the deacons. And I hope to have my lot together with them in God. Labour together with one another,

> compete together, run together, suffer together, lie down together, and be raised together as the household slaves, attendants and servants of God. Be pleasing to the one in whose army you serve, from whom also you receive your wages. Let none of you be found a deserter. Let your baptism remain as your weaponry, your faith as a helmet, your love as a spear, your endurance as a full set of armour.[30]

It is stirring stuff, made more compelling by his own imminent sacrifice which Ignatius wholeheartedly embraced.

Finally, in an interesting plea, Ignatius the Bishop of Antioch, the successor to the Apostle Peter, on his way to martyrdom in Rome, encourages Polycarp to take up more of a regional influence in the area. Thus, he writes this charge in the closing paragraph in view of recent divisions in Antioch:

> It is fitting O Polycarp, most blessed by God, for you to call a council that is pleasing to God and to elect someone whom you hold most dear and resolved, who can be called the runner of God. Deem this one worthy to go to Syria [Antioch] and glorify your resolute love for the glory of God. A Christian has no authority over himself, but is diligent for God. When you bring it to completion, this work belongs to both God and you. For by grace, I believe that you are prepared to do good deeds that are appropriate to God. Because I know the zeal you have for the truth, I have urged you just through these few words.[31]

There are several things to note here: the encouragement to Polycarp to take on a more regional leadership role; the acknowledgment by Ignatius of Polycarp's instinctive regard for the truth (a very Johannine trait); and the charge that he must not turn his back on this calling. In which case it is no surprise that Polycarp may have appointed an intermediary to be "the runner of God" to the church in Antioch; that he felt able to write a letter of encouragement to the Philippian church (perhaps one of several such letters); and that he went to Rome to strengthen his fellow Syrian, Anicetus, who had become Bishop of Rome (157-68).

Polycarp's letter to the Philippians may well have been an extended correspondence conflated to produce a single manuscript.[32] The Philippian church was the first to be formed in Europe during Paul's second missionary journey (Acts 16:6-40), and, as Polycarp says in his letter nearly a hundred years later (c.140), it "continues to abide and bear fruit in our Lord Jesus Christ".[33] Nevertheless, there were problems: some had been tempted to embezzle money;[34] wives were called to be affectionate towards their husbands;[35] widows "to pray without ceasing for everyone";[36] and deacons were to be blameless.[37] As for sex, they should remember that "neither the sexually immoral, nor the effeminate, nor male prostitutes will inherit the kingdom of God".[38] Alongside this call for righteous living was also one for doctrinal orthodoxy, and particularly the need to eschew the pitfalls of Gnosticism, such as the refusal to "confess that Jesus Christ had come in the flesh".[39] The way to do this, and this was a seminal thought for Irenaeus too, was "to leave behind the idle speculation of the multitudes and false teachings and turn to the word that was delivered to us from the beginning, being alert in prayer and persistent in fasting".[40] Conscious of their spiritual inheritance in the Apostle Paul who founded their church, and in the examples of Ignatius, Zosimius and Rufus, the Philippians are encouraged by Polycarp to endure. If Irenaeus knew this letter, there were principles to follow: reference to the authority of Scripture, emphasis on the Apostolic tradition, and a call for doctrinal orthodoxy, and for exposing Gnostic tendencies alongside true holiness of life.

A further example from Polycarp's ministry that may well have been influential for Irenaeus, was his journey to Rome to confer with his fellow Syrian and Greek speaker, Anicetus, Bishop of Rome from c.157-68. This consultation may well have been about the date of Easter, since the eastern church at Smyrna celebrated Easter on the fourteenth day of Nisan, as Passover, regardless of which day of the week it might fall on, while the Roman church celebrated Easter on the first Sunday following Passover. If this was part of their discussions, surely another part would have been the need to rebut both Marcionism in particular, and Gnosticism in general, to which we will come. It is thought that Polycarp went to Rome a year before his martyrdom in Smyrna on 23 February 157.[41] Marcion had arrived in Rome around 144 and his Gnostic views had become deeply influential. Polycarp and Anicetus must surely have talked about his destabilizing and heretical influence and how best to combat it.

By this time, Polycarp was in his mid-eighties, and despite having been the Bishop of Smyrna for over 40 years (he is addressed as bishop by Ignatius in c.107),[42] in one of their bouts of persecution in the reign of Antoninus Pius (138-61), the predecessor of Marcus Aurelius (161-80), the Roman authorities decided to arrest Polycarp and condemn him to death. The vivid tale of his arrest and martyrdom is told by Eusebius,[43] and is also in *The Apostolic Fathers*.[44] After initially hiding in a house in the countryside, Polycarp was found and arrested.[45] As we have seen, Polycarp refused to disown his faith and blaspheme. Showing extraordinary courage, he was tied to a stake in a pyre which was then set alight. The flames formed a kind of ark around his body not consuming him, whereupon he was pierced and killed by a sword or dagger, but not before offering a prayer of praise and thanksgiving.[46] His martyrdom would be an inspiration to the Christian community for centuries to come.

It is possible that Irenaeus, if not among the crowd in the arena, was in the city that day. As a late teenager or young adult in his early twenties,[47] he found in Polycarp an inspiration for his life and future ministry. Some thirty years later, in 180, Irenaeus recalls the early and abiding influence of Polycarp. Indeed, there has been some scholastic revision of the significance of Polycarp as a theologian in recent years. Previously Polycarp was mainly appreciated as a pastoral bishop and martyr, with his contribution to orthodox theology in rebutting Gnosticism and in particular Marcionism, which rejected the Old Testament, somewhat overlooked. More recently, Charles Hill has made a strong case that Polycarp might have been the author of the *Epistle to Diognetus*.[48] Furthermore, Polycarp had a positive view of the piety of the Old Testament, which provided the groundwork for Irenaeus' hermeneutic of "humanity's growth towards perfection" through the struggles recorded in the Old Testament.[49] Indeed, Irenaeus records Polycarp's rejection of Marcion in *Against Heresies*. Thus, he writes seminally in Book III of his greatest work:

Polycarp was not only instructed by Apostles, and conversed with many who had seen Christ, but was also, by Apostles in Asia, appointed bishop of the church in Smyrna, whom I also saw in my early youth, for he tarried (on earth) a very long time, and, when a very old man, gloriously and most nobly suffered martyrdom, departed this life, having always taught the things which he learned from the Apostles, and which the Church has handed down, and which alone are true. To these things all the Asiatic churches testify, as do also those men who have succeeded Polycarp down to the present time—a man who was of much greater weight, and a more steadfast witness of truth, than Valentinus and Marcion, and the rest of the heretics. He it was who, coming to Rome in the time of Anicetus caused many to turn away from the aforesaid heretics to the Church of God, proclaiming that he had received this one and sole truth from the Apostles—that, namely, which is handed down by the Church. There are also those who heard from him that John, the disciple of the Lord, going to the bath at Ephesus and perceiving Cerinthus (a Gnostic) within, rushed out of the bath-house without bathing, proclaiming, "Let us fly lest even the bath-house fall down, because Cerinthus, the enemy of the truth, is within". And Polycarp himself replied to Marcion, who met him on one occasion, and said, "Dost thou know me?" "I do not know thee, the first-born of Satan." Such was the horror which the Apostles and their disciples had against holding even general communication with any corrupters of the truth; as Paul says, "A man that is an heretic, who after the first and second admonition, reject: knowing that he that is such is subverted, and sinneth, being condemned of himself." There is also a very powerful Epistle of Polycarp written to the Philippians, and those who choose to do so and are anxious about their salvation, can learn the character of his faith, and the preaching of the truth. Then again, the church in Ephesus, founded by Paul, and having John remaining among them permanently until the times of Trajan, is a true witness of the tradition of the Apostles.[50]

There could not be a more important quotation establishing the Apostolic link, so vital to Irenaeus, through Polycarp to the Beloved Disciple, John himself, who may well have had a hand in Polycarp's appointment to Smyrna. The passage makes clear the early influence of Polycarp on Irenaeus, but also that Polycarp was active in advocating Apostolic truth or orthodoxy over against Gnosticism and its main proponents, Marcion and Valentinus. Furthermore, it demonstrates the extreme caution of John, Polycarp and Irenaeus in associating with the Gnostic leaders. The story of John fleeing the baths while Cerinthus was there is taken up by Eusebius in his history of the Church from the Apostles to Constantine.[51]

The other reference tying Irenaeus to Polycarp is Irenaeus' letter to Florinus, which is recorded by Eusebius in his *History of the Church*.[52] Florinus was, or had been, a presbyter in Rome, but had previously grown up with Irenaeus in Smyrna where they were both taught by Polycarp. But Florinus had subsequently become a Gnostic. In his letter, Irenaeus challenges Florinus to give up Gnosticism. By 150, Gnostic influences abounded in Rome, and Florinus had been swayed by their teaching and now held to some bizarre tenets, in particular the notion of the Ogdoad. This was an Egyptian Gnostic notion that four pairs of gods, male and female, existed prior to the material creation and embodied such concepts as darkness, absence, infinity, fertility (female), water and invisibility. As a consequence, Irenaeus writes to his old friend seeking to dissuade him from any association with this Gnostic gobbledygook. He recalls their shared boyhood and their mutual devotion to Polycarp, and more especially to Polycarp's teaching and how he would undoubtedly have reacted to the Gnostic teaching to which Florinus now subscribed. Irenaeus writes in these terms:

> Such notions, Florinus, to put it mildly, do not indicate a sound judgement. Such notions are out of harmony with the Church, and involve those who accept them in beliefs well-nigh blasphemous. Such notions not even the heretics outside the Church have ever dared to propound. Such notions the presbyters of an earlier generation, those taught by the Apostles themselves, did not transmit to you. When I was still a boy, I saw you in Lower Asia in Polycarp's company, when you were cutting

a fine figure at the imperial court and wanted to be in favour with him [Antoninus Pius, AD 138-61]. I have a clearer recollection of events at that time than of recent happenings—what we learn in childhood develops along with the mind and becomes a part of it—so that I can describe the place where the blessed Polycarp sat and talked, his goings out and comings in, the character of his life, his personal appearance, his address to crowded congregations. I remember how he spoke of his intercourse with John (the Apostle) and with others who had seen the Lord; how he repeated their words from memory; and how the things that he had heard them say about the Lord, His miracles and His teaching, things that he had heard direct from eyewitnesses of the Word of Life, were proclaimed by Polycarp in complete harmony with the Scripture. To these things I listened eagerly at that time, by the mercy of God shown to me, not committing them to writing but learning them by heart. By God's grace, I constantly and conscientiously ruminate on them by heart, and I can bear witness before God that if any such suggestion had come to the ears of that blessed and Apostolic presbyter he would have cried out and stopped his ears, exclaiming characteristically: "Dear God, for what times Thou hast preserved me, that I should endure this!" And he would have fled from that very place where he had been sitting or standing when he heard such words. The letters he sent either to the neighbouring churches to stiffen them, or to individual Christians to advise and stimulate them, furnish additional proof of this.[53]

This could not be a more important quotation. Charles Hill suggests from other uses of the Greek word for "boy" that it may well refer to a youth of about 17 years old.[54] It shows that Florinus, who had by now been drawn in by the Gnostic Marcion in Rome, was a little ahead of him, "cutting a fine figure at the imperial court". At the same time, it appears that Florinus had an underlying impressionability which made him vulnerable to Gnosticism. Irenaeus remembers being entranced by Polycarp's recall of the Apostle John's teaching about the ministry and teaching of Jesus. To have someone recalling first-hand the unique experience of being one of the inner group of disciples that followed Jesus, and furthermore that person being the Beloved Disciple, must have been unforgettable. Irenaeus' experience of hearing Polycarp talk about the Apostle John's teaching and his memories of Christ must have been an integral part of his own formation and faith journey. Indeed, Irenaeus says this teaching received from Polycarp was cause for "constant and conscientious rumination". Overall, this excerpt from Irenaeus' letter to Florinus, together with the statement that Irenaeus was delighted by the recounting by Polycarp of "certain matters" in Smyrna,[55] demonstrates the historical roots of his faith. Irenaeus was also no doubt inspired both by the martyrdom of Polycarp and also by his emphasis on following that which was true, a continuous thread in John's writings also.

The early years in Smyrna prepared Irenaeus for his future ministry. He was well educated in the best that classical training could provide, Smyrna being one of the leading university centres in the Eastern Mediterranean. He had been given an example in church leadership second to none. He imbibed with his spiritual milk the Johannine emphasis on the love of truth (2 John 1-2; 1 John 2:20-3; John 1:17; 8:31-2; 14:15-20; 16:13). It was with this training and from these examples that he was ready to take on the noxious substance in the Church that was Gnosticism. Hard to define, let alone pin down, it had grown like ivy around the tree of the Church, threatening to suffocate it in its pervasive and parasitical tendrils. Irenaeus, seeing its danger, sought to understand it as best he could, before writing his major work against it, not in Smyrna, but in the Roman city of Lugdunum to which he went in c.165.

Notes

[1] Philip Mansel, *Levant: Splendour and Catastrophe on the Mediterranean* (London: John Murray, 2010), p. 16.
[2] Bowie, "Literature and Sophistic", p. 899.
[3] See the account of Augustine's schooling in his *Confessions* Bk 1., xiv, tr. Henry Chadwick (Oxford: Oxford University Press, 2008), p. 17.
[4] Robert M. Grant, *Irenaeus of Lyons* (London: Routledge, 1997), p. 41.
[5] Pliny the Elder, *Natural History* 2.14, cited by Grant, *Irenaeus of Lyons*, p. 44.

6. Grant, *Irenaeus of Lyons*, p. 44.
7. Grant, *Irenaeus of Lyons*, p. 29.
8. Irenaeus, *AH*, IV.28.3.
9. Irenaeus, *AH*, IV.26.1.
10. Grant, *Irenaeus of Lyons*, p. 32.
11. *HE* III.1, op. cit., p. 65.
12. *HE* III.23, op. cit., p. 83.
13. *AH* II.33.2.
14. *AH* III.4.
15. *HE* III.24, op. cit., p. 87.
16. *HE* V.24.
17. See Charles H. Hill, "The Man Who Needed No Introduction", in Paul Foster and Sarah Parvis (eds), *Irenaeus: Life, Scripture, Legacy* (Minneapolis, MN: Fortress Press, 2012), pp. 95, 96.
18. Sebastian Moll, "The Man with No Name", in Paul Foster and Sarah Parvis (eds), *Irenaeus: Life, Scripture, Legacy* (Minneapolis, MN: Fortress Press, 2012), p. 89.
19. *The Martyrdom of Polycarp* 9, in *Apostolic Fathers I*, Loeb Classical Library, Vol. 24 (Cambridge, MA: Harvard University Press, 2003), p. 381.
20. *HE* III, op. cit., pp. 97ff.
21. Ignatius, *To the Smyrnaeans* 9.1b, in *Apostolic Fathers I*, Loeb Classical Library, Vol. 24 (Cambridge, MA: Harvard University Press, 2003), p. 305.
22. Ignatius, *To the Smyrnaeans* 7:1,2, op. cit., p. 303.
23. Ignatius, *To the Smyrnaeans* 1:1, op. cit., p. 297.
24. Ignatius, *To the Smyrnaeans* 1:2, p. 297.
25. Ignatius, *Letter to Polycarp*, 1.2, in *Apostolic Fathers I*, Loeb Classical Library, Vol. 24 (Cambridge, MA: Harvard University Press, 2003), p. 311.
26. Ignatius, *Letter to Polycarp* 1.3, op. cit., p. 312.
27. Ignatius, *Letter to Polycarp* 2, op. cit., p. 313.
28. Ignatius, *Letter to Polycarp* 4, p. 315.
29. Ignatius, *Letter to Polycarp* 4, p. 315.
30. Ignatius, *Letter to Polycarp* 6, p. 317.
31. Ignatius, *Letter to Polycarp*, op. cit., p. 319.
32. See Introduction to the Letter, op. cit., pp. 326-8.
33. Ignatius, *Letter to the Philippians* 1.2, in *Apostolic Fathers I*, Loeb Classical Library, Vol. 24 (Cambridge, MA: Harvard University Press, 2003), p. 333.

34 Ignatius, *Letter to the Philippians* §4, op. cit., p. 337.
35 Ignatius, *Letter to the Philippians* §4.2, op. cit., p. 339.
36 Ignatius, *Letter to the Philippians* §4.3, op. cit., p. 339.
37 Ignatius, *Letter to the Philippians* §5.2, op. cit., p. 339.
38 Ignatius, *Letter to the Philippians* §5.3, op. cit., p. 341.
39 Ignatius, *Letter to the Philippians* §7.1, op. cit., p. 343.
40 Ignatius, *Letter to the Philippians* §7.2, op. cit., p. 343.
41 See Charles E. Hill, *From the Lost Teaching of Polycarp* (Tübingen: Mohr Siebeck, 2006), p. 73.
42 *HE* III.36, op. cit., p. 97.
43 *HE* IV.14, op. cit., pp. 116-23.
44 *Apostolic Fathers I*, Loeb Classical Library, Vol. 24 (Cambridge, MA: Harvard University Press, 2003), pp. 367-401.
45 *Epistle of Barnabas* 6,7, op. cit., p. 375.
46 *Epistle of Barnabas* 14, op. cit., p. 387.
47 Hill, *From the Lost Teaching of Polycarp*, p. 74.
48 Hill, *From the Lost Teaching of Polycarp*, pp. 98ff.
49 Hill, *From the Lost Teaching of Polycarp*, pp. 86,87.
50 *AH* III.4.
51 *HE* III.28, op. cit., pp. 91,92.
52 *HE* V.20, op. cit., p. 168.
53 *HE* V.20, op. cit., pp. 168,169.
54 Hill, "The Man Who Needed No Introduction", pp. 100ff.
55 *AH* I.31.1.

4

The Threat of Gnosticism

At some point in his early Christian development, Irenaeus must have recognized the threat to the Church posed by Gnosticism, the definition of which we must return to. As far as we know—and the evidence is sketchy—Irenaeus stayed in Smyrna until the early 160s, when he moved as a missionary presbyter to Lugdunum, having presumably been invited by the church there. He was therefore sent as a kind of missionary presbyter by the church in Smyrna to the Greek-speaking congregation in Gaul. He probably travelled there via Rome, where by 160 the effects of Gnosticism were rife. Irenaeus would then remain in Lugdunum for the rest of his life, apart from at least one further journey to Rome. We do not know when he died, but it is likely to have been in the late 190s.

Whilst in Lugdunum, around 180, he wrote his great work, with its full title being *On the Detection and Refutation of Knowledge Falsely So Called*. The important words here are *detection*, *refutation* and *knowledge* which is *false*. These key words summarize the content of the book, if not doing justice to the positive presentation of Christianity found in the final two parts of the work. The work—which runs into five separate books and covers 400 pages of closely worded argument with numerous Scripture quotations—is written in Greek, although there are surviving manuscripts in Latin and one partial text in Armenian, together with some original Greek fragments. The original work was meant for the whole Church Empire-wide and was directed especially against the Valentinian Gnostics, one branch of this multi-headed heretical hydra.

Against Heresies, to give its common and shortened title, is on the one hand a refutation of false knowledge, in which Irenaeus was well grounded, and on the other hand a fresh iteration of the essence of Christianity in terms both systematic and novel. The fruits of Irenaeus' classical education and his brief apprenticeship to Polycarp can be seen in this seminal piece of writing.

Gnosticism, so called, was based on the Greek noun *gnosis*, meaning knowledge. In some of its aspects, notably the concept of redemption related to Jesus, it approximated to Christianity, itself a newcomer to the religious scene of the ancient world. The other commonly understood religions, by virtue of their age and insight (wisdom) among the ancient Western nations were Greek wisdom, exemplified by Plato and particularly his influential work on the universe, *Timaeus,* and *Phaedo* on the soul; paganism, with its myriad gods arising from Greek and Roman culture and their literatures; Judaism; and other ancient religions of Egypt and the Near East. Apart from Judaism, these other philosophies and religions offered a cosmology that, even if varied, was well entrenched in the culture, onto which the newcomer Christianity was grafted by Gnostic leaders seeking to create a new religion of the marketplace, however esoteric. Gnosticism was, therefore, a syncretistic religious potpourri which reflected the attempt to fuse Christianity with other very different cosmologies from a variety of sources. It was thus by no means a single conception, but rather a collection of thoughts and divinities found in several different localities and crafted into a *smorgasbord* of religious concepts.[1]

There are scholarly arguments about labelling these mystic religions Gnostic in the first place. The word was first applied by the seventeenth-century writer Henry More (1614-87) in his description of all the types of religious doctrines attacked by Irenaeus in *Against Heresies* in the second century.[2] Some scholars would prefer dis-application of the term, and favour the simple expression *mystical religions of the ancient world*, but this is unlikely to take hold,[3] for the term Gnosticism has stuck.

There was no single Gnostic sect, but at least 12 sects who were often in bitter rivalry. What these mystic religions have in common is a dualism separating the spiritual from the material, with priority given to the spiritual, as well as complex creation narratives with numerous emanations of the deity spawned by a supreme god, the Invisible Spirit. This god is himself beyond knowing and his many emanations or *aeons* dwell in a Pleroma or Entirety disconnected from the material universe. The possibility of salvation for humans comes through redemption offered by Christ and through possessing *a secret knowledge* and responding to it in ritual baptism. This secret knowledge involves the use of magic passwords that facilitate the movement of the soul towards the entirety.[4]

In effect, these varieties of mystical knowledge became streams of Gnosticism with differing leaders from the past or the present, such as Simon Magus, his disciple Menander, Marcion, Valentinus, Basilides and Carpocrates, of whom we will hear more.[5] Each relied on particular sources, many of which, rightly or wrongly, came to be termed the Gnostic Gospels. The aim was to generate a spark of knowledge in the hearer (*gnosis*) which would have saving effects; and in that respect, Gnosticism was purported to be a religion of salvation. What Irenaeus set himself to do in *Against Heresies* was to detect and refute this *false knowledge*, whilst at the same time demonstrating the revealed truth of Christianity.

In fact, there were warning signs from Apostolic times, some sixty years before Irenaeus, of the upsurge of a *false knowledge* emanating from both Jewish and Greek sources. The Apostle Paul warns Timothy, at that point a young pastor in Ephesus, not far from Smyrna, saying, "Timothy, guard what has been entrusted to your care. Turn away from godless chatter and the opposing ideas of *what is falsely called knowledge*, which some have professed and in so doing have wandered from the faith" (1 Timothy 6:20-1). The Epistle to the Colossians has more than a hint of Gnostic disturbance of the church there, and of teachers promoting worship of intermediate celestial and angelic powers capable of *giving greater fullness to those who follow an ascetic lifestyle* (Colossians 1:15-23; 2:9-12,16-19). Furthermore, the Apostle John repeatedly underlines in his writings that Jesus really came *in the flesh*. He is saying this to a culture deeply imbued with the Greek philosophical idea that the fleshly, material life is prone to evil influences, and that it cannot possibly mingle with the divine. Hence the Incarnation is impossible, or, if it is possible, Jesus and Christ represent two different parts of a human-divine nexus.

Against this, John pronounces the notion of the divine taking on flesh at the very beginning of his Gospel. Writing in Ephesus in *c*.90, John proclaims that, "*The Word became flesh* and made his dwelling among us" (John 1:14), and in his letter he writes, "This is how you can recognize the Spirit of God: every Spirit that acknowledges that Jesus Christ *has come in the flesh* is from God" (1 John 4:2,3). To deny that Jesus took on truly human flesh is to undermine everything that Jesus came to do and was. This is at the heart of Irenaeus' positive argument in *Against Heresies*.

The roots and myths of Gnosticism

At root, Gnosticism and its main texts are an attempt to explain the origins of the universe and the problem of evil. Much ancient philosophical and religious literature, apart from the purely pagan narratives about the gods, is taken up with these themes. Indeed, the Gnostic myth is "a bold attempt to ... proclaim human salvation through a combination of the Jewish Scriptures, Platonist mythological speculation and (it seems) revelatory meditations on the structure of the human mind".[6] Not only this, but Gnostic writers create a cast of invented make-believe gods or powers (*aeons*) said to rule and interact with humans and the creation at large. This leads to the bestowal of god-names as seemingly complex and comic sounding as Barbēlō (meaning, from an Egyptian context, the Great Emission), Bithyus, and Yaldabaoth. In essence, the Gnostic "system" is a disassociation *between* the great, invisible god who is supreme and unknowable, the sphere of entirety or Pleroma in which intermediate *aeons* of consequence exist, *and* a fallen, evil, material and corporeal world. The salvific or therapeutic purpose is to bring the human as part of this creation into a relationship with the source of its being and "ameliorate its condition of attachment to the body and its passions".[7]

In this sense, Gnosticism borrows from Christianity the notion of redemption offered by Jesus Christ, through which people are delivered from a fleshly, evil, corrupt existence into the life of the Pleroma or Entirety. As Henry Chadwick writes, "The content of the Gnostic Gospel was an attempt to rouse the soul from its sleep-walking condition to make it aware of the high destiny to which it is called."[8] The means by which this connection between humans and the source of their being might be made is through the intellect, which is the faculty necessary for the contemplation of God. In this, both the writers of Gnostic literature and Platonists are more or less at one. In summary, Gnosticism is a combination of myths from Eastern religions, with aspects of Judaism and Platonism bolted onto a Christian notion of a spiritual redemption.

Creation is fallen, and prone to evil because of the way in which it has been created. Sophia or Wisdom is the lowest of the 24 *aeons* which make up the entirety or Pleroma. Wisdom produces a thought of her own without the consent of her male consort, which leads to dissonance and the opportunity for evil. The result of this is an imperfect thought or pseudo-aeon, the first divine being that does not belong to the entirety of immortals. This misguided power, named Yaldabaoth, proceeds to contaminate creation, making it weak and evil. Wisdom's power enters Adam, who is able to stand upright and seek higher principles. However, a female revelatory principle becomes active when Eve is created, and she becomes separate from him. The rulers attempt to rape the spiritually endowed Eve, resulting in the births of Cain and Abel, but a more spiritually enlightened ancestor is created by Adam and Eve in the person of Seth.[9] Gender is an important driving, and at times ambiguous, principle in Gnostic thought. For the most part humanity is dominated by rulers who face them with the temptations of sex, judge them with the catastrophe of the flood, and fascinate them with the possibilities of precious metals. This rather confused context provides the locus of enlightenment.

The ruler-of-all or supreme deity is the Invisible Spirit. The Invisible Spirit is essentially *divine thought*, who devolves his power into a Pleroma or Entirety, a sphere in which the *aeons* exist.[10] The *aeons* are a multifaceted realm of divine qualities, including such concepts as will, thought, life, grace, truth, form, insight, perception, memory and others, numbering 24 in all.[11] Foremost among the *aeons* is the second principle, created by the Invisible Spirit, and described in *The Secret Book of John* as Barbēlō or Forethought,[12] or the Mother–Father.[13] This Barbēlō then becomes the *aeon* from whom Christ is created. Christ, or the Self-Orginate, becomes a kind of pivot between the Invisible Spirit, the Barbēlō, and the other *aeons* in the Pleroma or Entirety.[14] He is the one who can provide *gnosis* (knowledge), and in particular of the four archetypes (like Plato's perfect "forms") that accompany Christ.[15]

What we have thus far are various beliefs which characterize and underpin Gnosticism. The details may vary according to the different types of Gnostic literature, which in turn project differing sects of Gnosticism, but the overarching system is consistent. There is a great unknowable, invisible supreme God. There is a hierarchy of *aeons* of which Barbēlō is the principal being. These *aeons*, which are divine emanations, represent the main ideas of life. The lowest of the *aeons*, Sophia, is involved in the process of creation. A negative and corrupting influence in the person of Barbēlō is responsible for a material world that is damaged and broken. The descendants of Seth, however, have an opportunity for enlightenment, which comes through accepting teaching which once again restores spiritual life from mere material existence. This event finds focus in a ritual baptism which is not Christo-centric or focused on Christ's death and resurrection, but rather one in which knowledge is sealed into a person. Thus, *The Apocalypse of John* states, "I raised and sealed that person, with the light of the water of five seals, so that from henceforth death might not have power over that person."[16] The five seals may be the five steps in baptism, namely enrobing, washing, enthroning, glorying and being caught up to luminous places. Or it might simply mean five ways of being anointed with oil. In any event, it is the moment in the Gnostic's life in which an individual is gathered up through knowledge into the life of the Pleroma, thereby reversing the ill effects of creation. This baptism is "the central and defining moment".[17] And the *gnosis* which the candidate experiences is an acquaintance with God in this mortal life and an ascent, as with Platonism, to higher levels of spiritual existence. Here erotic desire might well be transformed from desire for a beautiful body into desire for a beautiful soul, as was the case in spiritual interpretations of *The Song of Songs* or in the Gnostic book of *Zōstrianos*.

Gnosticism divides humanity in terms of its response to this saving knowledge obtainable through Christ or other forms of knowledge, be they Jewish or Greek, into three categories. There are the *pneumatikoi*, the spiritual ones who fully embrace this salvation by *gnosis*; the *psychikoi*, i.e. those who can attain some kind of salvation through partial knowledge and good works; and the *hylikoi* (who typify only a material or fleshly response) and who have no possibility of redemption. Once again, the basis for salvation seems to have been greatly altered from the teaching of the New Testament (see John 17:3; Ephesians 2:8 and Acts 16:31), making divisions that cannot readily be drawn from its teaching. The *pneumatikoi*, however, adopt a binary response to the corruption of the flesh and material life in general: some choose a deeply ascetic life, turning their back on all activities of the flesh, not least sexual intercourse and procreation (which only sustain corrupt material life), while others see no danger from the flesh, given its inferior status, and incorporate feasting and orgies into their way of life. This binary response to saving knowledge is a characteristic of Gnosticism. Furthermore, others see the Old Testament—its creation narratives and description of violent human life in the nation of Israel—as the work of a separate entity not related to the Father of Christ and therefore turn their back on its history and teaching. This is the principal teaching of Marcion.

These then are some of the common tenets, but to consider Gnosticism in any way a watertight system in which there is more than a basic consistency would be to overstate its integrity. Its texts have a measure of harmony, but they can be known as much for their dissimilarities. What binds them together is the attempt to deal with the existence of evil in the created order, a doctrine in which the Invisible Spirit is at odds with the creation and disassociated from it, in which matter is regarded as malevolent, and salvation is experienced in a moment of enlightenment or gnosis unrelated to forgiveness emanating from the Cross and the Incarnation of Christ in real flesh and blood. These are the basic features of Gnosticism and the heart of the divergence from orthodox Christianity.

The varieties of Gnostic texts

Studies in Gnosticism were given enormous stimulus by the discovery of many manuscripts close to the Nile at Nag Hammadi in Egypt. Indeed, the discovery of a cache of Gnostic Gospels and other writings in 1945 did for Gnostic studies what the discovery of the Dead Sea Scrolls at Qumran in 1946 did for the study of the Jewish Scriptures. The cache was found at the bottom of a majestic cliff, the Jabal al-Tarif, which was in turn a few kilometres from Nag Hammadi on the Nile and near the sites of two Pachomian monasteries.[18] Clearly there had been Christians nearby, and it may have been monks or virgins who hid these manuscripts in leather pouches in a stone jar beneath a large boulder,[19] where they rested for nearly two millennia.

The discovery galvanized interest and understanding. The Nag Hammadi find included nearly fifty texts written in the Coptic or ancient Egyptian language, still used in Coptic worship and liturgy, but not spoken. Other discoveries, such as the Berlin Gnostic Code, the Codex Tachis and other fragments were discovered in a garbage tip in the city of Oxyrhynchos. A fourth-century text records the intense monastic activity in the city of Oxyrhynchos in the Thebaid, somewhat downstream from Nag Hammadi, and close to Luxor. In one such text a pilgrim records:

> We also visited Oxyrhynchos, a city in the Thebaid, whose wonders beggar description. So full is it of monasteries inside that the monks themselves make the walls resound, and it is surrounded outside by other monasteries, so that there is another city outside the city.... There are twelve churches in it, since the city is very large.... There was no hour by day or by night in which they did not carry on divine service; indeed, there was no heretic or pagan inhabitant in the city, all the citizens alike were faithful and under religious instruction, so that the bishop was able to give the kiss of peace in the main square... Who could state the number of monks and virgins, which was immemorable.[20]

Although there is more than a touch of hyperbole about this description with its estimation of 10,000 monks and 20,000 virgins, there was nonetheless a considerable monastic presence. Admittedly, this account is from the late fourth century, but the roots of the movement might well have been in the late second century.

The almost fifty Nag Hammadi texts give a good idea of the range of Gnostic literature. Produced mostly in the second century but used thereafter in succeeding centuries by the church in that area, they are written in Coptic for the most part, although no doubt translated into

Greek for further circulation. Some are heavily laden with the Gnostic myth. Others are either contemplations or embellishments of the Gospel narratives used in worship or instruction. *The Prayer of the Apostle Paul* at one end of the spectrum has just faint traces of Gnosticism, such as the use of the word fullness or Pleroma, while others, such as *The Secret Book of John*, are more full-blooded in their Gnostic understanding.

The Prayer of the Apostle Paul, written on the front flyleaf of the Nag Hammadi Codex I, appears to be a kind of introduction to the other texts in the form of a contemplative prayer. It begins:

> Grant me your (mercy), (my) Redeemer, redeem me, for I am yours: I have come from (you). You are (my) mind bring me forth. You are my treasury: open for me. You are My fullness (Pleroma): accept me. You are my rest: give me incomprehensible perfection. I call upon you, you who existed and pre-existed, in the name exalted above every name (Philippians 2.9), through Jesus Christ, (Lord) of Lords, King of eternal realms. Give me your gifts, with no regret, through the Son of Humanity (or Son of Man), the Spirit, the Advocate of (truth). Give me authority, (I) ask of you, give (healing) for my body, since I ask you through the preacher of the gospel, and redeem my eternal enlightened soul and my spirit, and disclose to my mind the first-born of the fullness of grace.[21]

While the *Prayer of the Apostle Paul*, purporting to be Apostolic, although most certainly not written by Paul himself, has nuances of Gnosticism mixed with biblical material and a sense of the doctrine of the Trinity, other Gnostic texts in the Nag Hammadi cache are much more prescriptive.

Such a one is the *Tripartite Tractate*, a title given by modern scholars to a text which originally had none ascribed. The work follows many of the tenets of Valentinian Gnosticism: an unknowable Father or Infinite Spirit; emanations of the *aeons* from his seed which seek his power and presence; and a Spirit which pervades the Pleroma or Entirety and keeps harmony.[22] In this work, the Church is seen to correspond to the Pleroma as a congregation of *aeons* which in God's mind predated the creation of the evil world and is part of the story of the fallen *aeon*.[23] The Logos or fallen *aeon* experiences passion, from which comes a multitude of rebellious powers, especially the powers of materiality. However, the Logos then repents and asks for help, whereupon the *aeons* collectively send the Son-Saviour, who comes to manifest the totality or Pleroma on earth and save those who are enlightened. There is much attention given in this text to psychical humans activated by a redeemer, in turn sent by the Logos and the demiurge ruler, who have the capacity to recognize the Saviour and escape mortal existence.[24] The Logos then experiences a further emotion of joy and the Church becomes the image of the Pleroma, for which end it was destined.

A further text, *The Treatise on Resurrection*, probably written in the second half of the second century, might have been authored by Valentinus, while the recipient is one Rheginus.[25] The content of this text is distinctly Valentinian, but nevertheless diverges from some of the main precepts of that particular Gnostic myth,[26] further demonstrating the loose way in which most Gnostic teaching was communicated and meriting the title of a "ragbag".[27] In this text, the Invisible Supreme God is termed the Father. Christ is acknowledged as the Son of Humanity who came from above, "a seed of truth" who "swallowed death" and "laid aside the perishable world and exchanged it for an incorruptible eternal realm".[28] Those who respond will be saved, and their thoughts and minds will be taken into the Pleroma or Fullness. The body, however, will not be saved; only thought and the mind will continue.[29] The text affirms the resurrection, concluding, "it is more appropriate to say that the world is an illusion rather than the resurrection that came into being through our lord Jesus Christ".[30] What is clear in all this is the Gnostic aversion to the body, to material creation, and their rejection of the notion that it would have any part in the future, or in their terms, the Pleroma.

Finally, there are two texts which bring us closer to the life of Jesus but remain within the overall Gnostic framework. They are *The Secret Book of John* and *The Gospel of Thomas*. *The Secret Book of John* is the most widely known of the so-called Sethian tracts, i.e., those texts which identify the third child of Adam as the one who carries forward the spark of enlightenment and which most probably comes from Gnostic groups in Egypt. The basis of *The Secret Book of John* is teaching supposedly given by the post-resurrection Jesus to the Apostle John.[31] Jesus is described as a mother-father figure who has already raised up the seed of Seth to the Father's many-roomed house (i.e., the Pleroma, which includes the four eternal *aeons* prepared before the creation of the world). The *parousia* is expected shortly. Further teaching is given by the Saviour Jesus about the One or the Invisible Spirit. The One (a Platonic title), is described apophatically as, "illimitable, unfathomable, immeasurable and invisible".[32] He is superior to the *aeons* and full of majesty and purity. Barbēlō is the first emanation from this Invisible Spirit, and is described as feminine and as the Forethought of All: "Her light shines like the Father's light; she the perfect power, is the image of the Perfect and Invisible Virgin Spirit."[33] Often Barbēlō is described in Gnostic texts and by Irenaeus as the mother-father principle: one stage removed from the Great Invisible Spirit. Barbēlō resides among the *aeons*, one of whom, Sophia, has rebelled against the Invisible Spirit and gives birth to Yaldabaoth, who in turn gives birth to a plethora of fallen powers.[34] Later Sophia repents and is restored to the *aeons*.

From Yaldabaoth a fallen creation is formed and a fallen humanity created, beginning with Adam and Eve.[35] Marriage is instituted between Adam and Eve, but Yaldabaoth defiles Eve and Yahweh and Elohim are born. The Saviour is sent into this *mêlée* to bring redemption to those who respond. He says to John, "I entered the midst of darkness and the bowels of the underworld, turning to my task. The foundations of chaos shook as though to fall upon those who dwell in chaos and destroy them. Again, I hurried back to the root of my light so they might not be destroyed before time."[36] All this is given to John by the resurrected Jesus to pass on to the disciples that they might understand and respond. But what we have in essence is Gnostic myths and cosmology into which Jesus has been inserted. They are seemingly bizarre and far-fetched, but nonetheless these ideas had made considerable inroads into the Church by 150.

Finally, in our pick of the Gnostic texts found in the Nag Hammadi cache and displayed in the Coptic Museum in Old Cairo is *The Gospel of Thomas*. There are two extant manuscripts, or part manuscripts, for this text. A fragment in Greek is dated from the second century, while the Nag Hammadi text is from the fourth century, as indeed are many others.[37] Further Greek copies have also surfaced in the British Library and the Bodleian. Some scholars suggest the Greek texts were part of the source Q (from the German word *Quelle* for source), one of the main sources for the New Testament, but this is as yet unproven. The text is ascribed to the disciple who doubted the resurrection until confronted by Jesus directly in the upper room (John 20:24-9), and who, having been convinced, took the gospel to India, founding Mar Thoma, the Syrian Church of South India.

Unlike *The Secret Book of John*, Thomas' is "a sayings Gospel". In other words, it is a list of sayings in the tradition of the book of Proverbs in the Old Testament, except taught by Jesus and recorded, it claims, by Thomas. Almost all of the sayings are given by Jesus, and several are close verbatim repetitions of the Gospel. So, for instance, the ninetieth saying is "Come to me, for my yoke is easy and my mastery is gentle and you will find rest for yourselves", which closely resembles, even if it is not quite identical to, Matthew 11:28-30. Given this format, and as one would expect, the text does not have all the Gnostic cosmology which is so strongly present in *The Secret Book of John* and *The Tripartite Tractate*. What we can deduce from the presence of this book in this cache of literature, which is mostly described as Gnostic, is that monastic communities in that area were nourished by a combination of Scripture, strongly Gnostic writings, and some texts which were not canonical (i.e., not incorporated into the writings of the New Testament), but that were related to those canonical Scriptures, and used in either worship or teaching or both. The presence of *The Gospel of Thomas* illustrates the range of what is generally called Gnostic teaching. The truth is that, quite understandably, some texts are more Gnostic than others, but they all exist within a framework of acceptance of a large amount of the Gnostic system, a system that undermines the simplicity, power and truth of the gospel. And it was to uphold this simplicity and the Apostolic teaching about the redemption found in Christ, making man or woman fully human, that Irenaeus wrote his great work, *Against Heresies*.

The response of Irenaeus to Gnosticism

As far as Irenaeus was concerned, the Gnosticism of which he was most aware, and which he had taken the trouble to study, was first found in Egypt and taught in the school of Ptolemy, itself a "spin off of the highly influential system of Valentinian Gnosticism as described in *Against Heresies*".[38] It therefore seems clear that the ideas from the twelve or more rival sects which could broadly be described as Gnostic, and with which Irenaeus was most familiar, was this Valentinian system, closely followed by the teaching of Marcion.

The Valentinian system, as we have discovered, revolves around the existence of 30 *aeons* beneath the unknowable Great Invisible Spirit, which are separate cosmic entities and exist in quasi-sexual pairs descending in hierarchal order from the topmost entity, called Bythos (depth or abyss) until they reach Sophia (wisdom), from whom creation comes about through the disruptive and corrupting influence of Yaldabaoth. Escape back into the Pleroma, and into a truly spiritual existence no longer imprisoned by the body and the evil material world, can only come about through an epiphany of knowledge or at least through the release of trapped knowledge inside a person. This is enabled through baptism and thereafter by eschewing a flesh-driven existence. As we will see, when we come to evaluate Irenaeus' great work *Against Heresies*, he uses a combination of Scripture, philosophical reasoning, sarcasm and telling irony to show the emptiness of what the Gnostics propose.

The other Gnostic system with which Irenaeus was familiar was that of Marcion (although some scholars dispute that Marcion is really Gnostic).[39] It is a simpler system and less devoted to esoteric cosmology, but still destructive of true Apostolic faith. Marcion's thesis is that the Old and New Testaments come from different sources, different gods. The Old Testament god is a corrupt demiurge who creates a fallen world and humankind, and is also responsible for the corrupt god of the Hebrews. Jesus, by contrast, is the representative of the true supreme being who comes to bring salvation through redemption. Marcion thus deems the Old Testament and sections of the New Testament corrupt. His canon only includes a shortened version of Luke's Gospel and ten Pauline Epistles. The rest of the New Testament he discounts. Once again

Irenaeus has his work cut out to refute these theories which had, as we shall see, gained considerable traction in Rome.

When Irenaeus' refutation came, it needed to include a welter of Christian rebuttal of Gnosticism and a redefining of the essence of Christianity, no less. He had to make the case that the supreme Invisible God was the same as the creator of the universe and humankind, and that there was no dissonance between the two. He had to make the case for creation as originally good, and only subject to futility because of the inroads of human sin or self-will and the malevolence of the Devil. He had to make the case that the material and the corporeal world were not inferior to the spiritual or to the soul, but were one and the same creation, each needing the other. He had to make the case that Jesus really came in flesh or in a human body through the womb of Mary, and not in a make-believe humanity. He had to make the case that Jesus came as the eternal Son of God, to redeem and recapitulate humankind. He had to make the case that only what the Apostles and their legitimate successors taught was true, and the Church, properly formed, was the ark of salvation. He had to make the case that the Spirit guided the writing of canonical Scriptures, which in turn guided the Church. He had to make the case that the Old and New Testament were from the same divine source, not at variance with each other, but part of a single programme of revelation. He had to make the case that God would bring all things to completion, rewarding true faith and judging evil. He had to make the case that *humanity-redeemed* would reveal the glory of God. It was a lot to combine and deal with in a single work.

This was no small task, but in *c.*160, when Irenaeus moved from Smyrna to Lugdunum, and quite possibly via a religiously febrile Rome, the need for such a case was becoming daily more obvious. The church in Rome in 160 was fragmented and vulnerable. It needed to be called back to its vocation, and it needed a substantial rebuttal of false teaching and a restatement of true Christianity. A hundred years after the faith had been elaborated by the magisterial Epistle to the Romans (57), there needed to be refutation of false knowledge and a restatement of true knowledge. To understand the need for this work, we must grasp the fragmentation that had occurred in Rome as well as the danger that Gnosticism, however far-fetched in ideas, posed.

Notes

1. Chadwick, *The Early Church*, pp. 33ff.
2. David Brakke, *The Gnostics* (Cambridge, MA: Harvard University Press, 2021), p. 19.
3. Brakke, *Gnostics*, p. 19, 27.
4. Chadwick, *The Early Church*, p. 36.
5. *AH* IV.6.4, op. cit., p. 270.
6. Brakke, *Gnostics*, p. 52.
7. Brakke, *Gnostics*, p. 53.
8. Chadwick, *The Early Church*, p. 35.
9. Brakke, *Gnostics*, p. 66.
10. *The Secret Book of John*, in *The Nag Hammadi Scriptures*, ed. Marvin Meyer (San Francisco, CA: HarperOne, 2007), p. 111.
11. *The Secret Book of John*, p. 113.
12. *The Secret Book of John*, p. 110.
13. Brakke, *Gnostics*, p. 57.
14. Brakke, *Gnostics*, p. 55.
15. Brakke, *Gnostics*, pp. 56, 57.
16. *Apocalypse of John* 31:3-25, cited by Brakke, *Gnostics*, p. 74.
17. Brakke, *Gnostics*, p. 77.
18. Meyer, *The Nag Hammadi Scriptures*, p. 2.
19. Meyer, *The Nag Hammadi Scriptures*, p. 3.
20. *Historia Monachorum in Aegypto* 5, cited by Peter Parsons, *City of the Sharp-nosed Fish* (London: Weidenfeld & Nicolson, 2007), p. 193.
21. Meyer, *The Nag Hammadi Scriptures*, pp. 17,18.
22. Meyer, *The Nag Hammadi Scriptures*, p. 71.
23. Meyer, *The Nag Hammadi Scriptures*, p. 59.
24. Meyer, *The Nag Hammadi Scriptures*, p. 60.
25. Meyer, *The Nag Hammadi Scriptures*, p. 51.
26. Meyer, *The Nag Hammadi Scriptures*, p. 57.
27. Chadwick, *The Early Church*, pp. 33ff.
28. Meyer, *The Nag Hammadi Scriptures*, pp. 52-3.
29. Meyer, *The Nag Hammadi Scriptures*, pp. 52-4.
30. Meyer, *The Nag Hammadi Scriptures*, pp. 52-4.

31   John Turner, "Introduction", *The Secret Book of John*, in Meyer, *The Nag Hammadi Scriptures*, p. 104.
32   Meyer, *The Nag Hammadi Scriptures*, p. 108.
33   Meyer, *The Nag Hammadi Scriptures*, p. 108.
34   *Yaldabaoth's World Order*, in Meyer, *The Nag Hammadi Scriptures*, p. 115.
35   *The Creation of Adam*, in Meyer, *The Nag Hammadi Scriptures*, p. 119.
36   Meyer, *The Nag Hammadi Scriptures*, p. 131.
37   Meyer, *The Nag Hammadi Scriptures*, p. 136.
38   *AH* I.8.5 cited in Paul Foster and Sarah Parvis (eds), *Irenaeus: Life, Scripture, Legacy* (Minneapolis, MN: Fortress Press, 2012), p. 17.
39   Timothy Barnes, *Tertullian* (Oxford: Oxford University Press, 1985).

5

Division in Rome

When Irenaeus travelled to Rome *en route* to Lugdunum from Smyrna in *c*.160, it is very likely he went by ship, in which case he was following in the footsteps of the Apostle Paul, travelling from Asia to Rome, and Polycarp. After his lengthy stay in Caesarea, where he was tried by any number of rulers (see Acts 24-26), Paul went by ship to Puteoli (Acts 28:13), close to Herculaneum, which would be destroyed in the eruption of Vesuvius in 79 some seventeen years later. Normally a sea voyage would be preferable to a land journey, but in Paul's case there was a violent storm and shipwreck (Acts 27, 28).

Although there is no written evidence, it is likely that Irenaeus took ship from Smyrna to Ostia, the port of Rome, and broke his journey in the imperial city before continuing on a different ship to Marseille, and then up the Rhône to Lugdunum. This stopover would have given him the opportunity of conferring with church leaders in Rome, and also allow him to gauge the depth of the Gnostic threat to the church there, especially since, while in Lugdunum, he would write his great work, *Against Heresies*, no doubt stimulated by the rifts, divisions and false teaching that he had heard of in Rome itself.

It was now a hundred years since Paul's arrival in the city of Rome, where he had been held initially under house arrest (Acts 28:16,30), and where he would later be tried, imprisoned and executed (2 Timothy 4:6-8). Much had happened to the church there since then. Indeed, the trajectory of the church was greatly influenced by the characteristics of Rome itself, a city of over a million—more than twice the size of its nearest rivals: Alexandria, Antioch and Carthage. Moreover, Constantinople, New Rome, would not be founded as an imperial city for nearly 200 years. In Rome, many new buildings had come and gone. The Great

Fire of July 64 had led to the destruction of much of the city. Of the 14 neighbourhoods or districts, three were left completely devastated, and a further ten substantially destroyed. This led to a considerable rebuild firstly by Nero and then by the Flavians. The effect on Christian communities, by then meeting in the city, must have been severely disruptive, since they gathered in some of the worst-affected locations.

This dislocation, together with the growing spread of Christian communities in the city, meant the church in Rome was disparate from the start. Our best guide to its composition is Paul's great letter to the Romans, with its greetings to different households and individuals in the final chapter, which some have deemed the most interesting chapter in the letter. The greetings in Romans 16 indicate that five separate church gatherings or communities were known to him around AD 60: a group gathered in the household of Priscilla and Aquila (v. 3); another in the house of Aristobulus (v. 10); another in the household of Narcissus (v. 11) including quite possibly freed slaves; another in the household of Asyncritus and others (v. 14); and another gathered in the household of Philologus (v. 15). And if the remaining 14 people listed by Paul—some of whom were well known to him—were in at least one more church, it means that there could have been seven or more different church communities spread around the re-emerging city by the end of Paul's life.[1] Furthermore, we know from much later sources in the fifth century that there were churches or congregations meeting in the 25 *tituli* of Rome, and this must have been around the time that the city was sacked by the Goths in 410. (The word *tituli* refers to named hosts of each church gathering, such as Titulus Philologus.) Some scholars believe that 20 of these *tituli* churches existed before the reign of Constantine.[2] Cornelius records that by the middle of the third century, there were 46 presbyters in Rome, and if on average two or three of these worked in one parish or *tituli*, it means that by the third century, there were some 15 to 23 congregations throughout Rome.[3] Cornelius also notes that there were 17 doorkeepers, which probably corresponds with the number of churches then.[4] These numbers are significant as they show that, despite persecution, the Church was growing over these early centuries. However, they also show that, if widely spread over the city with only a loose overall connection, communities of Christians would have potentially been much more open to infiltration with erroneous teaching or practice.

These various congregations which existed in Rome by the end of the second century, and so towards the end of Irenaeus' life, were found, as you would expect, in a range of settings. It is clear from Paul's Letter to the Romans, which treats the relationship of the law to the gospel (especially in Chapters 3-8), and the destiny of Israel in Chapters 9-11, that the church in Rome was a very mixed Gentile and Jewish community, and that the possibility of separation between the two was very real. Paul therefore addresses the issue that the gospel does what the law on its own can never do (Romans 3:20 and 8:3): it gives to the faithful believer a righteousness which the law hints at but can never deliver (Romans 3:21ff.). In other words, faith in Jesus the crucified and risen Messiah creates a new human being: forgiven and reconciled to God filled with hope and the gift of the Spirit (Romans 5:1-11). Once again, the gospel does what the law can never do (see Romans 1:16,17).

With so much emphasis on this foundational teaching—informed by the nature of the church in Rome in the second half of the first century—it is no surprise to hear that with a strong mixture of Jew and Gentile, the church was closely connected to the synagogue and that this association sometimes even spilled over into violence between the two communities. This is what happened when Emperor Claudius banished all the Jews and Christians from Rome in c.49 because of one "Chrestus".[5] Hence there were Christians who were Jewish and there were other Christians who were drawn from the "god fearers", those who had foresworn paganism and were seeking God on the fringes of the synagogue. They were called *sebomenoi* (literally fearers of heaven) and are best described "as pagans favouring Jewish monotheism".[6] On the whole these *sebomenoi* were from the better-off classes, some even being of the *equites* class (or knights), that is, a class just beneath the elite senatorial or patrician class, but above the plebeian tradespeople and slaves. The fact was, as the content of the *Shepherd of Hermas c.*95 shows, there was great diversity in the Church: some elite, some poor, some slaves, influential women and widows.[7] Where were these different worshipping communities to be found?

Studies have shown the vicinities in which these congregations were to be found in contemporary Rome. Rome was divided into *vici*, which literally means a small city district. and was an administrative unit governed by four *vici* magistrates and served by four public servants.[8] These areas were defined by a certain number of inhabitants. There were 14 regions, and of these the most crowded was Trastevere on the west side of the Tiber. Each of the 14 regions of the city was classified in terms of the number of homes (*domus*), the number of rental apartments or other dwellings (*insulae*), and the number of districts. In Trastevere, there were 150 homes and 4,405 rented dwellings, by far the largest of all the 14 regions.[9] And it was here that there was the greatest number of churches. Trastevere was also the area where the largest number of Jews were located and where the immigrant population from the eastern part of the Empire could be found.[10] Soon after Irenaeus' time in the reign of Caracalla (198-217), Christians would be found in the region along the Appian Way south of the main city, where the thermal baths of Caracalla would become the largest bathing facility in Rome for ordinary people. Here they would worship in the tombs of Pope Callixtus, for in the third-century persecutions, Christianity literally went underground in the catacombs. Much later, in the late fourth century, churches would be found in the Aventine region (Region XII), where many elite families could be found. Here churches with some very rich female members who were friends of Jerome (*c*.347-420) existed. The women who lived in this upmarket district, where the very first convent was set up in the city, included Albina and Marcella.[11] However, for the present, in the years close to Irenaeus, most of the churches (by which we mean household churches adopted by a particular leader or *tituli*) were in the poorest area of Rome in Trastevere, with perhaps a few in neighbouring Mars Field (Region IX), and along roads like the Via Appia, where catacombs would be found under S. Sebastiano and S. Callisto.[12]

To summarize, the church in Rome was clustered around 15 to 23 communities in the time of Irenaeus' projected first visit there in 160 on his way to Lugdunum. These communities were sponsored by an individual who gave his name to the meeting, literally placed over the door of his house (*domus*). They were thus household (*oikos*) communities, meeting at the invitation of the host.[13] Some of these communities would have been spun off from nearby synagogues and would have consisted of a number of Jews or God-fearers or *sebomenoi*. At times, conflict arose between Jewish and Gentile communities, to the point where the emperor himself banished both from the city, as Claudius had done in *c.*49, with Priscilla and Aquila arriving in Corinth as a consequence (Acts 18:2). Much of the content of Paul's Letter to the Romans was designed to facilitate harmony between the Jewish and Gentile parts of the church and was written especially with that in mind. Several members of the church in Rome were relatives of Paul (see 16:7,11). The church at first appeared to comprise a mixture of tradespeople like Aquila and Priscilla, freedmen and women, slaves and some homeowners, but by the third century, increasing numbers of the better-off and those in the higher social classes—the *decurions* and the *equites* and their well-born wives and daughters—belonged. And as this happened, so churches moved to the better-off areas like the Aventine in the late fourth century. Communities also clustered around the catacombs or burial grounds along the Appian Way. Such was the social, ecclesial and ethnic context of the church in Rome, formed like most churches in a structure which included an overseer or bishop, presbyters, deacons, sub-deacons, exorcists, readers, door keepers and, by the middle of the third century, the responsibility for "fifteen hundred widows and distressed persons".[14]

The church in Rome was most probably a loosely connected group of churches, meeting in predominantly poorer parts of the city but linked by a tenuous association with a presiding bishop who was only partially recognized. However, there was a discernible trend in the second half of the second century towards greater episcopal control and oversight, not least because of the winds of false teaching that were blowing through the churches in Rome, especially from Gnosticism. In fact, there is little evidence of overall episcopal oversight in Rome at the turn of the first century. When, at the beginning of the second century in the reign of Trajan, Ignatius wrote to the Roman church not to stand in the way of his martyrdom there, he said, "I am writing [to] all the churches and giving instruction to all, that I am willingly dying for God, unless you hinder me. I urge you, do not become an untimely kindness to me. Allow me to be bread for the wild beasts; through them I am able to attain God."[15] Surprisingly, given that Ignatius addressed bishops personally elsewhere in his correspondence and not least in Smyrna, there is no mention of a presiding bishop in Rome. And likewise, there is only the sketchiest knowledge of bishops in the first century, or about the author of I Clement, a letter written to the feuding church at Corinth, but only in the name of the church in Rome, and not in the name of the bishop.[16] Irenaeus himself seems confident, however, that this letter was written by Clement, who was the third bishop of Rome following the apostles Linus[17] and Anicetus. Linus is apparently the person mentioned in Paul's Second Letter to Timothy (4:21).

What we may say is that in the first century and in the early part of the second century, there was limited episcopal oversight in Rome, and that it would become stronger in the late second century, in part to combat the various false teachings that had come to the city. It is possible that at the outset authority in the church in Rome resided with a group of presbyters, but that this proved inadequate in the face of persistent false teaching. Episcopal rule began to strengthen in the middle of the second century, during the episcopacies of Anicetus (*c.*155-66), Soter (166-75), Eleutherius (*c.*175-89) and especially under Victor (*c.*189-99).[18]

The attraction of Rome

If we are right in thinking that Irenaeus came to Rome on his way to Lugdunum in *c.*160, he would have had ample reason to be provoked by what he discovered and experienced there, and to channel that provocation into *Against Heresies* once he arrived in Gaul. And this would have been even more the case if he found in Gaul or Lugdunum the same Gnosticism circulating there as in Rome. Because the churches in Rome were a loose collection of communities with many influences, often meeting in the poorer parts of the city, and also without a strong episcopal centre or oversight, they were peculiarly susceptible to incoming immigrant teachers, some with money. Rome attracted such people. It was the centre of the Western world. It was probably the largest city on earth at the time. If you wanted to gain traction for ideas or promulgate them, then Rome was the ultimate place to gain an audience and a following—even if you had to pay for the attempt with your life. In the first part of the second century, there were three main figures who came thus to Rome: two were leading and influential Gnostics and the third was a talented Christian philosopher who would gain a martyr's crown. There were other voices and figures circulating in Christian circles with unsettling ideas by the early third century, not least about the Trinity, but the main three then were Valentinus, Marcion and, as he would be known, Justin Martyr.

Although we cannot be certain of dates in this rather shadowy post-Apostolic era, it is thought that Valentinus taught in Rome from the late 130s to the mid-160s.[19] He had received an education in Alexandria and was part of the early Christian community there, following one Theudas who had Gnostic tendencies. Theudas in turn had been a follower of the Apostle Paul. Some of Valentinus' writing had been collected by Clement of Alexandria, adding plausibility to the argument that he spent his early life there. Valentinus had then come to Rome seeking advancement both for himself and for his ideas. In Rome, he swiftly emerged as a prominent Christian spokesman; indeed, he even sought to become Bishop of Rome and only narrowly failed in his bid to be elected.

In *Orthodoxy and Heresy in Earliest Christianity*, a classic work on early Christianity, Walter Bauer posits the idea of there being "a Great Church" in line with the teaching of the Apostles Peter and Paul, and suggests this was most probably the church Valentinus hoped to lead as bishop before being narrowly defeated.[20] Nevertheless, Valentinus seems to have remained in Rome in the hope of giving his beliefs greater traction, until vanishing into the mists of history. If Irenaeus really did visit Rome on his way to Lugdunum, he would have found a church (whether the Great Church itself or other home churches in Trastevere) deeply affected by Valentinian teaching and the near miss of having him as bishop. Eusebius tells us that in the early years of Emperor Antoninus Pius (138-61) and while Hyginus was bishop (c.138-42), "Valentinus, who introduced a heresy of his own, and Cerdo (another Gnostic) who was responsible for the Marcionite error were both prominent in Rome". Eusebius says that "Irenaeus most effectively exposes the limitless depths of Valentinus' most erroneous system, and brings his wickedness, hidden out of sight like a reptile lurking in a hole, to the light of day".[21] It is a graphic image full of sinister jeopardy.

So, what was it that Valentinus taught that was so beguiling to much of the Christian community in Rome? It was a heady Gnostic cosmology, a reinterpretation of spiritual knowledge and reality from the perspective of both the Gospels and Pauline teaching, with appealing esoteric liturgies of baptism, along with some sexual innuendo.

The cosmology Valentinus espoused was much like other Gnostic approaches and similar to the *Tripartite Tractate* found among the cache of Gnostic literature at Nag Hammadi.[22] Equally, Valentinus may have been closely associated with *The Gospel of Truth*.[23] Indeed, in *Against Heresies*, Irenaeus directly associates Valentinus with this work.[24] While the *Tripartite Tractate* gives us the broad cosmology, *The Gospel of Truth* has a greater focus on the Gnostic Jesus. It is probable that, along with other Gnostic thinkers, Valentinus in general taught an ultimate, unknowable God or Father. He is singular (not Trinitarian), incomparable, immutable, unchangeable and eternal.[25] Below him is a state of entirety or Pleroma in which *aeons* exist which lay between the Father and the fallen material creation.[26] These *aeons* or emanations are from the Father, but the last, Sophia, turns away from or rebels against this "mother" of creation. Thus, the material world, which is fallen and evil, is born. Valentinus also subscribes to the idea of Yaldabaoth, who now oversees the world in its error and ignorance.

This is the cosmological context from which the origin of evil is explained and from which only *gnosis* or revealed knowledge can save a person mired in materiality. Thus, the idea of being saved or delivered through revelation, and in particular through Jesus, who is able to reveal the sweetness of the Father, is central to Gnostic thought, but the redemption Jesus offers is linked to occultist ceremonies in which this knowledge is imparted. The "believer" then moves from a category of being a mere bodily person (*soma*) to a person of the soul (*psyche*), before finally belonging to the truly elect (*pneuma*). If Valentinus did not himself teach this categorization, his pupil Ptolemaeus certainly did.[27] The ceremony of baptism was couched in mystery and visually impressive, intended to appeal especially to women because of its seeming seriousness and use of colour and fragrance. Eusebius records one such baptism in the following way: "Some of them fit out a bridal chamber, and celebrate a mystery with invocations on those being initiated, declaring that what they are doing is a spiritual marriage on the pattern of the unions above (in the Pleroma)."[28] And as if to corroborate this rather exotic and persuasive ceremony, an inscription with some missing words was found near graves close by the Via Latina, which reads suggestively:

> Longing for the fatherly light, O sister bride, my Sophie,
> In the ablutions of Christ anointed with imperishable holy balsam
> You have hastened to gaze upon the divine countenances of the *aeons*,
> Upon the great angel of the great counsel, the true Son,
> You have gone to the bridal chamber and ascended to
> The ... Fatherly ... And
>
> This deceased did not have a usual ending of life;
> She died away and lives and sees a truly imperishable light.
> She lives to the delight of the living, is really dead to the dead.
> O earth, why are you astonished about this type of corpse?
>
> Are you terrified?[29]

There is no doubt that Valentinus had a following. He was an erudite and persuasive speaker. He almost became a principal leader and nearly the Bishop of Rome. But he was not the only one in this period to be a siren voice leading the flock astray. There was Marcion as well.

Marcion (*c*.85-160) came to Rome somewhat earlier than Valentinus. He was a shipbuilder (*naukleros*) from Sinope in Pontus on the Black Sea. As a businessman, an entrepreneur, and something of a self-taught theologian with a practical bent, he was not so well educated, at least in ideas, as Valentinus. Being by trade a man who built seaworthy ships, by instinct he sought a plausible, "rationalist" faith tethered to the nostrums of the broadest and least doctrinaire Gnostic cosmology and the freedom to jettison (throw overboard!) anything that was difficult and not in keeping with the Kingdom of the loving shepherd of the New Testament.

Marcion certainly made waves in Rome.[30] Arriving with money, he promptly gave 200,000 sesterces to a church whose members accepted him as a teacher. This sum was enough to buy a house in Rome and turn its recipient into a comfortable middle-class householder (*domus*). Yet Marcion's acceptance by the church was not long-lasting, and by 144 he was leading his own independent church, having had his money returned.³¹ Nevertheless, his ideas spread quickly, as far afield as Asia and probably Gaul. Indeed, such was his influence that both Tertullian, writing in Carthage, and Irenaeus, who would soon be writing in Lugdunum, were to combat his ideas in 208 and 180 respectively. Like Irenaeus' *Against Heresies*, one of Tertullian's longest works, *Adversus Marcionem*, is comprised of five books: the first tackles Marcion's philosophical arguments; the second demonstrates the identity of the creator versus Marcion's Good God, the Father of Jesus; the third disproves Marcion's Christology; the fourth examines his gospel; and finally, the fifth treats Marcion's version of the Pauline epistles.³² The fact that both Tertullian and Irenaeus spent so much of their time rebutting Marcion only underlines the popularity of his thinking.

At root Marcion wanted to abandon anything that seemed to contradict the notion that only Jesus reveals the will and knowledge of God. This seems reasonable until we understand Marcion's back workings. Like the Gnostics, he believed in some form of ultimate God whom he calls the Stranger, but with whom, unlike Yaldabaoth, there can be no relationship. For Marcion, there is no relationship between the Stranger and creation. Maricon's distinct creator god is an intermediate being between this great transcendent ultimate Stranger God and creation itself. The nature of the creator god is that of an unyielding and unrelentingly just and punitive deity. As with the Platonists and Gnostics, the Stranger or ultimate god is an utterly transcendent divine being, who, until the arrival of Jesus, is unknown to the created order.³³ And until Jesus' coming, the created order is subject to the unrelenting demands of this demanding creator god who lacks the compassion of the Stranger.

The way these concepts work out in relation to the Bible is that, broadly, the Old Testament is deemed the work of this demiurge creator god, whose name is Yahweh, and is quite separate from the New Testament revelation of Jesus, who, by his partial Incarnation alone brings knowledge of the compassion of the Stranger God, now revealed as a Father. Jesus' Incarnation is not material, however, since like many Gnostics and Platonists, Marcion has a low regard for material existence. To back up his ideas, Marcion envisages a different canon of Scripture in which there is no place for the Old Testament, only a shortened version of Luke's Gospel and ten selected Epistles of Paul. Armed with this truncated canon, Marcion set out to form a new church.

The church in Rome was awash with contradictory ideas. If by 160 Marcion had left the city, it may well be that Valentinus was still there, as we are told that Valentinus "grew in influence under Pius [the emperor], and remained until Anicetus" [the bishop 155-165].[34] Furthermore, in his projected stopover *en route* to Lugdunum, Irenaeus may have heard, first hand, of the teaching of Valentinus, met Christians who were followers of Marcion, and also heard of our third chief incomer to the church in Rome, Justin the Apologist.[35] Michael Slusser makes the case that Irenaeus in all probability heard Justin Martyr in the city before he was executed and martyred some five years later in 165.[36] If Irenaeus had heard Justin, doing so would have in all likelihood been influential in his own determination to use all means theological and philosophical to combat heresy.

Justin (*c*.100-165) is an intriguing figure in second-century Christianity. He went to live in Rome as an immigrant during the reign of Antoninus Pius (138-61), taking with him a colourful intellectual back story. He was born into a pagan family in Flavia Neapolis in Samaria, now the city of Nablus on the West Bank. He had the benefit of a pagan philosophical education and was first a student of a Stoic school.[37] He then became a pupil of a peripatetic teacher who put him off further study by demanding payment following a single day's tuition.[38] After this he attached himself to a "very famous Pythagorean", but failure to complete examinations in music, astronomy and geometry meant he did not qualify for the class.[39] From there he found a Platonist teacher who appears to have satisfied his thirst for a more contemplative enquiry of the divine: "[I] improved myself as much as possible from day to day. The spirituality of the incorporeal interested me very much; the contemplation of ideas inspired my thinking.... [and] I cherished the hope of contemplating God directly, for this is the aim of Plato's philosophy."[40] Sometime after this he met a Syrian Christian through whom he was converted, which led him to regard his experience of Plato as a kind of prefiguring of his faith in Christ, since he considered the Word was revealed partially through Moses, but also, and particularly, in Plato. This was to be a common theme in Clement and Origen's thought in Alexandria also, and in Augustine of Hippo's journey to faith, as described in his *Confessions*.[41]

Primed in this way, Justin came to Rome with a defence (apology) of the faith both for Jew and pagan Greek or Roman. After all, as the Apostle Paul said, "Jews demand miraculous signs and Greeks look for wisdom, but we preach Christ crucified: a stumbling block to Jews and foolishness to Gentiles, but to those whom God has called, both Jews and Greeks, Christ the power of God and the wisdom of God" (1 Corinthians 1:22-4). Justin's aim was to persuade his listeners that a Christian was as rational, moral and pious as any contemporary Roman pagan—in fact more so—and that Christians make loyal and fruitful citizens, even if they eschew gladiatorial combat, spectacles, and pagan ceremonies and worship.

Wearing philosopher's garb and taking his own premises, Justin set about enlightening Christians and persuading pagans.[42] Philosopher's dress, a distinctive mantle Tertullian would also later wear and write about in *De pallio*, signified in the public mind that the wearer was not a priest or presbyter, but rather saw himself as a Christian philosopher, a new category of teacher in the public sphere, and as such an apologist for Christianity. Justin held court "above Myrtinus' baths",[43] and it was from here that he instructed his pupils: both pagans seeking to understand Christianity and Christians seeking a deeper understanding of their faith and its connections to the Greek philosophers, especially Plato. Justin's works reveal his close acquaintance with Plato. He refers to at least nine passages in Plato's *Timaeus*, mostly indirectly, as he had become acquainted with Middle Platonism, a later development of the Platonic tradition better known in Rome.[44] Justin's aim was to make Christianity seem more reasonable to his contemporaries and as such he commended Christianity as an apologist and as something of an evangelist to Roman society, right up to the emperor himself.

Justin's main works were *Dialogue with Trypho a Jew* and *Two Apologies* addressed to Emperor Antoninus Pius, the fourth of the so-called Five Good Emperors, the last being Marcus Aurelius, the Stoic. The *Dialogue* may have been with an actual person, or it may have been in the contrived Platonic style with an imaginary partner representing the other side of the argument. After an account of his own conversion, Justin then maintains that left to itself, the soul cannot see God. In brief, he goes on to demonstrate the inadequacy of the Law, circumcision and the sabbath;[45] the necessity of the Incarnation and the Cross;[46] and the point that true righteousness must come through faith in Christ.[47] Although a little diffuse at times, it is nonetheless a clear rendering of Pauline theology as expressed in Romans and Galatians, with some references to the limitations of Greek philosophy. Irenaeus may have known of its existence, but we cannot be sure.

What Irenaeus would have known were the two *Apologies* addressed to Emperor Antoninus Pius, who died in 161, around the time Irenaeus probably visited Rome. These *Apologies*, especially the first, seek to change Rome and the emperor's view of Christians as atheists,[48] arguing that they serve God rationally,[49] and are good and loyal citizens.[50] Christ himself is predicted in the Jewish scriptures and both heals and restores people through his power.[51] Justin called on the emperor to change his attitude to Christians or face God's judgement. Despite all this, or perhaps because of it, together with six friends, Justin faced trial, probably at the beginning of Marcus Aurelius' reign in *c*.162 and was executed on the orders of Junius Rusticus, Prefect of Rome from 162 to 168. Still, Justin had opened up a new front of intellectual reproach for the increasingly irrational persecution of Christians by the pagan state, even though such persecution still had a further century and a half to run.

When Irenaeus set sail from Rome to Marseille, he must have carried with him first-hand experience of the corrosive effects of Gnosticism and false teaching on the Church, as represented by Valentinus and Marcion. He also took with him some of Justin's arguments, which he reproduced in *Against Heresies*.[52] And perhaps there was already gestating in his mind the outline of the great book that was to set out clearly the deficiencies of Marcion and Gnosticism, and, in an original way, show how Christ offered true salvation.

Notes

[1] Peter Lampe, *Christians at Rome in the First Two Centuries: From Paul to Valentinus* (London: T&T Clark, 2003), p. 359.

2 Lampe, *Christians at Rome in the First Two Centuries*, p. 361, citing the work of J. P. Kirsch.
3 Lampe, *Christians at Rome in the First Two Centuries*, p. 361.
4 *HE* VI:4.11, op. cit., p. 216, cited by Lampe, *Christians at Rome in the First Two Centuries*, p. 362.
5 Suetonius, *The Twelve Caesars-Divus Claudius* 25, tr. Robert Graves (London: Penguin, 2007), p. 195 and Acts 18:2.
6 Lampe, *Christians at Rome in the First Two Centuries*, p. 69.
7 Lampe, *Christians at Rome in the First Two Centuries*, p. 90.
8 Lampe, *Christians at Rome in the First Two Centuries*, p. 51.
9 Lampe, *Christians at Rome in the First Two Centuries*, p. 54.
10 Lampe, *Christians at Rome in the First Two Centuries*, pp. 55ff.
11 Lampe, *Christians at Rome in the First Two Centuries*, p. 59.
12 Lampe, *Christians at Rome in the First Two Centuries*, pp. 31-3.
13 Lampe, *Christians at Rome in the First Two Centuries*, p. 374.
14 *HE* V.43, op. cit., p. 220, from Pope Cornelius' Letter.
15 *Ignatius's Letter to the Romans* 4:1 in *Apostolic Fathers I*, Loeb Classics, Vol. 24 (Cambridge, MA: Harvard University Press, 2003), p. 275.
16 See *Apostolic Fathers*, I, pp. 21-3.
17 *AH* III.3.3.
18 Lampe, *Christians at Rome in the First Two Centuries*, pp. 396ff. See also Allen Brent, "How Irenaeus misled the Archaeologists", in Paul Foster and Sarah Parvis (eds), *Irenaeus: Life, Scripture, Legacy* (Minneapolis, MN: Fortress Press, 2012), pp. 935ff.
19 Brakke, *Gnostics*, p. 100.
20 Walter Bauer, *Orthodoxy and Heresy in Earliest Christianity*, tr. Paul Achtemeier (Philadelphia, PA: Fortress, 1971), cited by James D. G. Dunn, *Christianity in the Making*, Vol. III (Grand Rapids, MI: Eerdmans, 2015), pp. 141, 151.
21 *HE* IV:11, op. cit., p. 113.
22 Meyer, *The Nag Hammadi Scriptures*, pp. 58ff.
23 Meyer, *The Nag Hammadi Scriptures*, pp. 31ff.
24 *AH* III.11.9.
25 Meyer, *The Nag Hammadi Scriptures*, pp. 62ff.
26 Meyer, *The Nag Hammadi Scriptures*, pp. 69ff.
27 Morwenna Ludlow, *The Early Church* (London: I. B Tauris, 2009), p. 58.

28 *HE* IV.11, op. cit., pp. 113-14.
29 John Behr, *Irenaeus of Lyons: Identifying Christianity* (Oxford: Oxford University Press, 2015), p. 33.
30 Barnes, *Tertullian*, pp. 124ff.
31 Justin Martyr, 1 *Apology* 26.4, cited by Ludlow, *The Early Church*, p. 51.
32 Barnes, *Tertullian*, p. 127.
33 Brakke, *Gnostics*, p. 97.
34 *AH* III.4.3.
35 Pierres Nautin, *Lettres et écrivains chrétiens des IIe et IIIe siècles* (Paris: Éditions du Cerf, 1961).
36 Foster and Parvis, *Irenaeus: Life, Scripture, Legacy*, p. 15 and fn. 214, and Michael Slusser, "How Much Did Irenaeus Learn from Justin?", *Studia Patristica* XL (2006), pp. 515-20.
37 Justin Martyr, *Dial.* 2.3.
38 Lampe, *Christians at Rome in the First Two Centuries*, p. 257.
39 Justin Martyr, *Dial.* 2.4ff.
40 Justin Martyr, *Dial.* 2.6; Apol. 2.121; 13:2.
41 Augustine, *Confessions*, Book VII.
42 Justin Martyr, *Dial.* 1.1; Eusebius, *HE* IV.11.
43 From *Acta Iusta* 3.2ff., cited by Lampe, *Christians at Rome in the First Two Centuries*, p. 259.
44 Lampe, *Christians at Rome in the First Two Centuries*, pp. 262ff.
45 Justin Martyr, *Dial.* xi, in TANF, Vol. 1 (Grand Rapids, MI: Eerdmans 1975), p. 199.
46 Justin Martyr, *Dial.* xcv, op. cit., p. 247.
47 Justin Martyr, *Dial.* xxix, op. cit., p. 209.
48 Justin Martyr, *Dial.* viii, op. cit., p. 165.
49 Justin Martyr, *Dial.* xiii, op. cit., p. 166.
50 Justin Martyr, *Dial.* xvii, op. cit., p. 168.
51 Justin Martyr, *Dial.* xlviii, op. cit., p. 178.
52 *HE* IV.18, p. 125, citing *AH* IV.11.2; V.26.3.

6

An Asian presbyter in Gaul

It is likely that Irenaeus travelled by ship from Rome to Massilia, present-day Marseilles. He would have embarked at Ostia, the port of Rome, made famous in Christian history by the death of Monica, the mother of Augustine of Hippo, when he was on his way back with her from Milan to Carthage in 388.[1] Her death in Ostia had a profound effect on Augustine. Much earlier, in the second century, the port city of Ostia had been greatly expanded, and now numbered some 50,000 inhabitants and was the principal grain port for Rome. The annual grain fleet from Carthage, the Cura Annonae, kept Rome in food, and Rome lived, we are told, on bread and circuses. The voyage to Massilia from Ostia of about 800 km would have taken just a few days. Irenaeus would not have felt a complete stranger when disembarking at the formerly Greek colony of Massilia, since Greeks or Phoenicians had settled there from the sixth century BC onwards.

In fact, it was a well-worn path for a Greek to come from the Eastern Mediterranean as far west as Massilia and many others would follow in the future, not least the monk, John Cassian, who was to found a monastery called St Victor on the nearby island of Lérins in 415. But all that was far ahead. From Massilia, Irenaeus almost certainly took one of the river boats of the type to be seen in the Roman museum in Arles, which plied the river Rhône from its mouth to the burgeoning capital of Gaul at Lugdunum. He arrived there in approximately 160 after his visit to Rome. This was also within a year of the Stoic philosopher and imperator, Marcus Aurelius, becoming emperor (161-80).

Lugdunum had been developing as the principal Roman city of Gaul for some time, much of which was due to the emperor, Claudius, who had been born there. Following the conquest of Gaul by Julius Caesar in

103

58-50 BC, which involved, it is said, the slaughter of over a million Gauls and the defeat of tribes such as the Helvetii, the Suebi, the Veneti, and the Nervii, Gaul had been created a province of the Roman Empire in 27 BC by Augustus. It was later divided into the *Tres Galliae* provinces, which consisted of Belgica, Lugdunensis, and Acquitania, with Narbonensis a further province outside of Gaul covering mostly present-day Provence. In 48, Claudius made the case in the Roman Senate for greater inclusion of Gaul into the Empire and in particular his own birthplace of Lugdunum. His proposal was that Gauls who already had Roman citizenship should be eligible for entrance into the Roman Senate.[2] As far as the Romans were concerned, however, these Gauls were still almost beyond the pale. They were even referred to by Claudius as "long-haired, unfamiliar and ill known".[3] A number of *canards* about the Gauls still circulated frequently around Rome: that they practised human sacrifice, that a Gaul called Brennus had once captured the Capitol in 390 BC, and that they were uncouth. It was hard to change these stereotypes.

Perhaps not surprisingly, Claudius' proposal was turned down and it would take a further 50 years for prejudices to be overcome and for the senatorial class in Rome to accept that Gallic magistrates could be admitted to the Senate. This came about, although still sparsely, during the rule of the Flavians, although even in the time of Hadrian there was little interest in Gaul.[4] Gaul was still disparaged by the ruling class in Rome. Although Pliny the Elder praised the agriculture in Gaul, his nephew Pliny the Younger was surprised to hear that his books were read in Lugdunum. He patronizingly said, as we have noted, "I never dreamed there were bookshops in Lyon."[5] Nevertheless he did keep up an interesting correspondence with a citizen of the colony. But it was not until the advent of Ausonius (310-395), a teacher of rhetoric in Bordeaux and tutor of the young Paulinus Bishop of Nola, that Gaul became a real intellectual centre.

The potential of Gaul was vast. Recent surveys have revealed just how many agricultural settlements there were—innumerable small towns or communities called *agglomerations sécondaires*.[6] Some of these were equipped with sanctuaries and public baths, and eight had their own theatres. Most were agricultural, but some were associated with mines and craft activity.[7] Vineyards began to flourish around Bordeaux, Dauphiné,

Burgundy and further north in the Rhineland.[8] Amphorae to transport the wine, which were such a tell-tale sign of Roman culture, were made in at least 60 sites around the three provinces. The first century was also a period of embellishment for the regional capital. All 23 theatres of classical design were built in the first century and many of these in the reign of Domitian. At the same time as this rolling out of Roman imperial edifices, the names of towns gave up their classical nomenclature to revert to more Gaulish tribal names, thus the rather unwieldy Durocortorum became Reims after the Remi, and Autricum took the name Chartres after the Carnutes.[9] However, the Roman imprint was still abundantly clear in the plethora of monuments that grew up around the provinces, and the space devoted in cities to accommodate them.

Like Gaul itself, Lugdunum would take time to find its stride as a provincial capital and as the most important city in the province, to be matched later only by Trier in the north during the rule of Constantine and his father Constantius, by Arles in Narbonensis, and by Bordeaux in Aquitaine. But lying, as it increasingly did, at the hub of routes from all over Gaul, and patronized by the Emperors Augustus and then Claudius, the city's star rose steadily. It was one of the largest sites for a capital city, measuring some 300 hectares and rising above the confluence of the Saône and the Rhône on the hill of les Fourvières. The city centre boasted a significant temple devoted to the worship of the emperor; indeed, the imperial cult lay at the heart of the development of Gallo-Roman cities. Not only that, but a temple was also built to serve the federal cult of the Three Gauls, a piece of carefully fabricated paganism designed to pull together the three regions of Gaul in an imperially sponsored cult. A huge limestone temple was built in Carrara marble on the hill of Fourvière under Claudius or the Flavians, perhaps by Italian craftsmen.[10]

Overall, no expense was spared to build Lugdunum into an imperial capital of the cult of Gaul, even though there was another grand federal sanctuary of the Three Gauls on its doorstep at Condate.[11] Alongside the temples, and beneath them, were two handsome theatres, an amphitheatre capable of holding 10,000, and an *odeon*, or smaller theatre, which could hold 5,000. Lugdunum therefore had all the ingredients for a significant imperial city. It had good roads spanning out into the interior to bring trade, produce and people. It guarded the entrance to the Alps, and its great rivers provided a ready combination of river traffic to the north, and from the Rhône, an outlet to the Mediterranean Sea and the rest of the Empire to the south.

How might Lugdunum have seemed to Irenaeus on his arrival in 160 or thereabouts? Goudineau imagines in a *jeu d'esprit* what a visitor from Italy would have made of the capital of Gaul:

> Language wasn't a problem anywhere. Almost all the Gauls have enough Latin for a traveller's needs. The province of Narbonensis is much the same as the north of Italia. Both the towns and countryside are very similar, and so was the cooking and the local costume. They even had the same sort of monuments there, dating back to the time of the early emperors. I travelled up the Rhône, which impressed me even more than the Po in terms of the strength of the current and the amount of shipping on it. The shops of Vienne are as good as those of Ostia, and the dockside at Lugdunum was piled up with amphorae and barrels.[12]

For Irenaeus, Lugdunum would not have seemed so strange, even with its chill winds from the Alps and the dark nights of winter. The climate was much colder than his hometown of Smyrna. But what was also familiar, as was the case throughout the Empire, were the struggles the Church was facing: storms of persecution that seemed to break out from nowhere, as much from an indignant populace as from repressive magistrates and prefects, and the ongoing struggle against the false knowledge of the Gnostics and others which had deeply penetrated the Church. These things were as much to be found in Gaul as they had been in Rome, Asia or Alexandria.

The Church in Gaul

Very little is known of the church in Gaul in this immediate post-Apostolic era, but if there was to be a church anywhere, it was most likely to be found in Lugdunum, the religious and economic hub of the three provinces, and possibly of Narbonensis as well. It would have been like the church in Rome, founded not by Apostolic mission but by Christians moving to the city for reasons of trade, migration or family. The church must have been composed largely, but not exclusively, of immigrants, and most probably the majority were Greek speakers. The meetings for worship and instruction were most likely held in private houses, as was the case in Rome, and would have been similar in form to those meetings described by Justin Martyr in his *First Apology*.[13]

Irenaeus would have been welcomed as a renewed link with the church in Asia and Rome, with whom many in the congregation would have had connections. Indeed, he would have represented continuity with the Apostolic tradition, having been taught by Polycarp, and probably ordained by one of Polycarp's associates. The fact that Polycarp had himself been instructed and taught by the Apostle John would have given a unique authority and immediacy to Irenaeus' teaching. It gave Irenaeus a direct link with the Apostle John. Such a pedigree, linked to Irenaeus' inherent gifts of teaching, study and pastoral diligence, made him a significant catch for this aspiring church in an important location. Not only that, but he would become involved in shaping the response of the entire Church to the false teaching threatening the Church throughout the Empire.

Irenaeus' day-to-day ministry in the city would have been much the same as in any other area. He would have led services as a presbyter in support of the bishop whom we know from Eusebius was called Pothinus.[14] By the time Irenaeus arrived, Pothinus was in his mid-seventies and was to face martyrdom in his nineties, much like the blessed Polycarp.[15] This persecution underlines the fragility of the Church's position in society at large: there was no support from the magistracy, and at any moment Christians could be hauled before the courts and ordered to worship the emperor by burning incense or giving him the divine title. Failure to do so, as in the case of Justin and his associates in 165, could lead to immediate execution with no appeal. Also, it was all too easy to fall foul of the local population who often despised Christians for refusing to get involved in Roman spectacles such as gladiatorial combat or the killing of animals in amphitheatres for entertainment. Tertullian in North Africa would inveigh against these activities in writings such as *De spectaculis*, warning Christians not to take part. In a word, Christians were as vulnerable to the whims of local populations and magistrates as to the edicts from the emperor himself. What also became clear was that different emperors took either a relaxed or a neurotic view of Christians in the Empire. Trajan showed himself unwilling to hunt down Christians, as seen through his instructions to Pliny the Younger in Bithynia, while later, Decius, Severus and, much later, Diocletian, saw the maintenance of paganism as integral to a successful empire, and therefore the repression and persecution of Christians whom they called "atheists" was considered good statecraft.

In point of fact, Irenaeus arrived in Lugdunum at the same time as a change in emperor, for following his death, Antonius Pius was succeeded by two adopted heirs who were to be the last of the so-called "Five Good Emperors". It was the first time that two emperors had co-ruled the Empire, although from 268 Diocletian was to constitute this arrangement more formally. These two co-emperors were Marcus Aurelius (161-80) and Lucius Verus (161-9). As far as the Empire was concerned, both were well chosen and able to work effectively together, although of the two, Marcus Aurelius was granted more authority. Much of Verus' rule was spent campaigning against the Armenians and Parthians in Armenia and Cappadocia, until his transfer to the provinces along the Danube where he died of illness while fighting against the Marcomanni in 169. Marcus Aurelius was particularly known in his lifetime as a philosopher-king, educated principally by the rhetorician Fronto, while today his meditations are still widely read and quoted.[16] He was steeped in the second sophist movement, which had revived Greek studies and philosophy.

Despite possessing a strong irenic quality, it was Marcus' misfortune to spend most of his days campaigning against German tribes along the Danube. Although there were regional outbreaks of persecution against the Church during his reign, not least south of Lugdunum at Vienne on the Rhône, this was not the intention of Marcus Aurelius himself. Indeed, in Eusebius, a Christian source named as Clement of Alexandria is quoted petitioning Marcus Aurelius as follows, "You sir, hold the same views on this matter as they did [i.e., his forbears Trajan and Hadrian], but with much more human sympathy and philosophic insight so we are the more convinced that you will whole-heartedly accede to our request for greater security."[17] But this was not to be, since the emperor was not prepared to give Christians imperial protection, which then left them vulnerable to regional waves of mob violence, directed against them as scapegoats for the ills of society. This was nowhere more evident than in Vienne.

Persecution in Vienne

Vienne lies about 35 kilometres downstream from Lyon. In about 177, the Christians of Vienne and Lugdunum suffered violent persecution with many martyred, an account of which was movingly written and sent by the church in Gaul to their Christian brethren in Asia and Phrygia. The letter, which must have become well known in the churches of Asia, was then published by Eusebius in his *Church History* and reads as an account of heroic suffering by many for the cause of Christ.[18]

The persecution was not so much orchestrated by the authorities as a spontaneous outburst of violence against Christians. The report tells of the Christians, "heroically enduring whatever the surging crowds heaped on them, noisy abuse, blows, dragging along the ground, plundering, stoning, imprisonment, and everything that an infuriated mob normally does to hated enemies. Then they were marched into the forum and interrogated by the tribune and the city authorities before the whole population."[19] It appears to have been a city-wide event in Vienne. One Christian, Vettius, tried to speak on behalf of the Christians to the tribune, governor and population, by pleading their virtue much as Justin Martyr did in his *Apology* but he was howled down by the crowd.[20]

Other more recently believing Christians did not have the courage or wherewithal to withstand the persecution and wavered in their stance. The writers of the letter said these "were not yet ready, they had not trained and were still flabby, in no fit condition to face the strain . . . ten proved stillborn, causing us great distress and inexpressible grief, and damping the enthusiasm of those not yet arrested".[21] But while there were some who wilted under the pressure, causing its own kind of consternation, there were others who showed extraordinary courage.

The numbers of Christians caught up in this persecution were large: "all the active members who had done most to build up our church life" were arrested. Furthermore, some of the heathen domestics who served the better off Greek Christians were induced by the authorities to make false accusations against their masters, impugning their honour and accusing them of orgies, banquets and incest, which further incited the mob.[22] The writers of this report saw, therefore, the fulfilment of the Lord's words come to pass: "A time is coming when anyone who kills you will think he is offering a service to God" (John 16:2). In particular, the endurance of five martyrs was recorded at some length: Sanctus, Attalus, Blandina, Maturus and the bishop Pothinus. Sanctus, a deacon from Vienne, was especially praised. He faced "crushing force from the soldiers". He was severely tortured "but would not even tell his accusers his own name, race or birthplace, or whether he was slave or free. To every question he replied in Latin 'I am a Christian'". Consequently, his tortures became worse: ending up with the soldiers pressing "red-hot plates against the most sensitive parts of the body".[23] The writer of the letter drew this conclusion:

> His poor body was a witness to what he had suffered—it was all one wound and bruise, bent up and robbed of outward human shape, but suffering in that body, Christ accomplished glorious things, utterly defeating the adversary and proving as an example to the rest that where the Father's love is nothing can frighten us, where Christ's glory is nothing can hurt us.[24]

No doubt it was a lesson made known with satisfaction around Phrygia and Asia.

Blandina, too, demonstrated exceptional faith and courage. As the writer says, too often the sacrifices and courage of women were overlooked. But now she was taken into the amphitheatre and hung on a post for the wild beasts. "She looked as if she was hanging in the form of a cross, and through her ardent prayers she stimulated great enthusiasm in those undergoing their ordeal [elsewhere in the arena] who in their agony saw with their outward eyes in the person of their sister the One who was crucified for them."[25] The wild beasts took no interest in her at first, so she was taken back to prison overnight and led out again the following day together with a 15-year-old boy called Ponticus. Despite the age of the boy and the sex of Blandina, they were shown no pity. For her part, Blandina encouraged the young Ponticus to maintain his resistance to swearing by the heathen idols and to remain steadfast in suffering. Then Blandina faced her own sufferings: she faced whips, the beasts and the griddle and was finally dropped in a basket and thrown to a bull until she too "was sacrificed".[26] Her remains were guarded by soldiers in the arena for six days, after which they were burnt, and her ashes scattered on the Rhône.

And where was Irenaeus, the presbyter of Lugdunum in all this? It is most likely that he was in Rome with his newly completed work *Against Heresies*. Eusebius records that those who became martyrs had already recommended Irenaeus to the new Bishop of Rome, Eleutherius, ordained bishop in 175 after Soter and Anicetus, whom Polycarp had met. They wrote to Eleutherius, commending Irenaeus as follows:

> Greeting once more. Father Eleutherius: May God bless you always. We are entrusting this letter to our brother and companion Irenaeus to convey to you. We are anxious that you should hold him in high regard, as a man devoted to the covenant of Christ. For if we had thought that position conferred righteousness on anyone, we should have recommended him first as a presbyter of the church, which indeed he is.[27]

In fact, Irenaeus was very soon to be appointed Bishop of Lugdunum, no doubt to bind up the wounds following a vicious persecution that had so marked the fellowship and traumatized the congregation. Irenaeus would remain there until the end of his life, close to the end of the century. Nor did persecution of Christians abate in the Empire: indeed "the thirteen years of Commodus's rule, who succeeded Marcus Aurelius had a higher frequency of well-attested instances of persecution".[28] By this time, Irenaeus had become a leading author. Following Justin Martyr, and before Tertullian from Carthage, Irenaeus was to be the single most important Christian writer of the second half of the second century, and also what we might call the first polemical systematic theologian in the post-Apostolic era. *Against Heresies* was thus a seminal work. Running over five books, it refutes false knowledge, and through the framework of recapitulation, reworks the offer of the gospel. He does not write about withstanding persecution, but he does write about the internal attack on the integrity of the Church from the twin heresies of Marcionism and Valentinian Gnosticism, whose effects he had seen first-hand in Rome and almost certainly in Lugdunum as well. He saw these teachings as a sustained and corrosive attack on the integrity of the gospel, and as dangerous, possibly more so, than outright persecution.

Notes

[1] Augustine, *Confessions* IX.
[2] C. Goudineau, "Gaul", in Alan K. Bowman, Peter Garnsey, Dominic Rathbone (eds), *Cambridge Ancient History, second edition, Vol. XI: The High Empire, AD 70–192* (Cambridge: Cambridge University Press, 2005), p. 463.
[3] Goudineau, "Gaul", p. 464.
[4] Goudineau, "Gaul", p. 462.
[5] Goudineau, "Gaul", p. 465, Epistle ix.2.2.
[6] Goudineau, "Gaul", p. 468.
[7] Goudineau, "Gaul", p. 469.
[8] Goudineau, "Gaul", p. 472.
[9] Goudineau, "Gaul", pp. 480-1.
[10] Goudineau, "Gaul", p. 487.
[11] Goudineau, "Gaul", p. 487.
[12] Goudineau, "Gaul", pp. 494-5.
[13] Justin Martyr, *First Apology*, ANF, Vol. I, lxv-lxvi (Grand Rapids, MI: Eerdmans, 1975), p. 185.
[14] *HE* V.I, op. cit., p. 143.
[15] *HE* V.I, op. cit., p. 143.
[16] Marcus Aurelius, *Meditations* (London: Penguin Classics, 2006).
[17] *HE* IV.26, pp. 133-4.
[18] *HE* V.1, op. cit., p. 139.
[19] *HE* V.1, op. cit., pp. 139-40.
[20] Justin Martyr, *First Apology*, op. cit., pp. 163ff.

21 *HE* V.1, op. cit., p. 140.
22 *HE* V1, op. cit., pp. 140-1.
23 *HE* V1, op. cit., p. 142.
24 *HE* V1, op. cit., p. 142.
25 *HE* V1, op. cit., p. 145.
26 *HE* V1, op. cit., pp. 147-8.
27 *HE* V1.5.4, op. cit., p. 150; VI.5.6, op. cit., p. 152.
28 Barnes, *Tertullian*, p. 155.

PART II

The glory of God

7

The true nature of God

Nothing was more important to Irenaeus than putting in place the fundamental building block of theology, which is the true nature of the one, Triune, Creator God. This was Irenaeus' purpose in his two surviving works.

Of all Irenaeus' writings, only two have come down to us. They are *Against Heresies* and *The Demonstration of the Apostolic Preaching*. The latter is a slim volume, most likely used for catechesis, while the former is the longest and most ambitious theological work since the Apostolic period, running to five books of densely written text and innumerable quotations from Scripture. In this respect, it is somewhat longer than Justin Martyr's *First Apology* (*c.*155-7). *Against Heresies* is both polemical and original. When Erasmus brought *Against Heresies* to light in the sixteenth century, he considered it demonstrated the vigour and power of the early Church.[1] It has remained ever since a foundation stone of Christian theology. The much smaller and later *The Demonstration of the Apostolic Preaching* is a summary of the rule of faith and is a kind of early catechesis for church leaders and candidates for baptism which seeks to demonstrate the truth of Christ's claims, especially through copious referencing from the Old Testament.

These two works came down to us through a circuitous route. *Adversus Haereses*, although originally written in Greek, survived in a Latin text quoted by Augustine in 421 in his *Contra Iulanium* 1.3.5 (*Patrologia Latina* 44, 644) and also in a few Greek fragments. There is also an Armenian text, dated variously from the fifth to the eighth century, which is more comprehensive, though still partial.[2] *The Demonstration of the Apostolic Preaching* also survived as an Armenian text, and was only discovered as recently as 1904.

The structure of *Against Heresies* has the first three books elucidating the nature of the heresies which Irenaeus calls in his title *Knowledge Falsely So-Called*, which he rebuts with extensive recourse to Scripture. Having dealt with the false hypotheses of the Gnostics and Marcion, he then sets out his own hypothesis, founded in the Scriptures, in Book IV, the longest of the books. This is the recapitulation (*anakephalaíōsis*) of humankind through Christ and God's plan (*oikonomia*) or the arrangement of salvation to that end, in which the glory of God is wonderfully shown. This recapitulation lies at the heart of Irenaeus' theology, in terms of which, not only are humans restored, but in the process, God demonstrates his own glory and sets humankind on a path of growth and eventual perfection, which is made clear in Book V. Irenaeus bases his argument on the Scriptures throughout, and especially the New Testament, except when he is refuting Marcion from the Old. It is in a church based on those Scriptures and led by those appointed *in faithful succession to the Apostles* that true knowledge of God and confidence in God are to be found.

From the outset, Irenaeus needs to demonstrate that there is one God who is Father of all, the maker of a creation which was originally and fundamentally good, although corrupted by the Devil and humanity's fall. In other words, he must overthrow the myths of the Valentinian Gnostics, which had become so prevalent and pernicious. The Gnostics used many of the same Scriptures as Irenaeus but included other literature to set the Jesus narrative within an overarching Gnostic myth which Irenaeus seeks to invalidate. Before reiterating this overall Gnostic myth, it is worth understanding why the Gnostics in general, and Valentinian in particular, held so strongly to a different creation narrative and a different concept of God from that of the Hebrew-Christian tradition.

The ancient world's view of creation and materiality

People in ancient societies lived in a world full of danger and with few or no rational or scientific explanations: death came too frequently to the young; plagues would sweep across communities and tribes; the natural word was full of horrors, such as earthquakes, floods and famines; disease or locusts destroyed crops; and war was all too common. In light of this, paganism developed a practice of propitiating various gods responsible for different areas of life: Jupiter or Zeus for the state, Ceres the goddess of agriculture, Neptune or Poseidon the gods of the sea, and Asclepius the god of healing. These are just a sample of the retinues of gods who between them controlled life and who needed to be consulted, sacrificed to or propitiated, if their own particular department of life was to flourish for a particular individual or community. Religion, therefore, was a constant uncertain round of consulting the auspices, sacrificing to deities, and assuaging the anger of these capricious beings to alleviate misfortune, disease and calamity.

Into these pagan and popular superstitions came the great Greek philosophic schools centred around Socrates (470-399 BC), Plato (c.427-348 BC), and Aristotle (384-322 BC) in the fourth-century school or academy in Athens. Rather than following the concept of a plethora of gods, Plato believed in "The Good" from which is derived wisdom.[3] This One or Good was the prime mover, creating the world from a substance already in existence, and investing it with meaning through the soul, form and reason. The One is unapproachable and unknown. All other things depend on this prime mover and become what they are intended to be. Thus, a distinction is to be drawn between that which is unchanging and that which is contingent, between that which *is* and that which is *becoming*. Famously, in *Timaeus*, Plato describes this relationship and process, which is also seminal to Irenaeus in his contention with the Gnostics, because it underlines the distinction that must be drawn between the creator and creation, between the changeless and the contingent. Plato makes the distinction as follows:

> If this is so, it must be agreed that one kind is the unchanging form, uncreated and indestructible, neither admitting into itself anything from anywhere nor itself entering anything anywhere, imperceptible to sight or the other senses, the object of intelligence; another kind is that which bears the same name as the form and resembles it, but is sensible, generated and is in constant motion, comes into being in, and vanishes from, a particular place, and is apprehended by opinion together with

sense perception; and a third kind is that space which is eternal and indestructible, which provides a seat for everything that comes to be, and which is apprehended without the senses by a sort of spurious reasoning and is hardly an object of belief—we look indeed in a kind of dream and say that everything that exists must surely be somewhere and occupy some space, and that which is nowhere in heaven or earth is nothing at all.[4]

While Plato's doctrine is not far removed from the Judeo-Christian idea of a good creator God, a prime mover who creates things that are themselves *becoming* and in a context of enduring physical space, it was not a concept that was taken up by the Gnostics. Their pessimism extended to all parts of creation, in which the greatest created beings, humans, were imprisoned in darkness until the spark inside them was released through true knowledge (*gnosis*). Not only this, but the pessimism found to a certain extent in Plato, and to a greater extent in Gnosticism and Marcionism, extended most especially to the material world, and to *the body in particular*.

In the days of Plato, the soul ruled. The inherent value of anything was imparted by the existence of the soul, which was attached to each separate living organism, and most especially to the human, in whom the soul pre-existed the material body and left in separation at death. The soul in Plato's thought provides self-motion, or vitality, as described in Phaedo. The three parts of the soul are identified as reason, spirit and appetite. Reason is found in the head, spirit in the chest, and the appetites in the belly. Reason is the highest part of the soul and is nourished by wisdom, beauty and truth; whereas the appetites or desires are a drag on the soul.

Plato's thought was to take root in the philosophic schools of Athens and elsewhere. In Alexandria, in the early part of the first century, Philo (*c*.25 BC-AD 50), a Jewish Hellenistic philosopher, used Hellenistic and Platonic ideas to interpret the Torah allegorically, so as to arrive, he thought, at a higher level of truth which combined both Hebrew Scripture and Greek philosophy, especially that of Plato. Philo posited a creator as the demiurge, artisan or fabricator of the world and a logos as a vivifying life force and archetypal wisdom. Thus, Philo's God, as for Middle Platonism, was an utterly transcendent Prime Mover who required intermediaries to engage with his creation. The Logos was the chief of these intermediaries and was described as the first-born of God. It was the object of the Logos to raise to life those who had become imprisoned in the calamity of the body.[5] The body was now a source of evil and dragged the soul into all kinds of desire, which could only end in destruction.[6] It was but a short step from this form of Neoplatonism—which was lodged in an allegorical interpretation of the Jewish Scriptures, and mixed later with Christianity—to the Gnosticism which grew especially in Alexandria by the second century AD. What Plato, Philo and Jewish ideas provided was a culture which was widely accepted and which would readily accede to Gnostic tenets and underpin much of Marcion's dualism as well. It was this composite thought that Irenaeus had to engage with, identify, explain and then refute, and which formed the starting point of his great work. He would also begin the process of freshly describing God as Triune, in which the Father creates, the Logos reveals and redeems, and the Spirit transforms, empowers and sanctifies. Indeed, from being eschewed or denigrated, sinful flesh is transformed through the Logos' Incarnation in true flesh and is then redeemed.

False knowledge

From the start, and particularly in the first two books of *Against Heresies*, Irenaeus sets out to describe the nature of false knowledge. It may have been that he intended to write only the first two books, before later developing it into a much longer work when he considered not only the need to expose and refute the false teachers, but also to restate the essence of the Christian faith in response.[7] He introduces the work in a serious and foreboding way:

> In as much as certain men have set the truth aside, and bring in lying words and vain genealogies, which as the Apostle says, "minister questions rather than godly edifying which is in faith" [see Titus 3:9], and by means of their craftily constructed

plausibilities draw away the minds of the inexperienced and take them captive, I have freely constrained, my dear friend [his correspondent] to compose the following treatise in order to expose and counteract their machinations. These men falsify the oracles of God, and prove themselves evil interpreters of the good word of revelation (§1.1 Preface).

As a result of his research, including the commentaries of the disciples of Valentinus, and in particular the disciples of Ptolemaeus, and through conversation with them, Irenaeus felt constrained to point out the pitfalls, indeed the grave dangers, of following their speculative, seemingly attractive, but specious theories. These teachers who also lived around the Rhône valley were wolves in sheep's clothing and were seeking to lead the unaware into "an abyss of madness and of blasphemy against Christ" (§2).

Apologizing for his lack of rhetoric as one living among the Celts and "for the most part using therefore a barbarous dialect" (§3), he hopes that the greater knowledge of his correspondent derived from this work will lead to a more thorough understanding of "the plausible system of these heretics" (§3).

Thus, having laid out his own intentions and offered caveats about his own abilities, Irenaeus embarked on a work which grew like Topsy and became one of the cornerstones of the post-Apostolic Christian world.

Irenaeus continues in this first book to describe "the plausible system of these heretics". In fact, they become less plausible and more fantastic the more he describes them. As we have seen, what drives "these plausible systems" is the deep pessimism that Gnostic theories have in general, and Valentinus and others have in particular, about the original goodness of creation, and indeed the vestiges of goodness left both in humanity and in creation following the Fall.

Initially, Irenaeus describes in a broad way some of the defining characteristics of the Gnostics or this "False Knowledge" circulating at the time of writing, before giving an account of the origin of these ideas and their genealogy or common relationship.[8]

The original uncreated God was known variously as the Propator, Bythus (commonly used in Egypt), or the demiurge (a Platonic description following the notion of a craftsmen or designer).⁹ He was beyond reach and knowledge. He existed outside the realm of created things and beyond the Pleroma in which the *aeons* existed. Furthermore, this Pleroma was divided into an Ogdoad (eight spheres), that is, seven heavens, and an eighth where the Propator dwelt, a Decad, and a Duodecad where a further thirty *aeons* dwelt. Dubious use of the Bible and stories from the New Testament were then used to justify these concepts, and numerology was often employed as well.¹⁰

More could be said, but the above gives a taste of the complexity of the Gnostic system (which is also far from uniform), of the separation of the divine from the created, and of the intermediaries involved. Indeed, so absurd do some of these speculations become in the Gnostic system that Irenaeus pokes fun at their invention. He describes a Pro-arche, or the foremost being, from whom twin powers emanate called the Gourd and Utter-Emptiness. Between them they produce a fruit "everywhere visible" called a giant cucumber or melon. He concludes, "these powers: the Gourd, The Utter-Emptiness, the Cucumber and the Melon brought forth the remaining multitude including the delirious melon of Valentinus!"¹¹ Irenaeus' point is that there is no end to absurd speculation when it becomes untethered from the Apostolic teaching of Scripture.

Irenaeus further undermines the claims of false knowledge by showing its inconsistency and its inherent contradictions and abuses. He does this by setting out a genealogy of false knowledge and then interjecting, at various moments, *the true rule or canon of truth*. Thus, he underlines,

> The Church, though dispersed through the whole world, even to the ends of the earth, has received from the Apostles and their disciples this faith: she believes in one God, the Father Almighty, Maker of heaven, and earth, and the sea and all things that are in them; and in Christ Jesus, the Son of God, who became incarnate for our salvation; and in the Holy Spirit, who proclaimed the prophets the dispensations of God.¹²

Irenaeus therefore interjects in a kind of credal form the essence of the Christian faith. And he makes the point that it is a catholic and universal faith and is therefore the same wherever the Church may be found: "For although the languages of the world are dissimilar, yet the import of the tradition is one and the same."[13] Nor does lesser or greater intelligence mean any variation of the truth; but rather the greater the insight or comprehension means the more clearly these truths may be explained, "in the general scheme of the faith".[14] Irenaeus will make clearer his idea that there is an unvarying Apostolic *oikonomia*, meaning an arrangement of the truth, and that false knowledge has no part in it.

From this firm platform and statement, Irenaeus goes on in Book I to further describe the teaching of Valentinus and his followers with all its convolutions. In these chapters, he describes the false practices of Marcus, a well-known Gnostic practitioner. Of Marcus, Irenaeus says,

> He is a perfect adept in magical impostures, and by this means drawing away a great number of men, and not a few women, he has induced them to join themselves to him, as to one who is possessed of the greatest knowledge and perfection, and who has received the highest power from the invisible and ineffable regions above.[15]

A combination of spurious knowledge, mysterious ceremonies, incantations and drama served to weave a mesmerizing spell over the adherents of Marcus, who believed that Charis, a female power in the Pleroma, "dropped her own lifeblood into the cup consecrated by Marcus".[16] The mysterious became mingled with the fantastic, the sensual with the sacrificial. It was with such claims, combining esoteric teaching with a seeming divine substance, that Marcus ensnared his flock. As they drank from the cup, they had these words said over them, "May that Charis who is before all things, and who transcends all knowledge and speech fill thine inner man, and multiply in thee her own knowledge, by sowing the grain of mustard seed in thee as in good soil."[17] It was all very heady stuff and the neophytes wanted to believe it. The associations were clear: from Holy Communion to the Parable of the Sower, to the idea of blessing through drinking, but the context had all been changed.

It is not Christ's liberating, saving death that is remembered, but a connection offered to an intermediary cosmic being who is the conveyor of knowledge through the ministrations of a self-seeking priest. In other words, Marcus is Gnosticism in action. Irenaeus then goes on to say, unsparingly, that Marcus possesses a demon as his familiar spirit, by means of which he seems to prophesy, and also enables as many as he counts worthy to be partakers of Charis to "go on themselves and prophesy".[18]

Irenaeus continues. He devotes himself especially to women, and those such as are well bred, and elegantly attired, and of great wealth, whom he frequently seeks to draw after him by addressing them in such seductive words as these:

> I am eager to make thee a partaker of my Charis, since the Father of all doth continually behold thy angel before his face. Receive from me the gift of Charis. Adorn thyself as a bride who is expecting her bridegroom, that thou mayest be what I am, and I what thou art. Establish the germ of light in thy nuptial chamber. Receive from me a spouse, and become receptive of him, while thou art received by him. Behold Charis has descended upon thee: open thy mouth and prophesy.

Initially reluctant, the woman is persuaded to utter whatever "nonsense" first comes into her head. She believes herself a prophetess; she believes she has received the gift of Charis. In response she offers him money and "yields up to him her person desiring in every way to be united to him, that she may become altogether one with him".[19] It seems the usual mix of a flattered ego, sexual innuendo, money, and the cult of an individual leader.

And so, the speculation continues. The female entity that surrounds the Bythus in profound silence, called Sige, in turn reveals Jesus to Marcus. And Jesus, who combines the numbers 888 and is also the Duodecad, since his name also spells out 12, is therefore ranked as a supercelestial being.[20] Another group called the Marcosians took a distinctively Platonic view of creation, believing that everything created was merely an image of something already in existence but invisible.[21] As Irenaeus goes on recording more and more "absurdities", he anticipates his friend's reaction: "I well know my dear friend, that when thou hast read through all this, thou wilt indulge in a hearty laugh over this their inflated wise folly! But those men are really worthy of being mourned over, who promulgate such a religion."[22] In other words, on hearing this "teaching" you do not know whether to laugh or cry!

Following this, Irenaeus proceeds to a pathology or genealogy of the false knowledge he is recounting, but not before reiterating once again what he calls the rule or canon of truth that, "there is one God Almighty who made all things by his word, and fashioned and formed, out of that which had no existence, all things which exist".[23] And this Almighty God is as much the Father of the patriarchs as the Father of Christ, which is in itself an early shot across the bows of Marcion to whose treatment Irenaeus will shortly come.

This genealogy of Gnostic deviation begins in Irenaeus' mind with Simon Magus, the magician of Acts 8:9ff., who practised sorcery and sought to buy the power and influence of the Holy Spirit with money. Next, Saturninus of Antioch and Basilides further developed the teaching of Simon to promulgate the view that there were two kinds of men: some irredeemably wicked destined for destruction, and others (presumably the enlightened ones) destined for salvation. You were either in one camp or the other. Furthermore, Christ was the offspring of "Nous", who in turn was an emanation of the unknowable Father. Christ did not himself die, but was replaced by Simon Cyrene as a substitute, and those who are saved by pursuit of *gnosis* are only saved in spirit, for the body, being corrupt, cannot inherit salvation.[24]

The genealogy of Gnosticism continues through many twists and turns. The Carpocrates believed that the world was created by angels and used magic.[25] They branded their followers in the lobes of their ears. They used images of Christ, purported to have been made by Pilate. They were known as Gnostics and apparently gained a multitude of followers in Rome.[26] Other groups followed, such as Cerinthus and the Ebionites, who were spurned by the Apostle John in Ephesus.[27] Cerinthus believed that since Christ was an impassable spirit and could not therefore suffer, a purely human Jesus was indwelt by a heavenly Christ until the passion and crucifixion.[28] From Cerinthus we come to Marcion, who will require substantial refutation throughout *Against Heresies*, and who taught that two separate gods were responsible for the Two Testaments or Covenants (Old and New): the one book being warlike, violent and evil, linked to the corrupt creator god of Gnostic thought, and the other being the record of the loving Jesus sent by the supreme unknowable Father. Both Father and Son were considered separate from fallen creation and its fallen intermediate creator. Marcion was readily believed by many, and Marcionism, as we have seen, had a wide following in Rome and quite possibly in Lugdunum also.

Finally other "false knowledge" sects added their pennyworth of error and practice. The followers of Tatian, the errant pupil of Justin Martyr, came to think of marriage as corrupt, declaring it "nothing else than corruption and fornication",[29] while at the other extreme, Basilides and Carpocrates indulged in promiscuous intercourse and kept a plurality of wives since the flesh and its activities were considered inconsequential.[30] Irenaeus then recounts the varied and bizarre cosmologies of the Barbeliotes and Borborians, who belonged to the Valentinian family of Gnostics that believed in Barbēlō, a timeless *aeon*.[31] Lastly, he describes the fantastic theories of the Ophites and Sethians, who believed that Christ was born of light emanating from Bythus which fertilized the first woman who then sprinkled light by ebullition on others. Once freed from the imprisonment of the corrupt body, these others could then find eternal light. But all the while they were subject to machinations of the evil genius of creation, Yaldabaoth.[32]

Irenaeus believed that setting out this system of false knowledge, if we can call it that, would reveal it as self-evident nonsense.[33] But nevertheless, he knew he had to refute this false knowledge both by refutation and a restatement of the truth. This refutation lies at the heart of Book II.

Rebuttal and refutation: Book II

While Book I is a fairly comprehensive statement of the nostrums of Gnosticism, especially those of Valentinian, which carried within them the seeds of their own absurdity and destruction, Book II is both a rebuttal and a refutation of Gnostic speculative theology. This refutation logically precedes Book III, which is a restatement of the essence of Christianity. Thus, the great work proceeds.

Book II contains three main parts: the reiteration of the one true God as the sovereign creator through his Word and the governor of his creation through his Spirit; the argument that Christ through his life and passion recapitulated humankind; and finally, the affirmation that true humanity consists in the redemption of *the entire human being*, physical, intellectual and spiritual.[34]

In refuting false knowledge of God, Irenaeus is at great pains to re-establish the theology of a single Godhead shown also to be three (which we shall come to), who is the creator and the initiator of redemption from the outset. He writes in the introduction to Book II that "I proved that there is one God, The Creator, and that He is not the fruit of any defect, nor is there anything either above Him, or after Him". With this aim in mind, he shows it could never have been otherwise and that there could never have been "any other fullness, or Principle, or Power or God, above him, since it is a matter of necessity that God, the Pleroma (Fulness) of all these, should contain all things in His immensity, and should be contained by no-one".[35] With this as his cardinal principle, all other agents are beneath him (if they even exist), including angels. Bythus and the 30 *aeons* can never be the creator.[36] Nor do these *aeons* have anything created in their image,[37] nor is Sophia and her thought (*enthymesis*) an agent of creation.[38] In fact, most of these ideas are taken from the heathen or pagans.[39] And in contradistinction to the Gnostics, as Irenaeus continually drives home, there is only one Creator God, who as we shall see, is Triune.

Having refuted the cosmology of the Gnostics and restored the reality of a Creator God who embraces his creation and will redeem it, in the second part of Book II, Irenaeus shows the spirit in which people should learn from the ministry of Christ.

Once again Irenaeus must disassociate the story of Christ, his passion, and his miracles, from the false fabrications (*plasma*) of the Gnostics.[40] Thus, the passion of Christ is *not* a replica of the passion of an *aeon*.[41] Nor is Judas, the twelfth of the Apostles, a type of the suffering of an *aeon*. Judas is not simply the evil thought of Sophia, but a self-willed man, capable of making and being responsible for his own fateful decisions. The Apostles are not types of *aeons* either.[42] Rather, they are real people taking real, self-willed decisions.[43]

Refuting the idea that there are 30 *aeons* merely because Jesus was baptized in his thirtieth year, Irenaeus goes on to maintain that Jesus could only have become a mature teacher if he had continued into his fourth and fifth decade, erroneously adding that the Gospels and all the elders testify to this.[44] This mistake in thinking that Jesus became 50 during his ministry reflects not only the pressure of maintaining an orthodox faith in the midst of the Gnostic onslaught, but also the accepted view that age and wisdom often go together. It was also convenient for his theology of recapitulation, to which we will come.

Irenaeus then refutes the numerology which the Gnostics found in the name of Jesus and in the Ark of the Covenant to validate their own system.[45] At the same time, he argues that although the number five occurs frequently in Christian revelations, whether in looking at the Pentateuch, the five witnesses on the Mount of Transfiguration, or the five points of the Cross, there is no reason to extract from the existence of five *aeons*.[46] The arguments and methods of numerology may appear arcane to us, but this was the kind of theological milieu in which Gnostic speculation occurred. Irenaeus concludes that it is better not to indulge in such speculation, and that people should instead make the way of love the route to truth: for "knowledge puffs up, but love edifies".[47] Rather than look for secret riddles in the text of Scripture through numerology or rank speculation, people should reflect with humble minds and a prayerful attitude, since "parables should not be adapted to ambiguous expressions".[48] In other words, the literal interpretation of Scripture was to be preferred to the allegorical, otherwise, people might miss "the rule of truth", which was the all-important yardstick for Irenaeus, and consequently people would fall into ever more esoteric interpretations.[49] Irenaeus concludes his argument thus:

> Having therefore the truth itself as our rule and the testimony concerning God set clearly before us, so we ought not, by running after numerous and diverse answers to questions, to cast away the firm and true knowledge of God. But it is much more suitable that we, directing our inquiries after this fashion, should exercise ourselves in the investigation of the mystery and administration of the living God, and should increase in the love of him who

has done, and still does, so great things for us; but never should fall from the belief by which it is most clearly proclaimed that this Being alone is truly God and Father, who formed this world, fashioned man, and bestowed the faculty of increase on his own creation, and called upon him upwards from the lesser things to those greater ones which are in his own presence, just as he was born as an infant which has been conceived in the womb into the light of the sun, and lays up wheat in the barn after he has given it full strength on the stalk. But it is one and the same creature who both fashioned the womb and created the sun; and one and the same Lord who reared both the stalk of corn, increased and multiplied the wheat and prepared the barn.[50]

Irenaeus thus describes the nature of the only God, whom we shall also see as Triune. In recognizing his existence, we must also leave to one side questions which cannot be resolved now: whether scientific, i.e., about nature or the world, or theological.[51] But there will come a time when we will know what we are able to know. Until then false knowledge must be overthrown.[52] As Paul says, we should be content to know "in part" but later, much later, we shall know in full (1 Corinthians 13:12).

Before concluding Book II, which is Irenaeus' considered response to the Gnostic theories he has outlined in Book I, he prepares the ground for his description of salvation as principally the restoration of humankind, by introducing the idea of what is and is not the essence of being human. For this lies at the centre of Irenaeus' economy (*oikonomia*) or arrangement of salvation.

The Gnostics maintained a tripartite division of humanity into the material, the animal and the spiritual, a division originating from their creation. These three conditions of humanity are brought about by three creations: the last being through angels and the former two from "weariness and fear" and "impetuosity".[53] The first two parts of humanity will perish and be unable to enter the Gnostic intermediate sphere in which resides the Pleroma. Even more fantastic in the Gnostic system is that the creator herself is flawed and her creation pervaded by evil from the start. She (the mother and creator in the Gnostic system) may even be surpassed by spiritual humans who rise beyond her.[54] This spiritual person, described as "a superior person", is one who has been enlightened, in whom the spark of knowledge has flared, and who has been admitted and baptized according to the Gnostic baptismal rite. Essentially liberated from the flesh and the material existence which holds a person prisoner, they now exist in the Pleroma.

The Gnostics also held to a Platonic view that the soul may pass from any previous bodily existence by forgetting all that took place in the body previously: something called "a drink of oblivion".[55] Christ, however, taught that souls would inhabit remade bodies and continue to exist, such that they might be known and recognized.[56] As Irenaeus says, God is well able to do this as "he is not so poor or destitute in resources that he cannot confer its own proper soul on each individual body, even as he gives it also its special character".[57]

Having completed two books setting out the false knowledge of the Gnostics and followed by its overthrowal, Irenaeus cannot finish there. Like John Milton who, having finished his epic poem *Paradise Lost* was encouraged to write *Paradise Regained*, Irenaeus wanted to show from Scripture and from the "Rule of Truth" the way God works for the restoration of humankind. However, before this next great theme in his work we must reiterate the nature of the Triune God Irenaeus stood by, and the *recapitulation* of humankind that he worked.

Irenaeus and the Triune God

It is worth emphasizing that Irenaeus had no trouble in believing in a Triune God of Father, Son and Holy Spirit. Although this is quite clear in *Against Heresies*, as we shall see, he also makes his belief in the Trinity plain in his brief summary of the faith in *Demonstration of the Apostolic Preaching*. Along with the so-called Great Church (i.e., the catholic or universal orthodox Church) of the post-Apostolic age, Irenaeus believed there was a natural ascription of divinity or eternity to each member of the Trinity. This seemed to be the plain teaching of the Gospels and the Pauline Epistles, which, by the year in which Irenaeus was writing (*c*.170), were widely received as authoritative for the belief and conduct of the Church. Incidentally, this was only 70 or 80 years after the writing of the last Gospel by John in Ephesus, as Irenaeus himself makes clear.[58]

The later complexities and heresies surrounding the way to express the biblical teaching of the Trinity still lay ahead. Broadly speaking, false representations of the Trinity fell into two camps: they were either modalist or subordinationist. Modalists such as Sabellius, a third-century Roman presbyter, stressed the unity of the Godhead, but saw the Son and the Spirit as different expressions or emanations of the One God, who reveals himself and acts in three ways or modes of being. Subordinationists acknowledged the Son and Spirit as separate beings, but held that they are, and always have been, subordinate to the Father, who alone is eternal and uncreated. For those who stressed the monarchy of the Father in different ways, the essential oneness and supremacy of the Father was non-negotiable.[59] The most well-known example of this position was Arius, who sparked the fourth-century Trinitarian controversy leading to the First Council of Nicaea (325) and later to the Council of Constantinople (381).

If Irenaeus likewise wanted to stress the One-ness of God, particularly against the idea of many divine emanations taught by the Gnostic Valentinus, or the two-god theory of Marcion, one of the Old Testament, the other of the New, he would never do so at the cost of downgrading the divinity of the Son or the Spirit. He would have been content with his near contemporary Tertullian's assertion about the Trinity, i.e., that "there is One God in Three persons".

First of all, Irenaeus stresses the distinct divine activity of each person in the Trinity, highlighting the activity, or what theologians call the "economy" of the Trinity, whilst at the same time upholding that they are of one substance or being (*ousia*). This is what theologians call the immanence of the Trinity, although this vocabulary of *substance* and *ousia* was scarcely used in 170. Thus, in reference to the sacrament of baptism, Irenaeus speaks of the economy or activity of the Trinity:

> And for this reason, the baptism of our generation proceeds through these three points: God the Father bestowing on us regeneration through His Son by the Holy Spirit. For as many as carry in them the Spirit of God are led to the Word, that is to

> the Son; and the Son brings them to the Father; and the Father causes them to possess incorruption. Without the Spirit it is not possible to behold the Word of God, nor without the Son can any draw near to the Father: for the knowledge of the Father is the Son, and the knowledge of the Son of God is through the Holy Spirit; and according to the good pleasure of the Father, the Son ministers and dispenses the Spirit to whomsoever the Father wills and as he wills.[60]

These words almost precisely foreshadow those used by Gregory of Nyssa 200 years later in combatting Arianism. And for us today they show the interdependence of the Trinity in unity of purpose and being.

Furthermore, Irenaeus sees the interweaving of the Trinity in establishing the Kingdom of God through the ages as also manifesting this economy, and this through both the Old and New Testaments. Thus, he says:

> And David refers even more openly and clearly to the Father and the Son when he says "your throne, O God, is for ever and ever; you have loved justice, and hated iniquity, therefore God has anointed you with the oil of gladness above your fellows" (Psalm 45.6). For the Son, because he is God, receives from the Father, that is from God, the throne of the eternal kingdom, and the oil of anointing above his fellows. And "oil of anointing" is the Spirit, with which he was anointed, and "his fellows" are prophets, and the just, and the Apostles, and all those who receive the fellowship of his kingdom, that is, his disciples.[61]

The foundational rock on which Irenaeus builds his theology, in contradistinction to both Valentinus and the Gnostics as well as to Marcion, is the affirmation that there is one God who alone is Triune, in three persons who together were and are responsible for creation. Far from being the product of evil intention as in Gnostic doctrine, the creation is good. But in an open system in which freedom existed for angels and humans, the advent of evil was still a possibility. God is a three-person deity of Father, Son and Spirit. He is intimately involved with his creation but distinct from it. He is the only *being*, to use Platonic language, taken from *Timaeus* (27D-28A), while the creation and not least humankind are to *become* what they were intended to be.

The fact that humankind can only become what they were intended to be is the story of salvation through the Incarnation and consequent redemption. This is remaking humanity to the glory of God. For Irenaeus, as we shall see, the remaking of humanity comes about through recapitulation by Christ. But the theological platform on which everything is built is the doctrine of the Trinity and the creation that proceeds from God. His most brilliant and troublesome creation is man and woman, in whom the glory of God will eventually be fully shown, but whose path to glory lies through the Incarnation of Christ.

Notes

[1] Desiderius Erasmus, *Opus eruditissimum Divi Irenaei* (Basle, 1526), pp. 2-3.
[2] Denis Minns, *Irenaeus: An Introduction* (London: Continuum, 2010), p. 6.
[3] Bertrand Russell, *History of Western Philosophy* (London: Routledge, 2007), p. 110.
[4] Plato, *Timaeus*, tr. Desmond Lee (Harmondsworth: Penguin, 1977), p. 43.
[5] Paula Gooder, *Body: Biblical Spirituality for the Whole Person* (London: SPCK, 2016), p. 22.
[6] Gooder, *Body*, p. 22.
[7] Behr, *Irenaeus of Lyons*, p. 74.
[8] *AH* I.9.21; I.9.21 and I.22.28.
[9] *AH* I.1.2; I.12.1; I.8.2; II.3.1.
[10] *AH* I.3.3.
[11] *AH* I.11.4.
[12] *AH* I.10.1.
[13] *AH* I.10.2.
[14] *AH* I.10.3.
[15] *AH* I.13.1.
[16] *AH* I.13.2.
[17] *AH* I.13.2.
[18] *AH* I.13.3.

19 *AH* I.13.3.
20 *AH* I.15.2.
21 *AH* I.17.1-2.
22 *AH* I.16.3.
23 *AH* I.22.1, quoting John 1:3.
24 *AH* I.24.1; I.24.1-5.
25 *AH* I.25.1.
26 *AH* I.26.6.
27 *HE* III.28; IV.14.
28 *AH* I.26.1-2.
29 *AH* I.28.1.
30 *AH* I.28,2.
31 *AH* I.24.1.
32 *AH* I.30.5-9.
33 *AH* I.31.3-4.
34 *AH* II.10.2-6; II.24-30.8.
35 *AH* II.1.2.
36 *AH* II.2.1-4; II.3.1-2; II.4.1-3.
37 *AH* II.7.1-7.
38 *AH* II.12.1-8.
39 *AH* II.14.1-9.
40 *AH* II.23.1-2.
41 *AH* II.20.3.
42 *AH* II.21.1-3.
43 *AH* II.20.4.
44 *AH* III.22.5.
45 *AH* II.24.2; II.24.3.
46 *AH* II.24.3.
47 *AH* II.26.1.
48 *AH* II.27.1.
49 *AH* II.27.1.
50 *AH* II.27.1
51 *AH* II.28.2-3.
52 *AH* II.28.6-7.
53 *AH* II.29.3.
54 *AH* II.30.1-2.

55 *AH* II.23.1-5.
56 *AH* II.24.1-4.
57 *AH* II.23.5.
58 *AH* III.1.1.
59 Minns, *Irenaeus*, pp. 56ff.
60 *Demonstration of the Apostolic Preaching* §7.
61 *Demonstration of the Apostolic Preaching* §47.

8

God's troublesome and testing creature

William Shakespeare put these words into the mouth of Hamlet: "What a piece of work is a man, how noble in reason, how infinite in faculty. In form and moving how express and admirable, in action how like an Angel, in apprehension how like a god, the beauty of the world, the paragon of animals. And yet to me, what is this quintessence of dust?" (*Hamlet*, Act 2, Scene 2). Shakespeare captures the paradox at the centre of human existence: brilliant but tragic, beautiful but mortal; dust to dust. Irenaeus would have mostly agreed, perhaps recalling the words of the Psalmist, who also proclaimed man's calling, extolling human creation but posing a question as to human destiny.

> When I consider your heavens,
> The work of your fingers,
> The moon and the stars,
> Which you have set in place,
> What is man that you are mindful of him,
> The son of man that you care for him?
> You made him a little lower than the heavenly beings
> And crowned him with glory and honour.
> You made him ruler over the works of your hands;
> You put everything under his feet:
> All flocks and herds,
> And the beasts of the field,
> The birds of the air,
> And the fish of the sea,
> All that swim the paths of the seas.
> O Lord, our Lord,

How majestic is your name in all the earth (Psalm 8:3-9).

Irenaeus too will describe the origin, the fall and the destiny of human beings as the backdrop to the story of the rescue of humanity, which he will tell as a remaking of humankind through *recapitulation* by Christ. More of that to come. His starting point, as indeed for almost all the Church Fathers in their writings, is the creation narratives of Genesis, and in particular the creation of the human race in Adam and Eve. Many of the Fathers wrote on the six days of creation or the *Hexaemeron*. In later times, Ambrose, Augustine of Hippo, Basil of Caesarea, Gregory of Nyssa and John Chrysostom would all write their own accounts of these six days; and in so doing pave the way for later medieval writers such as Aquinas and Bonaventure. As far as humanity is concerned, human beings were the last creatures to be made in this sequence of six days, which we understand today as referring to six epochs (2 Peter 3:8), after which God rested on the seventh day, having described his creation as good (Genesis 1:25).

Man: the image and likeness of God

Humanity is given two creation accounts in Genesis (1:26-28 and 2:18-25), the second being a more extensive one of the creation of woman, and the relationship between man and woman before the Fall. Along with the other Church Fathers, Irenaeus took these creation narratives as the starting point for his own understanding of human nature and destiny. The phrase that defines the nature of humanity is "the image and likeness of God". This phrase could be said to be a *hendiadys*, which refers to a combination of two words or concepts giving a single meaning: such as "nice and warm", meaning comfortable, or "hand to mouth", meaning unregulated. For Irenaeus, the terms *image* and *likeness* were virtual synonyms for the essence and determinative characteristics of humanity. He was not always consistent in the way he rendered the meaning of image and likeness, however, and this arose from the fact that *Against Heresies* was a piece of polemical writing answering the Gnostics, rather than just a piece of systematic theology.

Irenaeus also makes plain that the image of God becomes perfect in a human being as a progression. A person is not perfect and complete from the outset. In this respect, a line may be drawn between Paul and Augustine and Irenaeus; the former two (Paul and Augustine) hold to a more perfect and complete creation of man in the first place. In pictorial terms, this is shown, for example, in Michelangelo's creation of Adam on the ceiling of the Sistine Chapel versus Dürer's depiction of Adam and Eve in the Prado, although admittedly after the Fall. Whereas the former figure is heroic and powerful, the latter is inevitably vulnerable, and, to use Irenaeus' word, plastic and in need of refashioning.

Indeed, Irenaeus is very conscious that Adam's flesh is the "ancient handiwork (*plásis*) formed out of the mud or dust by God for God, and it is [such] that John declared the Word of God [also] truly became".[1] Irenaeus makes the case that man *becomes perfect* only through his remaking and refashioning by Christ after the Fall, in much the same way that Christ himself became perfect following his own testing while on earth. This is not to suggest that Jesus was imperfect from the start, far from it, but that his perfection was untested, unproven and made complete by his own sufferings (see Hebrews 5:7-10). Indeed, "the notion that Adam was not created perfect, but rather created in the image of God and was intended to come to be in the likeness of God at the end of a process of development, is Irenaeus' most characteristic understanding of Genesis 1:26, and the one that most coheres with the rest of his theological system".[2] Furthermore, man's image, Irenaeus suggests, may only be fully known after the coming of Christ, who is himself the image of the true man.[3] Christ thus makes perfect that which was previously marred and incomplete (Colossians 3:10). Irenaeus writes the following telling words whilst reflecting on the man born blind who is then healed in John 9:

> For, as the Scripture says, he made man by a kind of process: "And the Lord took clay from the earth and formed man". Wherefore also the Lord spat on the ground and made clay, and smeared it upon the eyes, pointing out the original fashioning of man, how it was affected, and manifesting the hand of God to those who can understand by what [hand] man was formed out of dust. For that

> which the artificer, The Word, had omitted to form in the womb [viz., the blind man's eyes], he then supplied in public, that the works of God might be manifested in him, in order that we might not be seeking out another hand by which he was fashioned, nor another father; knowing that this hand of God which formed us at the beginning, and which does form us in the womb, has in the last times sought us out who were lost, winning back his own, and taking up the lost sheep upon his shoulders, and with joy restoring it to the fold of life.[4]

In other words, it is the Father through Christ and the Spirit who puts right what is incomplete in humanity and completes what is lacking and is as yet imperfect. It is the story of the progression of humankind from imperfection to completeness, retold in the sign of the healing of the man born blind that typifies Irenaeus' sense of progressive salvation.

Fundamentally, what makes humans human is that we are made in the image and likeness of God. This means we have reason, speech, language, social skills, artistic ability, self-reflection, creative and inventive ability, and the capacity to know God. All this is summed up in the concept of being made in God's image. We are made in his image and come, in the end, to share his likeness. This is Irenaeus' starting point, as it is of all Christian and Jewish understanding of humanity. Not only that, but in the context of his battle with the Valentinian Gnostics, Irenaeus re-establishes the fact that, unlike their teaching, and instead like that of the Apostle Paul, Adam is created in the image of God, and created by God after the pattern of Christ, who himself is the image of the invisible God (Colossians 1:15) and the eternal Word.[5]

Thus, in his *Demonstration of the Apostolic Preaching*, Irenaeus writes:

> But man, he formed with his own hands, taking from the earth that which was purest and finest, and mingling in measure his own power with the earth. For he traced his own form on the formation, that that which should be seen should be of divine form: for (as) the image of God was man formed and set on earth. And that he might become living, he breathed on his face the breath of life; that both for the breath and for the formation

man should be like unto God. Moreover, he was free and self-controlled, being made by God for this end, that he might rule all those things that were upon earth. And this great created world, prepared by God before the formation of man, was given to man as his place, containing all things within itself.[6]

Irenaeus goes on to say that Adam and Eve were "innocent" and "entire, preserving their own nature, since they had the breath of life which was breathed on their creation: and while this breath remains in its place and power, it has no comprehension and understanding of things that are base. And therefore, they were not ashamed, kissing and embracing each other in purity after the manner of children."[7]

However, in case humans think of themselves more highly than they ought, they were given a command which tested them, and showed them the limits of their freedom. This command, not to eat of the fruit of good and evil, reminded them that they were subject to God and were also subject to certain limitations. Thus, Irenaeus writes:

> God set him certain limitations so that if he should keep the commandment of God, he should ever remain such as he was, that is to say immortal: but, if he should not keep it, he should become mortal and be dissolved to the earth from whence his formation had been taken.[8]

The effects of the Fall

In answering the Gnostics in *Against Heresies*, Irenaeus makes plain his understanding (unlike theirs) that God was completely involved in creation, and that it was constructed in such a way that rebellion against God was possible, and indeed foreknown before the act of creation itself, especially of humanity (Genesis 1:26). Hence the pause in the narrative where the Godhead ponders his most costly creation. Man and woman are costly creations in the sense that their Fall will inevitably lead to the sacrifice of Christ for the refashioning and redeeming of humankind, which will itself result from the character of God as holy and loving.

Adam and Eve, representing humanity, are "entire", but are given a commandment, the keeping of which will prove their obedience and their love of the creator. But in this they fail. Irenaeus then goes on to describe the nature of their Fall, pinning the cause firmly on the Devil or Satan:

> This commandment [not to eat of the Tree of the Knowledge of Good and Evil] the man kept not, but was disobedient to God, being led astray by the Angel who, (on account of) the great gifts of God which he had given to man, was envious and jealous of him and both brought himself to nought and made man sinful, persuading him to disobey the commandment of God. So, the Angel, becoming by his falsehood the author and originator of sin, himself was struck down, having offended against God, and man he caused to be cast out of Paradise.[9]

Irenaeus goes on to call this rebellious angel the Apostate, Satan, and the Slanderer. The effect of this was to bring "anxious grief", sorrow, toil, lamentation, murder and death into the world, and furthermore through this intervention, sexual relations with women, "concupiscence, constraints of love, spells of bewitchment and sorcery" occur.[10] The origin of evil in creation is attributed simply to two things by Irenaeus: the reality of the Devil, a fallen angel, and the disobedience of Adam and Eve.

For Irenaeus, the very concept of the Devil denotes something real and critical. The Devil is no equal and opposite force to God, who alone is the creator. In this, Irenaeus is far removed from the later Manichees (*c.*260), themselves a Gnostic sect. Their understanding of the universe lay in twin forces of good and evil struggling in history with an uncertain outcome. Instead, Irenaeus believed in "God's unlimited supremacy over the Devil".[11] Indeed, the life that the Devil has now been permitted by God himself results from his creator, who is now his enemy.[12] The defeat of the Devil is ultimately certain, but until then the struggle must be taken seriously, just as it was for Christ, who was tempted, delivered, crucified and exalted in his struggle with Satan. The cause of the Devil's enmity with humankind is his envy of their status and their destiny in

God's Kingdom.[13] This causes him to ruin, or attempt to ruin, what God has created.

Furthermore, not only does humanity in the persons of Adam and Eve fall into the lies and snares of the Devil, but through acting on his lies rather than following God's commandment, they fall into a form of slavery which Paul calls in Colossians the "dominion of darkness" (Colossians 1:13). This slavery has the effect of preventing the development of humankind, keeping them in a kind of stasis or state of spiritual stagnation. As Wingren says, "[Humanity's] growth is destroyed through the circumstances of his attachment to evil, and the child ceases to progress towards his destiny which has been appointed by God. Man is created to conform to the *imago* and *similitudo* of God, but in actual fact fails to achieve his destiny."[14]

Accepting the Devil's suggestion that Adam and Eve will not die by eating the fruit, "for God knows that when you eat of it your eye will be opened, and you will be like God, knowing good and evil" (Genesis 3:4) was the first step towards the catastrophe of the Fall. The second step is plain disobedience. The Devil convinces them that God has withheld something good and beneficial which will make them like God. So, following this conviction, they want everything, and they want it at once. Thus, when the Devil in the form of the serpent offers them the chance to become like God, they quickly seize it. They take that which is forbidden. What happens in this symbolic act of disobedience is the disruption of the whole divine economy (*oikonomia*). For in their disobedience, Adam and Eve are not behaving towards the Creator in a way that is consonant with their created and dependent status, but rather, in taking there and then something that is promised in the destiny of humankind, they crash the whole of creation, including themselves. About this very point, Irenaeus writes as follows:

> How, then, will that be God which is not yet a human being? [i.e. which has not yet come to maturity and perfection]. How will that be perfected which had just begun? How will that be immortal which in its mortal nature did not obey its creator? You ought first to keep within the bounds of humankind and then from there partake in the glory of God. For you do not make

> God, rather it is God who makes you. If then, you are the work of God, await the hand of your fashioner who does all things at the due time—the due time for you, that is, who are being created. Offer him a soft and pliable heart and retain the shape which your fashioner gave you. Retain the moisture he gives you, for if you turn dry and hard you will lose the imprint of his fingers. If you retain the shape he gives you, you will advance to perfection. The mud in you will be hidden by the handiwork of God. His hand created your substance; it will overlay you, inside and out, with pure gold and silver and so adorn you that the king himself will desire your beauty (Psalm 45.11). But if you become hardened, and reject his handiwork and become ungrateful to him because he made you a human being—ungrateful that is to God—you will have lost at once both his handiwork and life. For creating belongs to the generosity of God; being created belongs to the nature of humankind. If therefore you offer him what is yours, that is faith in him and subjection, you shall be the recipient of his handiwork and shall become a perfect work of God.[15]

Here is the substance of Irenaeus' hypothesis which is set in a polemical context of an answer to Marcion and the Gnostics. He describes the Fall as an untimely reaching for something forbidden by God at the instigation of a jealous Satan. At the right time, that forbidden thing is to be part of our human calling, which is to know good and evil, not from personal experience, but through wisdom and understanding. As a matter of interest, the Greek Fathers of whom we would have to say Irenaeus is one (though living in the Western Empire when writing *Against Heresies*) in general describe the Fall with a softer landing than the Western Latin Fathers of whom Augustine, 200 years later, would be the leader. As we have seen, Irenaeus depicts the Fall as a substantial block in the progress and development of humankind, as opening the door to pain, grief, sin and death in a way that God has not planned; although he must have foreknown it from the beginning even if he did not will or predestine it. Indeed, as humans, we are given freedom to choose to obey or not. Whereas Augustine, principally writing in the heat of the Pelagian controversy from *c*.410, strikes a more Pauline note. Adam and Eve were created perfect (Romans 5:12-21), but lost their perfection, that is their similitude to God, whilst retaining their image of God—severely marred but still intact and present. For Irenaeus, the image must be restored, although humans are not perfect from the start. *Adam is innocent from the beginning but not perfect, since they are unproven.* Thus, he writes:

> If, however, any one says, "What then? Could God have exhibited man as perfect from the beginning?" Let him know that, inasmuch as God is indeed always the same and unbegotten as respects himself, all things are possible to him. But created things must be inferior to him who created them, from the very fact of their later origin; for it was not possible for things recently created to have been uncreated. But inasmuch as they were not uncreated, for this very reason do they come short of perfect. Because, as these things are of later date, so are they infantile; so are they unaccustomed to, and under-exercised in, perfect discipline. For as it certainly is in the power of a mother to give strong food to her infant, (but she does not do so), as the child is not yet able to receive more substantial nourishment; so also, it was possible for God himself to have made man perfect from the first, but man could not receive this perfection, being as yet an infant. And for this cause our Lord in these last times, when he summed up all things into himself, came to us, not as he might come, but as we were capable of beholding him.[16]

In these senses, Irenaeus has a strong doctrine of accommodation.

Conclusions

The main building block in Irenaeus' doctrine of humanity, which also answers the Gnostics, is that *humanity is God's creation*. It is hard to overstress the cardinal importance of this teaching in the face of the Gnostics. Humanity is part mud (*humus*) and part breath of God. Indeed, God himself could not have been more intimately involved in the creation of humanity, requiring as it did a pause for reflection in the

Godhead before this most costly creation, costly to God himself and therefore to each member of the Trinity. It is often the case in Irenaeus' writing that the hands of the Father are the Eternal Word and the Spirit, through whom humanity was first made, and then recreated. As Irenaeus writes, "Now shall God be glorified in his handiwork, fitting it so as to be comfortable to, and modelled after, His own Son. For by the hands of the Father, that is by the Son and the Holy Spirit, man and not merely a part of man, was made in the likeness of God."[17] A line may be drawn from this act of creation to the Incarnation, the crucifixion, the resurrection and Pentecost—the receipt of the Spirit. Far from abhorring the flesh, God was himself incarnate in the self-same flesh, in which he also suffered, although without sin (Hebrews 4:15), thus proving that he neither then, nor in the future, despises our flesh. It will be a point of argument with the Gnostics *that the flesh is a worthy recipient of the Spirit* and not to be despised because of its weakness or its subjection to change, as the body so often is in Platonism.

The merit of the flesh is a continuing source of tension with aspects of Greek culture. Indeed, Tertullian needed to write a treatise maintaining that the resurrection of the believer means a bodily resurrection of the flesh, remade and reworked (1 Corinthians 15:35-49).[18] Likewise, both Tertullian and Irenaeus (and later Athanasius in *De Incarnatione*) had to contend for the fact that Christ the Eternal Word also took on *real human flesh* and did not come in just the appearance of the flesh which was a Gnostic heresy. This heresy is called Docetism (from *dokein*, meaning to seem) and Tertullian wrote against it in his *On the Flesh of Christ*,[19] something which the Apostle John was already contending for in his own lifetime when he was writing his Epistles in *c.*80-90 (see 1 John 4:1-3).

In *Against Heresies*, Irenaeus also affirms that humanity may be recapitulated by Christ (which we shall come to) and be made ready to receive the Kingdom of God. Irenaeus wrote towards the end of *Against Heresies* these words: "When the spirit here blended to the soul is united to God's handiwork [the flesh], the man is rendered spiritual and *perfect* because of the outpouring of the Spirit, and this is he who has been made in the image and likeness of God."[20]

When Adam and Eve leave the Garden of Eden, exiled by God himself for their disobedience (Genesis 3:23-24), they are under more than a cloud. They experience a sentence of death which enters the world (several of the Church Fathers speculate as to what life would have been like if there had been no death and no expulsion from the garden). But they are now under the control of sin or selfish egotism; relationships between men and women have become distorted and discordant; there is pain in childbearing; and work has become toilsome and hard. Although in some kind of spiritual captivity, men and women are capable nevertheless of independent action.[21] God then begins to enact his plan for humanity's liberation and reinstatement, whilst showing his true glory. After oscillating between regret and judgement (Genesis 6-9) the plan unfolds: a family is chosen through whom God will reveal and display his will—the family of Abraham—and in time the Law is given through Moses to indicate God's ways and train Israel's conduct, however ineffective this proves.[22] Yet a new way must be found through a perfect and divine being who can restore the image of God in humanity, fashioning men and women in a true likeness to God while also demonstrating his glory. This way is through what Irenaeus calls recapitulation.

Notes

[1] *AH* I.9.3. See also Behr, *Irenaeus of Lyons*, p. 119.
[2] Minns, *Irenaeus*, p. 75.
[3] *AH* V.15.2.
[4] *AH* V.5.2.
[5] Gustaf Wingren, *Man and the Incarnation: A Study in the Biblical Theology of Irenaeus*, tr. Ross Mackenzie (Eugene, OR: Wipf & Stock, 2004), pp. 17ff.
[6] *Demonstration of the Apostolic Preaching* §11.
[7] *Demonstration of the Apostolic Preaching* §14.
[8] *Demonstration of the Apostolic Preaching* §15.
[9] *Demonstration of the Apostolic Preaching* §16.
[10] *Demonstration of the Apostolic Preaching* §§17-18. See Genesis 6:1-3; Enoch VII.1; *AH* IV.27.2.
[11] Wingren, *Man and the Incarnation*, p. 39.
[12] Wingren, *Man and the Incarnation*, p. 39.

13 *AH* V.24.1-4.
14 Wingren, *Man and the Incarnation*, p. 51.
15 *AH* IV.39.2-3.
16 *AH* IV.38.1.
17 *AH* V.6.1.
18 Tertullian, *On the Resurrection of the Flesh*, TANF, Vol. III pp. 545ff.
19 Tertullian, *On the Resurrection of the Flesh*, p. 521.
20 *AH* V.6.1.
21 Wingren, *Man and the Incarnation*, p. 61.
22 Wingren, *Man and the Incarnation*, pp. 50ff.

9

Salvation unfolded: The Incarnation

It is worth remembering that in 170, the New Testament as we know it, and the Bible as we have it, did not yet exist. Irenaeus, however, would have had its main constituent parts: the Septuagint, which was the Greek translation of the Jewish Scriptures made in Alexandria in the third century BC (and possibly other translations to be assembled by Origen in his *Hexapla,* for instance Aquila of Sinope and Theodotion of Ephesus), the Gospels and Paul's letters, which were then widely circulating. Some of these texts were recent. John's Gospel, his letters, and Revelation were only written at the very end of the first century; likewise some of the translations of the OT into Greek. Given that these were still in manuscript form and would not be in a single codex until the mid-fourth century, to own all these manuscripts you would need to be either a very wealthy individual or a well-appointed or well-resourced church. Since the Church was persecuted, as we have seen at Vienne and Lugdunum, and given that Christians consequently often met in private homes, or in the open air in summer, they were vulnerable to opposition and their resources, especially manuscripts, were all too susceptible to being confiscated or destroyed.

Furthermore, there was still a very undeveloped form of episcopal oversight in the mid-second century, even in Rome and Alexandria, and Constantinople as such did not exist! In other words, the Church in 170, when Irenaeus was writing, was still in a very rudimentary and embryonic stage, and with the Apostles no longer present. In this fragile state, the Great Church (by which is meant the orthodox universal catholic church) was continuously challenged by false teaching, as we have seen in the case of the Gnostics and their literature.[1] And in writing his polemical work against the Valentinians and Marcion in particular, it was necessary for Irenaeus to demonstrate there was a rule or canon (yardstick) by which God had revealed his salvation plan to humankind, and which also needed correct interpretation. This was central to his task, so that future generations, as well as his own, would find true spiritual life through the Word faithfully transmitted, and by the Spirit making Christ's presence real in the lives of believers, according to that teaching.

To this end, Irenaeus was at pains to stress that there is a canon or rule for recognizing the revelation that God has given. Indeed, Clement of Rome, Tertullian and Clement of Alexandria were all involved in answering the Gnostics and likewise maintained that there was a tradition of faith by which we know and correctly interpret the Scriptures.[2] Thus Clement of Rome (88-98, and not to be confused with Clement of Alexandria of 150-215) wrote, "Let us come to the glorious and venerable *canon of our tradition* and let us see what is good and pleasing and acceptable in the sight of our Maker."[3]

With this idea of a rule in mind, Irenaeus wrote that we are not to speculate about things beyond our knowledge and that, if Christians do not do so, they "shall continue without danger, and all Scripture, which has been given to us by God, shall be found by us perfectly consistent; and the parables shall harmonize with those passages which are perfectly plain".[4]

This rule or tradition will demonstrate God's progressive revelation in the Old and New Covenants. And the hypothesis latent in the Testaments is that this revelation is for the redemption of humankind in Christ. The Scriptures which Irenaeus endorsed are the Law and the Prophets in the Old Testament, and the Gospels and the teaching of Paul and the Apostles in the New. This plan of God for human salvation is now made clear in Books III and IV of *Against Heresies*. For the most part, Book III concentrates on the witness of the Apostles to the coming of Christ and its purpose. Book IV reverts to showing that the Old Testament is part of a single overarching revelation in which God is the Creator; that humanity is made in God's image; that the patriarchs and especially Abraham demonstrated the way of faith; that the Law must bring us to Christ; that the history of Israel is a warning about truly following God, as well as a preparation for the Messiah; and finally that the prophets demonstrate the true character and expectations of God as well as predicting and preparing the community for the coming of the Messiah. All of this was to both contradict and correct Marcion and his teaching which maintained erroneously and deceptively that the Old and the New Testaments come from different gods, and that only Luke's Gospel and the Pauline epistles were of any value.

From the Old and New Testaments, Irenaeus describes the arrangement or *oikonomia* for salvation. As far as he was concerned, the Testaments are not so much a collection of writings grouped by time, but two covenants in which humanity develops and progresses towards its goal. Once again the notion of progression in Irenaeus' theology was strong. The Old Testament describes a people held by Law, while the New Testament demonstrates humanity being offered liberation through Christ: his Incarnation, life, sacrificial death and resurrection. Nevertheless, the presence of Christ, though shadowy, is also to be found in the Old Testament as the Word not yet made flesh.[5]

The witness of the Apostles to Christ: Book III

Book III of *Against Heresies* sets out the teaching of the Apostles and their appointed successors concerning the Father, Christ and the Spirit in a positive manner, with just occasional rebuttal of various Gnostic sects or heresies on the way, e.g., the Ebionites, who taught that Jesus was the natural son of Joseph and Mary;[6] Marcion;[7] and the Jews who don't recognize their Messiah.[8] The authority for Irenaeus' teaching comes from a combination of Scripture and tradition. As such it is somewhat less polemical in style and content than the first two books. In the opening two sections Irenaeus gives the sources of the authority for his teaching.[9]

In a fascinating opening section, he states that he has learnt of God's plan of salvation from the Apostles, who first proclaimed their teaching in public, then handed it down through the Scriptures. He goes on to say how Matthew wrote, "for the Hebrews in their own dialect".[10] (Was there an original Hebrew or Aramaic version of Matthew?) He records that Mark was the interpreter of Peter and "wrote down in writing what had been preached".[11] Luke, also "the companion of Paul recorded in a book the gospel preached by him"; and finally John, "who leaned upon Christ's breast [i.e., the Beloved Disciple of John 13:23], did himself publish a Gospel during his residence at Ephesus in Asia". These Gospel writers were inspired by the Spirit and declared that there was one God and Father and one Christ, the Son of God.[12]

If the Apostles and their associates taught these things, then so did tradition. The tradition appears to be in part the oral tradition before the teaching was written down in Gospel form, and out of which Scripture arose. For there was probably a gap of some thirty to seventy years from the ascension of Christ and the last Gospel being written. This gap required faithful leaders to steer the Church before Scripture, tradition and continuing leadership were properly established. According to Irenaeus, leaders of the Church in Rome and Antioch in the first century were Linus, Anacletus and Clement in Rome; and Peter, Euodius and Ignatius in Antioch.[13] They covered the 70 years of church life until the completion of the Gospels. Hence, tradition and Scripture mingled together. Irenaeus continues to list other early church leaders and his own beloved Polycarp whom he knew as a boy or young man. Thus, Irenaeus states that it is in the Scriptures and this Apostolic tradition, guided by the Spirit, that truth may be found.[14]

Irenaeus continues in this vein for most of Book III in both answering the false teaching of the Gnostics in their various sects and at the same time restating the teaching of the Apostles. There are some specific rebuttals of false interpretation of statements by Paul by the Gnostics: not least his phrase "the god of this age" (2 Corinthians 4:4) which they take to mean a "god" separate from the Creator.[15] Likewise, it was necessary to make clear to the Gnostics that the phrase "ye cannot serve God and mammon" in Matthew (6.24) does not refer to a separate god called mammon who is equal to the Creator.

In other words, the Gnostics were seeking to explain either creation or the work of salvation as depending on several gods apparently named in the Scriptures, most of which Marcion nonetheless abandons. One might say Irenaeus' method was to rebut false interpretation and keep restating the central hypothesis of the Bible, which is that there is a single creator, that humanity is his creation and that the eternal Word became the incarnate Christ in order to restore humanity, the created order and his Kingdom. To interpret the Scripture in any other way would be to violate the meaning of the Apostles and the rule of faith.[16] One might say these years from 100-170 were years of struggle about the correct interpretation of Scripture.

Not only does Irenaeus state this rule of faith, and state it again and again, but at one point he intersperses it with a heartfelt prayer to "the Lord God of Abraham . . . who is the Father of our Lord Jesus Christ".[17] This prayer recognizes that establishing the truth and seeing off Gnostic distortions was and is a spiritual battle. So, he concludes his prayer, "Grant, by our Lord Jesus Christ, the governing power of the Holy Spirit; give to every reader of this work to know thee, that thou art God alone, to be restrengthened in thee, and to avoid every heretical, and godless and impious doctrine."[18]

Having set out the need for a tradition and for teaching that stems from the Apostles and also a line of Apostolic succession in the church leaders, particularly in Antioch and Rome, and especially in the first century and until his own day, Irenaeus continues to affirm the consistency of the Gospels and Paul's writings in their themes of salvation. All of them, that is the four Gospel writers and Paul, agree that there is but one God in three persons spoken of in the Old Testament, including by the patriarchs, Moses and the prophets. Matthew in his Gospel affirms that the God of Abraham was the Father of our Lord Jesus Christ.[19] Furthermore, he tells us that the same Spirit who inspired the prophets (see especially Isaiah 11:1-2) descended on Jesus at his baptism to equip him for his ministry.[20] Likewise, Irenaeus underlines Luke's account of the nativity as the essential prerequisite to "Christ winning back to God that human nature which had departed from God". Human beings are taught to worship God after a new fashion, not another God, "because there is but one God, who justifies the circumcision by faith, and the uncircumcision by faith".[21] "Mark too picks up the prophecy of Isaiah at the outset of his Gospel that the Messiah, the Son of God (Mark 1:1-3), would be announced by a voice crying in the wilderness (Isaiah 40:3)".[22] And finally, John is quoted at length from the Prologue to demonstrate that Jesus is none other than the eternal Word made flesh for the salvation of humankind. He is the creator who became incarnate (John 1:14).

All this was in complete contrast to both Marcion and Valentinus.[23] Finally, in a simple piece of numerology which Irenaeus cannot resist, he suggests that four is the complete number: there being four directions in the world (north, south, east and west), four principal winds and four faces to the cherubim (a lion, a calf, a man and an eagle).[24] Likewise, four Gospels give a complete account of the ministry of Christ.

Having endorsed the consistency of the Gospels in their teaching about the status of Christ as both God and Man, and as the Incarnate Word, Irenaeus continues his argument about the consistency of Scripture through a survey of Acts and Paul.[25] Summarizing the preaching in Acts, Irenaeus shows the distinction between preaching to the Jews and Gentiles: "to the Jews, indeed they proclaimed that Jesus who was crucified by them was the Son of God, the Judge of the quick and the dead, and that he received from his Father an eternal kingdom in Israel, as I have pointed out: but to the Greeks (as in Athens in Acts 17) they preached one God, who made all things, and Jesus Christ his Son".[26] Once again Irenaeus' aim is the same: to show the consistency of the message and in a word that the Creator God is also the Redeemer. Redemption or recapitulation comes about through the Incarnation of the eternal Word in flesh, to redeem humankind and remake its marred image. Having shown this hypothesis and this arrangement of salvation spread through the Old and New Testaments, Irenaeus can now show how the Incarnation fits this great scheme, indeed is its fulfilment, and how the glory of God may once more be shown in humankind.

The Incarnation

In Chapter 16, halfway through Book III, Irenaeus demonstrates that Jesus was both perfect God and perfect man.[27] It is a fundamental chapter and one of the longest in the work. If anything, the Gnostics maintained a form of adoptionism which meant that they believed that the fullness of Christ's divinity descended from the Pleroma and inhabited a man whom God had selected, and that this happened when the Spirit descended on Jesus like a dove at his baptism.[28] Indeed, they make Christ and Jesus two separate beings, combined for a time of earthly existence. In this sense, there is no full Incarnation, and some Gnostics only went so far as saying *it seemed that God took on flesh*, but he did not *really*, which was Docetism.[29] Irenaeus writes that the Incarnate Word was empowered and equipped by the Holy Spirit.[30] He rebuts entirely this theory of "appearance only" and indeed of a heavenly Christ combining with an earthly Jesus, by drawing on the nativity passages of Matthew and Luke, and the teaching of the Apostle Paul in Romans and Galatians (see Romans 1:1 and Galatians 4:4).[31]

Irenaeus then alights upon a piece of powerful parallelism: the pre-existent Word is the paragon for Adam, while the human but faithful Mary is the paragon for Eve. The Word is the pattern for all humanity, including innocent but untested Adam; while Mary is the pattern for the originally innocent but untested Eve. Nowhere is this parallelism better put than in Book III, Chapter 18, where Irenaeus writes: "For as by the disobedience of the one man who was originally moulded from the virgin soil, the many were made sinners, and forfeited life; so was it necessary that, by the obedience of one man, who was originally born from a virgin, many should be justified and receive salvation."[32] And again, elsewhere he writes, "For what the virgin Eve had bound fast through unbelief, this did the virgin Mary set free through faith."[33]

Although the Incarnation comes after Adam in time, the incarnate Christ is nonetheless the pattern of life and paragon to which Adam is called. Thus, Irenaeus writes a little later in Book III:

> The Word, the creator of all, sketched out in advance in Adam the future economy of the humanity of the Son of God. God gave definition to the first, ensouled human being (*psuchikós*—Adam) with a view to its being saved by the spiritual human being (*pneumatikós*—Christ). For since the one who was going to save already existed, in order that he should not be a saviour to no purpose, there was need that (the one who) was to be saved should come into existence.[34]

For Irenaeus, the Word was always to be the Saviour, and the imperfect Adam from the outset was the one to be saved. As Augustine would later teach, God foreknew what he would have to do and would predestine those whom he foreknew to be saved. The Word would save them through his own recapitulation of human life (to which we shall come in the next chapter), but in particular, this would be achieved through the Cross, the sacrificial death of Christ. Jesus' descent to the Cross, for the purposes of freeing an enslaved humankind, is also made clear by Irenaeus:

> As it was not possible that that human being who had once been defeated and crushed through disobedience should strike back and win the victor's prize, and impossible, too, that the one who had fallen under sin should attain salvation, (so) the Son, who is the Word of God, achieved both these things: coming down from the Father, and becoming flesh, and descending even to death, and bringing to its completion the economy of our salvation.[35]

Thus, Irenaeus rose to special heights in describing the suffering of the Word-in-flesh for the human race. He made clear that Jesus *really suffered* and that it was neither the mere *seeming suffering* of docetic Gnosticism nor the incapacity for suffering of *divine impassability*, but rather true suffering on behalf of an enslaved humanity. Thus, "Christ fought and conquered: for he was man contending for the fathers, and through his obedience doing away disobedience completely: for he bound the strongman, and set free the weak, and endowed his own handiwork with salvation, by destroying sin. For he is a most holy and merciful Lord, and loves the human race."[36]

Here, then, was the plan of salvation set forth through Christ, and the restoration of humanity which he would provide, and this is the note with which the fourth book of *Against Heresies* begins. The fourth book is the longest of the five books of Irenaeus' great work and Irenaeus introduces it as follows:

> By transmitting to thee, my very dear friend, this fourth book of the work which is entitled *The Detection and Refutation of False Knowledge*, I shall, as I have promised, add weight, by means of the words of the Lord, to what I have already advanced: so that thou also, as thou hast requested, mayest obtain from me the means of confuting all the heretics everywhere, and not permit them, beaten back at all points, to launch out further into the deep of error, nor be drowned in the sea of ignorance; but that

thou, turning them into the haven of truth, mayest cause them to attain their salvation.[37]

In so doing, Irenaeus adds weight to what has gone before and in place of further refutation gives greater traction and substance to his hypothesis of God refashioning humankind in Christ.

Book IV

As always with Irenaeus, this book consists of a restatement of the chief falsehoods of the Gnostics, with the particular intention of debunking Marcion's theory that the Old Testament is not consonant with the New. Indeed, far from the Testaments coming from different minds or sources, Irenaeus demonstrates that the New is but a development and progression of the Old. The idea of *progression* is common both to the relationship between the Testaments and to the development of humankind's perfection through Christ. In other words, God works over time to bring about his will in restoring humanity's image. Progress is thus a key concept in Irenaeus' theology.

At the outset of Book IV, Irenaeus hastens to restate that there is one God, though in three persons, who is the creator of a good creation.[38] And he prepares a people through Abraham and Moses for himself, although the Jews "departed from God in not receiving his Word".[39] Nonetheless, the patriarchs were called and the Law given as the background to the coming of the Messiah, the Son of God. The patriarchs, the Law, the priesthood, the sacrifices, the temple, the monarchy (the House of David), the prophets and the covenants all find their fulfilment in Christ.[40] As far as Irenaeus is concerned, both the Gnostics and the Jews have missed the mark, for the two Testaments fit together as promise and fulfilment for the benefit of humankind.[41] And Irenaeus' writing is all of a piece, for in his only other extant work, *Demonstration of the Apostolic Preaching*, he is at pains to show how the promises of the New Covenant are anticipated in the Old. In a work of 100 short paragraphs, 65 are spent in, more or less, showing that what was symbolized or promised in the Old Testament is fulfilled in Christ.[42] Above all Irenaeus demonstrates the consistent work of God, which is shown in a progressive revelation until it finds its fulfilment in Christ. Far from there being two gods, as Marcion argued so seductively, there was only one, who worked out his will through all the intractableness of human will.

Alongside this is the growing appreciation of God's overall grand plan which will be set out fully in the next chapter in all its glory and burnished excitement, but with it the steady witness of Irenaeus as to where the reality of these things may be found: in the true Church, or as have some have termed it in the *Great Church*—the fellowship of orthodox believers across the nations. It is to the Scriptures that people must go for sure instruction. Thus, he writes:

> If anyone, therefore, reads the Scriptures with attention, he will find in them an account of Christ, and a foreshadowing of the new calling. For Christ is the treasure which is hid in the field, that is, in this world; but the treasure hid in the Scriptures is Christ, since he was pointed out by means of types and parables .... When it is read by Christian [believers], it is a treasure hid indeed in a field, but brought to light by the cross of Christ.[43]

The Scriptures must be properly understood through the guidance of the Spirit and the faithful preaching and teaching of presbyters under leadership of the bishop. Therefore, Irenaeus goes on to explain the role of the presbyters as "people who possess the succession from the Apostles ... and together with the succession of the episcopate have received the certain gift of truth, according to the pleasure of the Father".[44] As he says epigrammatically and memorably, "for where the Church is there is the Spirit of God: and where the Spirit of God is, there is the Church and every kind of grace: but the Spirit is truth".[45]

The Spirit, the Scriptures, the faithful lives and teaching of presbyters in true succession of the Apostles, the oversight of a godly bishop like Polycarp, who Irenaeus once again mentions as an inspiring example of faithful and truthful preaching,[46] were all prerequisites for refuting heresies and establishing the truth. They must also be the essential pillars of the Church. Having given further weight to his previous books in Book IV, there is one more book to add, which he introduces as further teaching, especially taken from St Paul. Having looked closely at the relationship of the Old and New Testaments and developed the argument of their single source and inspiration, and having interpreted a number of parables prone to misinterpretation by Gnostics, Irenaeus now turns to the more explicit teaching of the Apostle Paul in his final book, Book V. But before we follow him there, we must properly highlight the great theme which lies scattered throughout all these books, which is the *recapitulation of humanity by Christ* and the refashioning of the image of God in humanity, or in an individual man or woman, so manifesting God's glory. It is the seam of gold that runs through the whole work, and it is Irenaeus' particularly distinctive contribution to theology.

Notes

[1] *AH* III.4.1.
[2] Behr, *Irenaeus of Lyons*, pp. 108-20.
[3] *1 Clement* 7.2-5.
[4] *AH* II.28.3.
[5] Wingren, *Man and the Incarnation*, pp. 65,66,71.
[6] *AH* III.15.1; Behr, *Irenaeus of Lyons*, p. 64.
[7] *AH* III.13.1.
[8] *AH* III.21.5.
[9] *AH* III.1,2.
[10] *AH* III.1.1.
[11] *AH* III.11.
[12] *AH* III.1.2.
[13] *AH* III.3.3.
[14] *AH* III.4.1.
[15] *AH* III.4.1.
[16] Grant, *Irenaeus of Lyons*, p. 48.
[17] *AH* III.6.4.
[18] *AH* III.7.4.
[19] *AH* III.9.1-2.
[20] *AH* III.9.3.
[21] *AH* III.10.2.

22. *AH* III.10.5.
23. *AH* III.11.2.
24. *AH* III.11.8.
25. *AH* III:12-14.
26. *AH* III.12.13.
27. *AH* III.16.1-8.
28. *AH* III.6.1.
29. *AH* II.19.1-3; III.22.1.
30. *AH* III.17.1. See also Isaiah 9.
31. *AH* III.16.2-6.
32. *AH* III.17.7.
33. *AH* III.22.4.
34. *AH* III.22.3.
35. *AH* III.18.2.
36. *AH* III.18.6.
37. *AH* IV.1.
38. *AH* IV.1.1; IV.6.4-6.
39. *AH* IV.7.4.
40. *AH* IV.9.1-3.
41. *AH* IV.18.4.
42. *Demonstration of the Apostolic Teaching* §37-100.
43. *AH* IV.26.1.
44. *AH* IV.26.2.
45. *AH* III.24.1.
46. *AH* IV.32.1.

1 0

Recapitulation and the glory of God

Scattered through the books of *Against Heresies* is Irenaeus' main idea about the purpose of Christ's Incarnation. This plan, or *oikonomia* of God's provision of salvation, Irenaeus describes in terms of the "recapitulation of humanity" by Christ—the Incarnate Word, fully God and fully Man.

The Greek word *anakephalaíōsis* literally means recapitulation or the remaking of something by summing up. It is a term that was often used in the literary criticism of the rhetorical schools, where a work (for instance, Homer's *Iliad*) would be summarized, or the narrative encapsulated by the teacher. In rhetoric, it meant summing up an argument by going over the main points or headings, again by way of summary.[1] As such, it may very well have been a term latent in Irenaeus' thinking from his own rhetorical education in Smyrna as part of the second Sophist movement of the first century AD. It may also have been a term which Justin Martyr used in his teaching,[2] and quite possibly Irenaeus came across it more theologically in Rome. He was to make it his own, and place it at the centre of his theological understanding.

Irenaeus took this idea of recapitulation and applied it to God's plan of salvation which finds its fulfilment in the Incarnation of Christ and his assumption of our humanity in order to refashion and redeem it. This is also a very Johannine idea, since the Prologue tells us that the Word assumed Adam's flesh (John 1:1-18), yet without sin, in order to rescue humanity from death and to give to Adam's descendants eternal life, through a response of repentance and faith.

The idea of recapitulation is also present in Paul's teaching in the Epistle to the Ephesians, where he writes, "For he has made known to us in all wisdom and insight the mystery of his will, according to his purpose which he set forth in Christ as a plan (*oikonomia*) for the fullness of time to recapitulate (*avakephalaiōsthai*) all things" (Ephesians 1:9-10). Or, as the NIV puts it, "to bring all things ... together under one head, even Christ" (1:10b). Thus, the term is implied in St Paul's argument about the reunification of all things in Christ, by being summed up and refashioned in him; and it is also used in the rhetoric teaching of the "schools" of the Empire. Irenaeus now goes to work using it in his restatement of Christian teaching and of God's overarching purpose, in opposition to the fragmented Gnostic theories he seeks to refute.

Although coming to a climax in the Incarnation and the life of Jesus, Irenaeus makes clear that recapitulation is present in the plan of God from the very beginning and through the successive covenants with Noah, Abraham, Moses and finally Christ. He summarizes this in his *Demonstration of the Apostolic Preaching*:

> Thus, he gloriously achieved our redemption, and fulfilled the promise of the Fathers, and abolished the old disobedience. The Son of God became the Son of David and Son of Abraham; perfecting and summing up this in himself, that he might make us to possess life. The Word of God was made flesh by the dispensation of the Virgin, to abolish death and make man live. For we were imprisoned by sin, being born in sinfulness and living under death.[3]

This idea, which only makes the barest of appearances in *Demonstration of the Apostolic Preaching*, is nonetheless scattered like gold dust across the pages of *Against Heresies*. In one way or another, the theme will be developed across the five books, and at least on one occasion Irenaeus, in his enthusiasm, will overstate his case by deeming Christ to have been at least 50 years old at his crucifixion, thus also recapitulating old age. Yet it remains a golden thread of his theology in answering the Gnostics and showing the purpose of the Incarnation. He uses it in particular to demonstrate how Christ in his Incarnation, life and passion refashioned human life by redeeming the Fall of Adam in a great reversal of its effects.

The first appearance of this term comes in the twenty-first chapter of Book III of *Against Heresies*, a book dedicated like the others to his unknown correspondent that he "may receive from me the means of combating and vanquishing those who are propagating falsehood ... For the love of God, being rich and ungrudging, confers upon the supplicant more than he can ask from it".[4] In Chapter 21, he concludes a section in which he recalls the prophecy of Isaiah that, "the virgin will be with child and will give birth to a son, and will call him Immanuel" (Isaiah 7:14) saying: "And he recapitulated in himself the ancient formation of man." In other words, Jesus, born of a virgin, in his own life, death and resurrection, begins that process of refashioning the image of God in man, as it was first in Adam but now perfected by Christ.

Irenaeus continues in the next paragraph: "The Lord took dust from the earth and formed man so did he who is the Word, recapitulating Adam in himself, rightly receive a birth, enabling him to gather up Adam into himself from Mary who was yet a virgin."[5] Irenaeus' argument here is against those who despise human flesh, such as the Gnostics and before them the Platonists,[6] saying it was right and proper for Jesus to take on human flesh through the Virgin Mary, herself a descendant of Adam (see Luke 3:37), and not to be born out of some new creation and so bypass the human flesh created in Adam. Irenaeus continues his argument thus:

> If he, Jesus, did not receive the substance of flesh from a human being [Mary], he neither was made man nor the Son of Man: and if he were not made what we are, he did no great thing in what he suffered and endured. But everyone will allow that we are composed of a body taken from the earth, and a soul, receiving spirit from God. This therefore, the Word of God, was made, recapitulating in himself his own handiwork; and on this account does he confess himself the Son of Man and blesses, "the meek, because they shall inherit the earth".[7]

Again, Irenaeus stresses the fleshly substance of Jesus' body, his descent from the human Mary and his dependence on material sustenance (e.g. food and drink), which together indicate his true humanity, which is like ours. And so, "for all these are tokens of the flesh which had been derived from the earth, which he had recapitulated in himself, bearing salvation to his own handiwork".[8] The whole theme of recapitulation is in fact a prequel to Gregory Nazianzen's famous dictum in his *First Letter to Cledonius the Presbyter*, where he writes, "The unassumed is the unhealed, but what is united with God is also being saved."[9]

It is through becoming incarnate and following the course of all life, from conception to grave (and for good measure, but wrongly, Irenaeus stretches Jesus' life into his fifties so as to recapitulate old age!) that Jesus is able to recapitulate the whole of human life, meaning that he not only refashions it but also restores the image of God. So, Irenaeus writes, "It was necessary, therefore, that the Lord coming to the lost sheep, and making recapitulation of so comprehensive a dispensation, and seeking after his own handiwork, should save the very man who had been created after his image and likeness, that is Adam."[10]

The way Christ, the second man, frees the descendants of Adam is "by binding the strong man, spoiling his goods and abolishing death, vivifying that man who had been in the state of death. For the first Adam became a vessel in his [Satan's] possession, whom he did also hold under his power that is by bringing sin on him iniquitously, and under the colour [the promise] of immortality entailing death upon him."[11]

As Irenaeus moves into the final books of *Against Heresies*, he underlines the recapitulation of Adam which Christ works, and does so particularly in the last book, Book V, as Book IV is mostly taken up with rebutting the theories of Marcion. In Book V, Irenaeus once again insists that Jesus took on Adam's flesh to refashion and restore it through recapitulation.[12] Later in the same book the idea of recapitulation is developed by drawing attention to the parallel of which Irenaeus is particularly fond between the Fall of Adam and the great reversal of that Fall by the Incarnation and mission of Christ. Thus Adam, we are told, disobeys God by eating the fruit of the tree of the knowledge of good and evil on a Friday; likewise, Jesus restores humankind through his death on a Friday. Adam eats from a tree; likewise, Jesus dies to redeem us on a tree.[13] Furthermore, "Eve, although a wife to Adam was still a virgin [there is no biblical evidence for this but it suited Irenaeus' parallelisms] when she disobeyed and became the cause of death to herself and through her to the whole human race. Likewise, Mary, though betrothed to Joseph, was still a virgin when by her obedience, she became the cause of salvation to herself and the whole human race. Mary untangled the skein that Eve knotted." Equally, "Eve was seduced by an angel into disobeying the Word of God, from whom she fled. Contrastingly when an angel proclaimed the good news to Mary, she obeyed the Word of God, and carried God in her womb."[14]

> Mary became Eve's advocate. The human race which had been bound to death by a virgin's disobedience found salvation by a virgin's obedience: virginal obedience weighed exactly in the balance with virginal disobedience. The sin of the first-fashioned human being was healed by the integrity of the first-born, the serpent's cunning was conquered by the simplicity of a dove and the chains by which we were bound to death were broken.[15]

Jesus, who himself bore the exact image of God (Colossians 1:15), takes on our flesh that he might in himself recapitulate our humanity, restoring it through faith. Hence, the image of God, as Paul describes, is being renewed by the Creator among all those who believe (Colossians 3:9-10).

The glory of God

At this point, it might be as well to summarize Irenaeus' thought, remembering that it was presented as a polemic and not as a piece of what we might call "systematic theology". It was a response to heresies which had made substantial inroads into the Church, and which Irenaeus had witnessed first-hand, both in Rome and then later in Gaul. At the outset, Irenaeus had to challenge the erroneous and at times fantastic cosmology of the Gnostic sects: the notion of God as always unknowable; the many emanations resulting in scores of *aeons*; the existence of the Pleroma, out of which creation was spawned by a wayward Sophia. From this wayward creation, the Gnostics argued, came a questionable material world, prone to evil and in need of redemption; and a humankind enslaved to its own flesh in which no good thing dwelt, and from which deliverance was needed in order to enjoy a true, and non-material or fleshly soul-spirit existence. Combatting all this, Irenaeus maintains there is always ever only one God who created through Christ and the Spirit, themselves like his two hands.¹⁶ It was God who directly and thoughtfully created Adam from earth's mud and the divine Spirit. The resulting humanity thereafter bore the likeness and image of God. This almighty and creating God was both three and one, and the creation was initially very good, with both angels and humans made in the image and likeness of God but with wills capable of disobedience. Humanity was tempted by the fallen angel Satan, fell from its exalted purpose and destiny, thence becoming damaged, prone to evil and sinfulness, and subject to death.

Into this material and fleshly existence comes Christ, the eternal Word, who takes on Adam's flesh to rescue Adam's descendants from the effects of sin and death. Christ comes as a saviour and by his perfect life, his sacrificial death and his victorious resurrection offers new life and hope. This is achieved through the *recapitulation* by which Christ reverses the effects of Adam's Fall and the Devil's enslavement of humankind. Jesus recapitulates in himself the birth, life and death of humankind, restoring thereby the image and likeness of God in them. "Irenaeus strongly emphasizes that the suffering and obedience of Jesus [as the second Adam] means the [eventual] abolition of sin, the destruction of the domination of disobedience and the expulsion of evil from humanity."¹⁷ Through Christ, victory is achieved and the hope of a new man established (1 Corinthians 15:42-57). Through redemption by this man of flesh, a new man with "a spiritual body" is raised to new Kingdom life (1 Corinthians 15:44b). The development of this new man in the flesh is begun by Christ in his resurrection and completed by him and the Spirit in the fellowship of the Church, where all are subject to Apostolic teaching and to the properly appointed presbyters and bishops in Apostolic succession. This then briefly is Irenaeus' scheme and both his hypothesis (his rule of faith) and his *oikonomia* (his arrangement of salvation).

If this, in broadest terms, is the direction of Irenaeus' theology, which is scattered through his great polemical work against the Gnostic sects, sprinkled through the work are a number of luminous statements which have been detached by themselves and are found in ongoing Christian thought: none more so than the famous statement in Book IV, the full quotation of which is this:

> For the Glory of God is a living man: and the life of man consists in beholding God. For if the manifestation of God which is made by means of the creation, affords life to all living in the earth, much more does that revelation of the Father which comes through the Word, give life to those who see God.[18]

Often the quotation has been curtailed to the phrase "the glory of God is a man or woman fully alive". What did Irenaeus mean by this? In many ways it is a fair summary of the trajectory of his theology.

Several questions arise from this statement: in what way or ways is the *glory* shown in a man or woman? What does *fully alive* mean for Irenaeus, and in what ways is a person able to *see God*? Answering or attempting to answer these questions should lead us deeper into what Irenaeus had in mind and how we might construe his meaning.

It is worth stressing at the outset that this statement, which is well known today in the Church, or becoming better known, occurs in Book IV, where Irenaeus is recapitulating (or summarizing) the argument for the unity of the two Testaments, Old and New, as coming from a single source, God himself, which he has been laying out. This, of course, is written specifically against Marcion who claimed that the Testaments came from different gods: with the Old Testament deriving from a god of violence, vengeance and wrath, quite unlike the God and Father of Jesus Christ.

Marcion had been teaching this doctrine and error effectively in Rome and no doubt had followers in Gaul as well. Irenaeus makes clear in answering Marcion that there is one God revealed in both Old and New Testaments.[19] He is known to Abraham.[20] Moses prophesies and makes mention of the coming of Christ, the Messiah.[21] The prophets prophesy the coming of Christ.[22] Irenaeus argues that the *natural law* which was at first written on the conscience (see Romans 1:20; 2:12-16) was later objectified and rendered in the Law of Moses and in particular the Ten Commandments.[23] In both Testaments, Irenaeus maintains that the way of salvation is the way of faith, although this became obscured by the sacrificial system and rituals of the Old Testament.[24]

Thus Book IV, Chapter 20, in which this famous quotation occurs, begins by reiterating the unity of the Godhead and likewise the progression of the Testaments emanating from a single source. He is the same God who took the clay of the earth and breathed his life into it. Indeed,

> It was not angels, therefore, who made us, nor who formed us [a Gnostic theory]. Neither had angels power to make an image of God, nor anyone else, except the Word of the Lord, nor any power remotely distant from the Father of all things. For God did not stand in need of these things, in order for the accomplishing of what he had himself determined with himself beforehand should be done, as if he did not possess his own hands. For with him were always present the Word and Wisdom, the Son and the Spirit, by whom and in whom, freely and spontaneously, he made all things, to whom also he speaks stating "Let us make man after our image and likeness".[25]

Having established again in Book IV Chapter 20 God's spontaneous and free creation of humanity, Irenaeus maintains that human destiny is "to see God". He goes on to explain what he means by this, admitting that although "the pure in heart" are promised that they shall "see God" (Matthew 5:8), he knows that in this life "no-one shall see [God] and live" (Exodus 33:20), and furthermore the Father is "incomprehensible", stressing thereby God's apophatic quality. Nevertheless:

> His love, and kindness, and his infinite power, even this he grants to those who love him, that is, to see God, which thing the prophets did also predict.... For man does not see God by his own powers; but when he [God] pleases, he is seen by men, by whom he wills, and when he wills, and as he wills. For God is powerful in all things, having been seen at that time indeed, prophetically through the Spirit, and seen too, adoptively through the Son; and he shall also be seen paternally in the kingdom of heaven, the Spirit truly preparing man in the Son of God, and the Son leading him to the Father, while the Father too, confers upon him incorruption for eternal life which comes to everyone from the fact of his seeing God.[26]

Here then is Irenaeus' idea of what it means to see God. He recognizes that it is a vision that develops through the sequence of God's revelation. It is a vision that begins with the prophets, continues through adoption by the Son and lastly is fulfilled by the Father in a finally and fully disclosed Kingdom. It is thus a "sequential seeing" through the eye of faith. So, Irenaeus continues, "It is not possible to live apart from life, and the means of life is found in fellowship with God; but fellowship with God is to know God, and to enjoy his goodness. We therefore shall see God, that we may live, being made immortal by that sight, and attaining even unto God."[27] In many ways, it is Irenaeus' doctrine of *theosis* underscored by the idea of progression.

This remark does seem like an early statement of *Theosis*, the doctrine of the Eastern Fathers especially found in Athanasius, Gregory of Nyssa and Basil of Caesarea, that through faith we are to become like God. For as Athanasius famously wrote in *De Incarnatione*, "He became man that we might become like he is" (§54). For Irenaeus the sequential revealing of God through the prophets and the Son would never be complete in this life. Nor would believing humanity have, in this present dispensation, any final knowing of God or God's final revealing of himself, until the end of this present dispensation in which our salvation may be grasped, but is far from complete. Irenaeus puts it memorably:

> For where there is a regular succession [i.e. sequence], there is also fixedness; and where fixedness, there is suitability to the period; and where suitability, there also utility. And for this reason did the Word become the dispenser of the paternal grace for the benefit of men, for whom he made such great dispensations, revealing God indeed to men, but presenting man to God, and preserving at the same time the invisibility of the Father, lest man should at any time become a despiser of God, and that he [God] should always possess something towards which we might advance; but on the other hand, revealing God to men through many dispensations, lest man falling away from God altogether, should cease to exist.[28]

The idea that God never-so-fully reveals himself now so that we have nothing further to advance towards is peculiarly like the spirituality of both Augustine and the Cappadocian Fathers which was to come some two hundred years later. As Gregory of Nyssa wrote in his reflections on the Song of Songs:

> The Soul, having gone out at the word of her Beloved, looks for him, though she cannot be reached by any verbal symbol, and she is told by the watchmen [the angels] that she is in love with the unattainable, and that the object of her longing cannot be apprehended. In this way she is, in a certain sense, wounded and beaten because of the frustration of what she desires, now that she thinks that her yearning for the Other cannot be fulfilled or satisfied. But the veil of grief is removed when she learns that the true satisfaction of her desire consists in constantly going on with her quest and never ceasing the ascent, seeing that every fulfilment of her desire generates further desire for the Transcendent. Thus, the veil of despair is torn away and the bride realizes that she will always discover more of the incomprehensible and unhoped for beauty of her spouse throughout all eternity. Then she is torn by an even more urgent longing.[29]

It is also at this point, following this line of argument, that Irenaeus introduces the statement for which he is best known:

> For the Glory of God is a living man and the life of man consists in beholding God. For if the manifestation of God which is made by means of creation affords life to all living in the earth, much more does that revelation of the Father which comes through the Word, give life to those who see God.[30]

From this great statement at least two fundamentals arise. Firstly, human life, a mixture of mud and spirit (or divine breath), comes from being created by God, just as recapitulation of human life comes through the reception of the Word who recapitulates us and who reveals the Father. Secondly, this results in a demonstration of the glory of God, *for the*

Glory of God is a man or woman fully alive. In other words, the glory of God is no more manifest than in his work of bringing back to full life the person whom he recapitulates or refashions following belief in the Word. The glory that is shown is the suffering love of God, the patience of God, the redeeming power of God, the forgiveness of God, and the resurrection power of God. It is not so much that in himself or herself man or woman is glorious, as that God has chosen to make his wayward creation, humankind, the theatre of his own greatest glory. That is where his Son's grace is most evident. Hence, the remaking of humanity lies at the heart of Irenaeus' theology.

As we have seen in Irenaeus' theology, the remaking of humanity so that it becomes fully alive is a process. It continues from the Garden of Eden to the present day in such a way that each individual, in response to God's grace, is in a permanent state *of becoming what he or she is intended to be.* As a person increasingly beholds the glory of God, as Irenaeus has explained,[31] so he or she becomes ever more alive. Perhaps this is simply another way of saying what the Apostle Paul describes in 2 Corinthians, where he says, "Now the Lord is the Spirit, and where the Spirit of the Lord is there is freedom. And we, who with unveiled faces all reflect the Lord's glory, are being transformed into his likeness with ever-increasing glory, which comes from the Lord, who is the Spirit" (2 Corinthians 3:17-18).

In the last chapters of Book IV, Irenaeus once again wrestles with the idea that human beings are vulnerable from the outset *being unoriginated from the beginning* (i.e., being creatures) and proving such by failing to become what they were intended to be. Instead, Irenaeus prefers the idea that human beings not being made perfect at first (in the sense that they are untested and incomplete, reflecting Hebrews 2:10 and 5:7-10) but are rather made as infants in need of becoming perfect as they develop through the grace of God. So, Irenaeus says:

> To the extent that they are unoriginated [i.e. created] they fall short of being perfect, for in as much as they have come into being recently, they are infants, and, in as much as they are infants, they are unaccustomed to and unpractised in perfect discipline. A mother cannot offer adult food to an infant, but

the infant cannot yet digest food suitable for someone older. Similarly, God, for his part, could have granted perfection to humankind from the beginning, but humankind being in its infancy, would not have been able to sustain it.[32]

Flaws, or at the very least questions, to do with Irenaeus' argument were to emerge over the coming centuries, not least in the controversy between Pelagius and Augustine. The point is that at the moment of creation humanity does bear the image and likeness of God. Human beings are innocent and in perfect fellowship as creatures with their Creator. But to Irenaeus they are deficient because they are unproven, untested. They are unproven, will be tested in their obedience, and will fail with catastrophic consequences. And so, Irenaeus argues, humanity at first *was innocent and yet not perfect and must gain perfection through a process in which recapitulation by Christ is central.*

Irenaeus outlines human progress in Christ as follows:

> Now it was necessary that man should in the first instance be created; and having been created, should receive growth; and having received growth should be strengthened; and having been strengthened, should abound; and having abounded, should recover from the disease of sin; and having recovered, should be glorified; and being glorified, should see his Lord. For God is he who is yet to be seen, and beholding of God is productive of immortality.[33]

Nothing could be more progressive than this. It is this process from disobedience to perfection that lies at the heart of Irenaeus' theology, in which the "the goal of Becoming from humankind is precisely this—never to cease becoming more and more like God. The perfection of humankind is to draw near to God and to share in his uncreated glory, especially through the bestowal of the gift of incorruptibility. The glory of the divine plan is that earth should be transformed and that, without ceasing to be a creature, should share the glory of its uncreated God."[34] It is in this sense that the glory of God is a human fully alive.

For Irenaeus, the glory of God is humanity fully alive with *that life* dependent on beholding God. This is both a process and an increasing revelation until there is full sight of God and full life for humankind in eternity. The process which begins with the refashioning of humankind in the recapitulation offered through Christ's life, death and resurrection will continue in the fellowship of the Church and reach a climax, in Irenaeus' estimation, in the millennial rule of Christ with the saints on earth. In this way, the process continues through the Church and in the victorious kingdom, which becomes the ark and the goal of this new humanity. The glory of God in humanity becomes more and more evident, but it can only begin with the recapitulation of humanity through Christ and be received through faith.

Notes

[1] Minns, *Irenaeus*, p. 108.
[2] Wingren, *Man and the Incarnation*, pp. 80-2.
[3] *Demonstration of the Apostolic Preaching* §37.
[4] Preface *AH*, Book III.
[5] *AH* III.21.10.
[6] See *Phaedo* 80:10-15.
[7] *AH* III.22.1.
[8] *AH* III.22.2.
[9] Gregory Nazianzen, *First Letter to Cledonius the Presbyter: On God and Christ*, ed. Lionel Wickham, Popular Patristics 23 (Crestwood, NY: St Vladimir's Press, 2002), p. 158.
[10] *AH* III.23.1.
[11] *AH* III.23.1.
[12] *AH* V.14.2.
[13] *AH* V.23.2.
[14] Minns, *Irenaeus*, p. 110.
[15] *AH* V.19.1.
[16] *AH* III.1.2.
[17] Wingren, *Man and the Incarnation*, p. 115, and my words in parentheses.
[18] *AH* IV.20.7.

19. *AH* IV.1; IV.5.1; IV.9; IV.12.
20. *AH* IV.7,8.
21. *AH* IV.10.
22. *AH* III.11.
23. *AH* IV.13; IV.15.
24. *AH* IV.17.4; IV.18.
25. *AH* IV.20.1.
26. *AH* IV.20.5.
27. *AH* IV.20.5-6.
28. *AH* IV.20.7.
29. *Commentary on the Song of Songs, PG*44.1029B-C.
30. *AH* IV. 20.7.
31. *AH* IV.20.
32. *AH* IV.38.1.
33. *AH* IV.28.3.
34. Minns, *Irenaeus*, pp. 89-90.

11

The Spirit, the Church and the Kingdom

There is no doubt that for Irenaeus the Church, properly constituted and taught, is where humankind moves from infancy into fullness of life, from the effects of the Fall to the glory of God. As early as the end of Book III, and before rolling out his teaching about recapitulation in Book IV, Irenaeus makes it clear that the Church has been gifted with the task of making its members mature and true in their faith. He writes:

> This gift of God [the Spirit] has been entrusted to the Church, as breath was to the first created man, for this purpose, that all members receiving it may be vivified; and the means of communion with Christ, has been distributed through it, that is the Holy Spirit, the earnest of incorruption, the means of confirming our faith, and the ladder of ascent to God. For in the Church it is said, "God hath set Apostles, prophets, teachers" (see Ephesians 4:11) and all other means through which the Spirit works; of which all those are not partakers who do not join themselves to the Church, but defraud themselves of life through their perverse opinions and infamous behaviour. For where the Church is there is the Spirit of God; and where the Spirit of God is, there is the Church, and every kind of grace; but the Spirit is truth.[1]

The Church is the place where life will be restored and where recapitulation will happen. For Irenaeus the Church replaces Israel, but nevertheless it is still a staging post until the full revelation of the Kingdom, which will only happen after the return of Christ at the Second Coming, and the inauguration of the Kingdom in his millennial rule with the saints on earth, to which we will come.

In his debates with Marcion, Irenaeus makes clear that God's will is revealed through the Law and the Prophets and that both find their fulfilment in the Messiah or Christ. Indeed, he believes that the promises of God are fulfilled only through the incarnate Christ. The inclusion of the Gentiles is predicted as early as the figure of Rahab welcoming the spies, who, in Irenaeus' typological interpretation of the Old Testament, represent the Father, the Son and the Holy Spirit.[2] Therefore, the rejection of Christ by the Jews, and especially by the institutions of Judaism, created a fissure which most of the early Church Fathers shared and which was deep, and frequently offensively expressed. In retrospect, it was the basis of a long-term denigration of the Jews that would have violent and awful consequences in Europe and further afield.[3] As with many others, Irenaeus interprets the destruction of the Temple and Jerusalem by the armies of Vespasian and Titus in AD 70 (after all, only a few generations before Irenaeus' birth) as God turning his back on the Jews and giving them over to destruction.[4] Jews who repent and believe in the Messiah can, like all others, be perfected in the community of the Church, which is the ark of salvation.

For Irenaeus, as with his contemporaries in Rome and Smyrna where he grew up, the Church is a community governed by the Word and Spirit and regulated by the oversight of church leaders, which includes presbyters and a bishop appointed in succession to the Apostles. The Apostles and their teaching are the foundations of truth in the Church and provide the rule or canon by which any church should be governed. Thus, Irenaeus writes:

> [A]fter our Lord rose from the dead, the Apostles were invested with power from on high when the Spirit came down upon them, were filled with all his gifts, and had perfect knowledge. They departed to the ends of the earth, preaching the glad tidings of the good things from God to us, and proclaiming the peace of heaven to men who indeed do equally and individually possess the gospel of God.[5]

In one of the earliest witnesses to the existence and circulation of the four Gospels by 150, which was only about 60 years after the writing of the last Gospel by John ("who published a Gospel during his residence in Ephesus in Asia" in *c.*90), Irenaeus goes on to say that this Gospel was written down by Matthew, Mark, Luke and John.[6] It is around this rule or canon of truth, which results from these Scriptures, that every true Church has its formation:

> Although the languages of the world are dissimilar, yet the import of the tradition is one and the same: for the churches which have been planted in Germany do not believe or hand down anything different, nor do those in Spain, nor those in Gaul, nor those in the East, nor those in Egypt, nor those in Libya, nor those which have been established in the central regions of the world. But as the sun, that creature of God is one and the same throughout the world, so also the preaching of truth shineth everywhere, and enlightens all men that are willing to come to a knowledge of the truth.[7]

We can safely say that for Irenaeus the integrity of the Church results from the Apostolic witness found in the commonly accepted Scriptures, which at that time especially meant the Gospels and Paul's Epistles. The Holy Spirit had directed the writing of the Scriptures and likewise these were now authenticated in the Church.

There is no doubt that throughout his writing Irenaeus emphasizes the work of the Spirit, recognizing him as part of the eternal Trinity and evident from the time of creation as one of the hands of God together with the Son.[8] Humanity was created by the hands of God, as Irenaeus says, "For it is the human being, and not part of the human being, which by the hands of God, that is by the Son and the Spirit comes to be the likeness of God."[9] And if the Spirit is present in humanity's creation, so too is he in human revivification through recapitulation by Christ and faith in his work. Thus, the two hands create and the two hands recreate in Christ the image and likeness of God in humanity. In this way, the glory of God is humanity fully alive through the work of the eternal Trinity in creation and redemption. The Spirit is responsible for guiding the Apostles and their associates, Mark and Luke, Gospel writers, in leading the Church into all truth. For Irenaeus, it is the comingling of Spirit and flesh that makes a human truly alive. Thus, he writes: "When this Spirit which is mingled with the soul is united with that which is moulded by the hand of God by means of the outpouring of the Spirit, then the spiritual and perfect human being comes into existence; and it is this that is made in the image and likeness of God."[10]

If the Spirit, therefore, is integral to the creation and recreation of a human life, the Spirit is also the one who helps perfect human beings in the context of the Church, which itself helps to mould their new lives. Thus, we consider

> those persons perfect who have received the Spirit of God, and who through the Spirit of God do speak in all languages [tongues] as he used himself to speak. In like manner we do also hear many brethren in the Church who possess prophetic gifts, and who through the Spirit speak all kinds of languages, and bring to light for the general benefit the hidden things of men and declare the mysteries of God, whom the Apostle terms "spiritual".[11]

With an eye to refuting the Gnostics, Irenaeus goes on to say that the truly spiritual person is not the person who is stripped of the flesh, but retains the Spirit, but the one in whom flesh and Spirit are properly comingled and who will go on to maturity and perfection. To summarize, or as Irenaeus would say, to recapitulate: the work of the Spirit is essential to the creation, salvation and perfection of humanity. He is the one who creates human beings with the Son; he revivifies humanity through the recapitulating work of Christ; he guides the writing of the Scriptures by the Apostles and their associates, and he it is who gifts the Church, which is the place of humanity's perfecting.

The final area of church life in which the Spirit works, Irenaeus explains, is in the sacraments of baptism and the Eucharist. Irenaeus calls the Spirit the water of life and the "dew of God", using the metaphor of water which is found in John's Gospel (John 7:37-8), which would have been so familiar to him, and to which he was especially connected by virtue of Polycarp's affiliation with the Apostle John.[12] As usual, Irenaeus is concerned most of all with the effect of the Spirit on our bodies, saying in a vivid metaphor:

> For as a compacted lump of dough cannot be formed of dry wheat without fluid matter, nor can a loaf possess unity, so in like manner, neither could we, being many, be made one in Christ Jesus without the voluntary rain from above. And as dry earth does not bring forth unless it receives moisture, in like manner we also, being originally a dry tree, could never have brought forth fruit unto life without the voluntary rain from above. For our bodies have received unity among themselves by means of that laver which leads to incorruption: but our souls by means of the Spirit... The Lord receiving this as a gift from his Father, does himself also confer it upon those who are partakers of himself, sending the Holy Spirit upon all the earth.[13]

For Irenaeus, the Spirit is conferred through and in baptism. Through the Spirit the body is cleansed. Through the Spirit unity is given to the body of Christ. Through the Spirit we are reconciled to God. Through the Spirit charismatic gifts of speaking in tongues, prophecy, discerning of spirits and exorcism are granted; and through the Spirit foreknowledge, seeing visions, seeing healings—even the raising of the dead—are given to the body of Christ.[14] Through the Spirit we are anointed, "so as to shine with the Glory of God".[15] Indeed, Irenaeus says, "It is not possible to name the number of the gifts which the Church, scattered throughout the whole world, has received from God, in the name of Jesus Christ who was crucified under Pontius Pilate and which she exerts day by day for the benefit of the Gentiles. She has received freely from God; freely also does she minister."[16]

This is a vibrant summary of the work of the Spirit in relation to baptism and witnesses to a vital church in Lugdunum in 170. It is also an answer to the counterfeit baptism offered as an esoteric and magic ritual to bequeath *gnosis* or secret knowledge by the Gnostics as in the case of Zostrianos.[17] And the thought must have been in Irenaeus' mind that true Christian baptism is more of a real revolutionary event in the life of an individual and the community than the proffered mysticism of the Gnostic rite.

Likewise, the Spirit is evidently at work in the Eucharist. We have seen that the very apex of the Church's life together in the Great Church in Rome, as recorded by Justin Martyr, was the celebration of the Eucharist with the bishop. It was both a community celebration and an evangelistic opportunity, demonstrating the heart of the church gathered around the sacrifice of Christ remembered. More than that, in Irenaeus' scheme it was "the chief means by which the members of the Church are prepared for their physical perfection".[18] Thus, Irenaeus declares that Gnostics and Jews cannot argue that,

> [t]he flesh which is nourished with the body of the Lord and with his blood, goes to corruption and does not partake of life. Let them, therefore, either alter their opinion, or cease from offering the things mentioned, but our opinion is in accordance with the Eucharist, and the Eucharist in turn establishes our opinion. For we offer to him his own, announcing consistently the fellowship and union of the flesh and Spirit. For as the bread, which is produced from the earth, when it receives the invocation [epiclesis], is no longer common bread, but the Eucharist, consisting of two realities, earthly and heavenly: so also, our bodies, when they receive the Eucharist are no longer corruptible, having the hope of resurrection to eternity.[19]

Once again Irenaeus' emphasis here, and even more so later,[20] is that the Eucharist is about uniting the physical with the spiritual, the earthly with the eternal and the corruptible being transformed by the incorruptible. Faced with the denigration of the flesh by his adversaries, Irenaeus maintains that humanity and its flesh is recapitulated by Christ, but is also prepared for the future by the Eucharist. It is, in that sense, the food of heaven which is taken from the earth and blessed by the Spirit for each pilgrim: heaven-destined and perfection-bound.

Irenaeus argues that just as wheat must go into the ground and die to become a plentiful crop (John 12:24), which is then used as bread for the Eucharist and is sanctified thereby, so likewise our bodies nourished by the Eucharist are sown after death in the ground but rise through the power of the Word of God to a resurrection, to the glory of God the Father. Thus, "he will secure immortality for what is mortal, and will bountifully bestow incorruptibility on what is corruptible" (1 Corinthians 15:53).[21]

Much of what Irenaeus teaches through his description of the Eucharist is polemical in the sense that he sees it as a further opportunity to state that it is through Christ's body and his blood—in other words through his *flesh* freely offered—that we are redeemed. And what is redeemed are the *souls and bodies* of the faithful. For Irenaeus' opponents maintained that the flesh "was not capable of incorruption".[22] But of course, Irenaeus maintains that we are saved through Christ's body and blood offered on the cross and that the Eucharist is a communion in his body and in his blood. This flesh of the Saviour who dies saves the flesh of the communicant who believes. Irenaeus summarizes it as follows: "He has acknowledged the cup which is part of creation as his own blood, from which he bedews our blood; and the bread, also part of creation, he has established as his own body, from which he gives increase to our bodies."[23] The Eucharist is therefore a reminder that just as the wheat in the Communion bread once died in the sowing but rises in the harvest, so our bodies receiving the benefits of the bread and wine are also "deposited in the earth, suffer decomposition there, and rise at the appointed time. The Word of God granting them resurrection to the glory of God even the Father who freely gives to this mortal immortality, and to this corruptible incorruption, because the strength of God is made perfect in weakness, in order that we may never become puffed up, as if we had life from ourselves."[24]

The Church, therefore, truly functioning and rightly taught, is the place where mortals begin to see God and in so doing become fully alive. In the Church, we may become what we were intended to be. In the Church, we are prepared for the future beyond death. In the Church, the image and likeness of God are further restored in humanity. In the Church, the Word guides humanity in the truth, and the Spirit fashions humanity for its resurrection life.[25] The Church must be rightly and faithfully governed by bishops and presbyters, appointed according to the Apostolic tradition and by their successors. Love and freedom are the hallmarks of the Church's life.[26] The Church is the waiting room or departure lounge for glory, which is yet to be finally and fully revealed.

The consummation of all things

Once again it is worth reminding ourselves that Irenaeus was writing *Against Heresies* around 180, perhaps only 90 years after the last Gospel, that of John, was written and circulated among the waiting Christian communities. John, we are told, wrote at the instigation of the brethren in Ephesus.[27] Then, with the addition of the Book of Revelation by either John the Apostle or John the Presbyter, many of the ingredients for Irenaeus' understanding of the "Last Things" were in place.[28] One of the defining characteristics of the Apostolic era was expectation of the imminent return of Christ. Indeed, some interpreted Christ's words to mean that his return to inaugurate and activate the Kingdom of God would occur during their lifetime (see Matthew 16:27-8).

At the very least, Christians should be ready for his return, although many fervently hoped for and expected it. Here the sharp persecution of the church in Vienne and along the Rhône heightened the expectations that these sufferings were the birth pains of a new and coming age (Matthew 24:8).

It is in this framework that we must understand the emphasis that Irenaeus gives to the "Last Things" or to eschatology in his scheme of the recapitulation of humanity into what it was created to be. In his confrontation with wave upon wave of Gnosticism in all its various forms, he reclaimed the biblical teaching of one God in three persons, who was responsible for creation. God deliberately and intentionally created humanity in his own image and in his own likeness. When first created, human beings were innocent but untested and must go through the Fall at the temptation of the fallen angel, Satan. God's foreknowledge meant that he knew the outcome of the creation of humanity from the outset and the costly deliverance it would entail. He nevertheless continued in that creation. Christ the eternal Logos, and latterly the incarnate Christ, entered the lists of humanity to recapitulate his troublesome and disobedient creature. Christ entered into all of human life to refashion and recapitulate it and did so through faithful Mary, the counterpoint of disobedient Eve. He did this through his whole life, from conception to the grave, and through his redeeming death and victorious resurrection. Those baptized into the faith of Christ are recapitulated, having now the image of God and the likeness of God restored in them. Thus, in the famous quotation from Irenaeus: "The Glory of God is a living man; and the life of man consists in beholding God."[29] Christ was the one true living God-man, but all who believe and are baptized become living humans as they behold God. The remaking of humanity as a process continues in the life of the Church: through scriptural teaching, through the presence of the Spirit, through the leadership of the Apostles and their successors, and through the sacraments of baptism and Eucharist. But finally, humanity completes the process of recapitulation in the ultimate consummation of all things. Many of Irenaeus' teachings on these events are laid out in Book V of *Against Heresies*.

The gateway to these "Last Things" is the resurrection, as our bodies are transformed to be like his glorious body (Philippians 3:20-1). Irenaeus paints the resurrection in vivid colours, writing: "Since the Lord has power to infuse life into what he has fashioned, and since the flesh is capable of being quickened, what remains to prevent its participating in incorruption, which is a blissful and never-ending life granted by God?"[30] This incorruption is a resurrected body, or as Irenaeus would say, the salvation of the flesh, redeemed by Christ with his own flesh, his body and his blood.[31] Furthermore, Irenaeus cites the examples of Elijah and the companions of Daniel in the fiery furnace as others whose flesh may be transformed and resurrected (Daniel 3; 2 Kings 2:11-12).[32] What Irenaeus is determined to underline is that the physical body is capable of resurrection, even if it is raised a spiritual body (1 Corinthians 15:35ff).[33] For Irenaeus, a human is a composite of body, soul and spirit; but it is the salvation of the body, together with soul and spirit, which is so unique to the salvation and recapitulation worked by Christ.[34] It is the down-payment of the Spirit in a Christian's life on earth that is the guarantee of future resurrection.[35]

If the resurrection from the dead for those who have been raised to life is the first step into these Last Things, the second and the third steps are the establishment of God's kingdom and the destruction of the Devil and his works, respectively. Both these doctrines are consonant with Irenaeus' view of the refashioning of the image and likeness of God in man through recapitulation by Christ, which process only comes to its ultimate fulfilment in the final coming of the Kingdom of God. This understanding also sits especially well with Chapter 20 of the Book of Revelation, which by then had been circulating as an Apostolic text among the churches for at least 60 years. Clearly Irenaeus taught the coming of God's kingdom in its entirety, at which point the recapitulation of the image and likeness of God in believing humanity will be complete. What is not so clear, and often disputed, is whether Irenaeus believed and taught a millennial rule of Christ on earth before the final inauguration of the Kingdom. This question is made more complex by the variation between the Latin Western text of *Against Heresies*, which has no reference to an explicit millennial rule on earth, and the Armenian text which does. Thus, Irenaeus in *that* text speaks of "[t]he seven thousand years of the kingdom of the just, in which the just shall grow accustomed to incorruptibility, when the whole of creation will be renewed for those who have been preserved for this".[36] For the sake of clarity, the 7,000 years refers to 6,000 years of a discernible and increasing Kingdom on earth before the Parousia, with the final thousand years being the rule of Christ on earth. The reason this does not appear in the Latin Western text may be that later Church leaders, such as Eusebius of Caesarea, did not approve of a literal millennium rule (although it had been supported by Papias), and so, presumably, the passage was dropped by copiers of the text in the West.[37] But in the final analysis, this must remain conjecture.

If, on the one hand, the Parousia precipitates the coming of the Kingdom and the full resurrection of the saints to share in the rule of the Lamb, it is on the other hand also the destruction of the Devil, the judgement of unbelievers and the bringing down of human empires. Much of this resonates with the prophets of the Old Testament, but more especially with the Book of Revelation and the writings of the Apostle John (see John 5:24-30), which had only recently been circulating in the churches of the West.

Throughout Irenaeus' writing, Satan or the Devil is depicted as the real enemy of God, and the means of defeating this adversary is only through the blood and death of Christ, the Son of God.[38] Unlike the

Gnostics, and in particular the third-century Gnostic sect of Manichees, this was not a struggle between two equal and opposite forces, for Satan had originally been, and was still, part of God's creation. In other words, he was God's Devil and always subject to God.[39] But, as with human beings, this angel had the capacity to rebel and did so, and through the Fall carried the rest of creation and especially humanity with him.

Satan has the capacity to spoil, to destroy and to traduce creation, but he did not have the capacity to create himself.[40] Until the final defeat of the Devil, which will be enacted in the Last Things, there will be perpetual struggle for the Church and for its members. And in his mission to release us from this power of the Devil, both in the Temptations and in Gethsemane, Jesus himself engaged in a real and deeply costly struggle with this fallen created being. Nevertheless, despite Christ's known victory over the Devil through the cross and resurrection, for an allotted time the Devil has the power to draw human beings into destructive behaviour, whether as individuals, groups or nations. Only in the Last Times and as part of the Last Things will the question about why it was that Satan rebelled against his Creator be answered. The cause seems to have been envy (*invidia*), and not simply envy of God, but also envy of human beings themselves, who have a higher destiny and more creative powers.[41] The object of Satan is to obliterate or at least corrupt the image and the likeness of God in humanity; the work of Christ through recapitulation is to restore that image and likeness to perfection, and eternally.[42]

Thus, in completing his account of the Last Things, Irenaeus is anxious to make clear the outcome for the Devil. Building his teaching especially on the Book of Daniel and Revelation,[43] Irenaeus sees the end of human empires although his time frame is of a more imminent Parousia, possibly in his own lifetime. The destruction of Satan and his minions is Irenaeus' main focus of judgement in the Last Things. This destruction is to be preceded by the coming of the Antichrist to Jerusalem for a period of three years and six months, when he will take his seat in the Temple of God, presumably rebuilt.[44] Somehow, Irenaeus identifies the Antichrist with the unjust judge of Luke 18:2ff. Then, following this period of turbulence, Jesus will return.[45] The Antichrist will be destroyed, the just will be raised into a renewed earthly Jerusalem, and the wicked will be judged.[46] Yet Irenaeus' focus, arising from his overall scheme, is more on the judgement and destruction of Satan than on the judgement of humanity, and his emphasis in human judgement is on granting to them what they have themselves craved in their earthly life, be it darkness or light. Judgement will be a separation between these two.[47]

But the outcome for those who have believed is a resurrection of body, soul and spirit, a perfection in them of the image and likeness of God. It is a celebration of the Son who took on our flesh to recapitulate our humanity so that in a clear-sighted vision the glory of God may be revealed to countless humans, now "fully alive".[48]

Notes

1. *AH* III.24.1, *op. cit.*
2. *AH* IV.20.12; IV.20.12.
3. Minns, *Irenaeus*, p. 123.
4. *AH* IV.4.1.
5. *AH* III.1.1.
6. *AH* III.1.1.
7. *AH* I.10.2.
8. *Demonstration of the Apostolic Preaching* §2.
9. *AH* V.6.1.
10. *AH* V.6.1.
11. *AH* V.6.1.
12. *AH* III.17.1.
13. *AH* III.17.3.
14. *AH* II.32.4.
15. Minns, *Irenaeus*, p. 129.
16. *AH* III.32.4.
17. Brakke, *Gnostics*, pp. 74-83.
18. Minns, *Irenaeus*, p. 131.
19. *AH* IV.18.4-5.
20. *AH* V.2.3.
21. *AH* V.2.2.
22. *AH* V.2.2.

23. *AH* V.2.2.
24. *AH* V.2.3.
25. Wingren, *Man and the Incarnation*, pp. 154ff.
26. Wingren, *Man and the Incarnation*, p. 174.
27. *EH* III.24-5, tr. G. A. Williamson (Harmondsworth: Penguin Classics, 1989), pp. 86-8.
28. *EH* VII.25, op. cit., pp. 240-1.
29. *AH* IV.20.7.
30. *AH* V.3.3.
31. *AH* V.2.1.
32. *AH* V.5.2.
33. *AH* V.6.1-2.
34. Minns, *Irenaeus*, p. 144.
35. *AH* V.81; V.12.2,4,6.
36. *AH* V.36.3, Armenian Text.
37. Minns, *Irenaeus*, pp. 140ff.
38. Wingren, *Man and the Incarnation*, p. 39.
39. *AH* IV.41.2.
40. Wingren, *Man and the Incarnation*, p. 39.
41. *AH* V.24.4.
42. Wingren, *Man and the Incarnation*, pp. 53ff.
43. *AH* V.26.1-2.
44. *AH* V.26.3-4.
45. *AH* V.28.2, 30.4.
46. *AH* V.32.1; 35.1-2; 36.2-3.
47. *AH* V.27.2.
48. *AH* IV.20.7.

12

A word for our times

There is no firm date for the death of Irenaeus. He died towards the end of the second century, possibly in the reign of Septimius Severus (193-211), the African emperor who adorned Libya with the city of Leptis Magna (Al-Khums). Alternatively, he may have died during the reign of Septimus' predecessor Commodus, the heir of Marcus Aurelius.

Marcus Aurelius (161-80), the famous emperor who fulfilled the Platonic ideal of a being a philosopher king, is still well known today, not least for his *Meditations* (174). He was the last of the "Five Good Emperors". Nonetheless, Marcus Aurelius' reign was marked out by its persecution of Christians. In Rome, Justin Martyr and his companions were condemned to death in 165 by the city prefect, Quintus Junius Rusticus. This was in response to Justin's *First Apology* (155), and its supplement, the *Second Apology* (c.157). They were together a defence of Christianity from a spiritual, intellectual and moral point of view, but met with uncomprehending disdain. Persecution in Rome replicated what occurred in Smyrna with the martyrdom of Polycarp (155), who, as we have seen, was such an influence on Irenaeus, and whom he considered his model. Likewise, in Marcus Aurelius' reign, the combination of mob violence and the interventions of Roman magistrates led to the martyrdom and torture of many Christians in Vienne and in the amphitheatre in Lugdunum.

As an educated Roman, and writing like Irenaeus in Greek, Marcus Aurelius gave us his *Meditations*, which "are not so much silent dialogues with a divided self, as admonitions and reflections the emperor addressed to himself and to which he seldom replies".[1] Irenaeus would have been able to help Marcus Aurelius with musings such as this one:

What a noble thing is the soul ready for its release from the body, if now must be the time, and prepared for whatever follows—extinction, dispersal, or survival! But this readiness must come from a specific decision: not in mere revolt like the Christians—but thoughtful, dignified, and—if others are to believe it—undramatic.[2]

There speaks the Stoic: confident of the soul, unsure of the afterlife, and in control of all emotions so that nobility might shine. However, all this self-studied introspection, self-sufficiency and classical erudition was to be violently overturned by his successor and son, Commodus.

Commodus (177-192)—so sinisterly portrayed by the actor Joaquin Phoenix in the film *Gladiator*, in part filmed at the amphitheatre in El Djem in present-day Tunisia—took the office of princeps or emperor back to the worst days of the Julio-Claudian dynasty under Caligula and Nero. He murdered his sister Lucilla, who had conspired against him, violated his other sisters and in other ways humiliated or attacked his officials.[3] He became besotted by gladiatorial combat. Having succeeded at the age of 18 and having settled with his father the Germanic or Marcomannic wars, he gave himself up to gladiatorial combat, which he always won, and to the slaughter of animals in protracted games in the Colosseum. We are told in the *Historia Augusta* that, "He engaged in gladiatorial combats, and accepted the names usually given to gladiators with as much pleasure as if he had been granted triumphal decorations. He regularly took part in games, and whenever he did, he ordered the fact to be inscribed in the public records. It is said that he engaged in gladiatorial bouts seven hundred and thirty-five times."[4] It is not surprising that he was poisoned and assassinated, and after a year of political upheaval Septimius Severus emerged as the new emperor. Perhaps it was in his reign that the aged Bishop of Lugdunum, revered both far and wide, died, firm in his faith and expectant of the resurrection of a body and soul recapitulated by Christ.

Septimius Severus had succeeded after another period of acute Roman instability in what is generally called "The Year of The Five Emperors". It surpassed by one emperor the period following the end of the Julio-Claudian dynasty in 68 with the death of Nero which precipitated "The

Year of The Four Emperors", ending with the accession of Vespasian and the Flavians taking power. Septimius Severus was no stranger to Lugdunum. Before his accession, he had been governor of the city, and his second marriage in 187 to the influential Empress Julia Domna, drawn from the pagan priestly family of Elagabalus from Syria, took place while he was Governor of Lugdunensis, which included most of eastern France.

Septimus eventually became emperor in 193. At the very least, Irenaeus would have known him from his years in Lugdunum as a governor or legate and military commander.[5] No friend of the churches, in his later rule Septimus legislated against conversion to Christianity.[6] It seems that for at least the early part of his reign (193-211), Irenaeus was still the Bishop of Lugdunum when he most likely died around 200. What Irenaeus left behind, quite apart from his faithful stewardship of the church in Lugdunum, was his great work *Against Heresies* and the shorter catechetical work *Demonstration of the Apostolic Preaching*. Themes from these works were to reverberate down the centuries. In a time when the New Testament Scriptures were being formed and where church leadership had not yet fully matured, his teaching would function as a seminal staging post in the development of Christian doctrine. Contemporaries like Justin Martyr and Tertullian were also to add their weight to this teaching, but his was, nonetheless, a singular contribution.

Irenaeus was very much a man of his age and might therefore be fairly called a representative of a more primitive understanding of Christianity. Like most of his era, he believed the creation of humanity in Adam and Eve was recent history. Nor is that so strange when we consider that as late as the seventeenth century, Archbishop Ussher (1581-1656) believed from the genealogies of Genesis that Adam was created on 22 October 4004 BC at 6 p.m. In an ironic review of Ussher's work, it was remarked that, "no closer would the archbishop commit himself!"

Following Papias, Irenaeus expected the millennial rule of Christ would begin at the start of the seventh millennium since the creation of humanity.[7] Again, in promulgating his teaching of the recapitulation of humanity through the Incarnation of Christ, Irenaeus believed Jesus lived till 50 years of age, since in this way he could be said to have recapitulated old age also—50 being advanced in years during that period.[8] Likewise, Irenaeus believed the number four was perfectly complete, and therefore four was the perfect number for the Gospels. If on the one hand Irenaeus was susceptible to such mild numerology or historical guessing, there is no doubt that on the other hand he left few stones unturned in his method of understanding the Gnostic myths. In the first two books of *Against Heresies*, he demonstrates his thorough research and understanding clearly, even of something as slippery and diffuse as Gnosticism in all its many forms. So, what especially does Irenaeus leave us?

At root, Irenaeus had to go back to the very basics of Christian theology to refute all the various theories and speculations of the Gnostic teachers, especially Valentinus and Marcion. Influenced by some of the Platonic teaching about the One who is unknowable, he had to retrieve the essential truths of Christianity that God is the Creator of the universe, itself originally good, and, far from being removed from his creation, God is instrumental both in its creation and its sustenance. Nor does God relate with either humanity or creation itself through a multiplicity of *aeons* or intermediaries. God is always the co-eternal Trinity of Father, Son and Holy Spirit; and thus, Irenaeus draws a very real line between Christianity and Judaism, which does not recognize the eternal nature of the *Logos* incarnate in Jesus. Evil entered the world through a malevolent fallen angel of great power and magnificence, who was jealous of the powers of human beings to be creative themselves, and whose destiny was likewise enviable. This opponent of God's created order, Satan or the Devil, was God's principal opponent and successfully suborned the obedience of Adam and Eve who represented the human family. At the time of their creation Adam and Eve were innocent but not yet perfect, in the sense of not being complete in either understanding or in their grasp of their vocation. The Fall, although catastrophic in its effects, was not yet regarded as so utterly marring, as in the later Augustinian account of the total corruption of the human will and the inability of a person to move unaided towards God in faith. That understanding drawn from the Apostle Paul was to come some 200 years later. But this restatement of the true nature of the Godhead was rightly the starting point of Irenaeus' theology, as indeed it is in the Bible. This was the first thing that needed to be refuted in the Gnostic system and is *the fundamental first step* in obtaining true knowledge of God and of ourselves.[9] Irenaeus had to unequivocally reiterate that God: Father, Son and Spirit is the Creator.

If establishing the true nature of God and his relationship both to creation in general and humanity in particular was the essential first step in Irenaeus' refutation of false knowledge, the second was to show how humanity could be rescued and reinstated to the position for which it was first created. This entailed the Incarnation, and the process of recapitulation. The eternal Logos freely became flesh in obedience to the Father in order to save humankind. The way this is done in Irenaeus' theology is through recapitulation, by which the image and likeness of God granted to humankind are to be fully restored. Recapitulation was a term originally used in the rhetorical and literary schools of the Second Sophist movement in Smyrna and elsewhere to summarize a classic text such as Homer's *Iliad* or *Odyssey*. Now Irenaeus re-employs the term with deeper theological intent. It is not just a summary of a text but the means whereby, through the life, death and resurrection of Christ, human bodily life *in its entirety* will be restored, and through faith in Jesus, become effective and operative in human beings, both singly and collectively.

Recapitulation, in effect, means the accomplishment of God's plan of salvation in history starting with the choice and training of Israel, but fulfilled in the life, death and resurrection of Christ. Jesus recapitulates Adam and Eve, and the humanity they represent. And since Christ took on flesh and was formed like Adam from the mud of the earth and the Spirit of God, he restores fallen humanity by reversing its disobedience with his own complete obedience. In this way Adam, and the humanity he represents, is restored to show the glory of God for which human beings were first made.[10]

Given the dynamic of Irenaeus' theology, it is not surprising therefore that he should come up with his famous dictum, "The glory of God is a living man [or man fully alive]; and the life of man consists in beholding God", which is becoming as well known as Augustine's saying that, "our hearts are restless till they find their rest in you".[11] The whole of Irenaeus' theology tends towards the glory of God shown in the restoration of humanity and the glory of God granted to humanity once restored. It is the whole direction of Irenaeus' thinking and indeed that of the Bible. This theology entails a restoration of the complete person: body or flesh, soul and spirit, and, given the Gnostics' indictment of the flesh, Irenaeus is at pains throughout to emphasize that God in Christ restores the flesh or body.

For Irenaeus, this movement from the imperfection consequent upon and evident in the Fall to the perfection made abundant in the final revelation of the Kingdom, is a process with different stages. Thus, at the outset, Adam and Eve, representatives of humanity, are vulnerable to disobedience by virtue of having the freedom of choice to disobey. The fact that humanity disobeys is due to their imperfection and ill-discipline. Irenaeus says that because of their moral immaturity they were readily vulnerable to Satan's temptation to disobedience, "Man was a child, not yet having his understanding perfected—wherefore also he was easily led astray by the deceiver."[12] This leaves humanity engaged in a process of becoming: from its recapitulation in Christ to its final perfection in the Kingdom of God. God alone is not in a state of becoming, but human beings are, for everything else is contingent upon him. Creatures are by definition in a state of becoming.[13] This is not only reflected in the teaching of the New Testament, that we become what we have been made in Christ (Philippians 3:12-14), but is reflected in the Platonic model that is so close to the theology of the Cappadocian Fathers, especially Gregory of Nyssa and later Augustine of Hippo. Both were deeply influenced by the Platonic model, recast by Plotinus and Porphyry.

If someone were to ask, "Could not have God brought into existence a perfect being incapable of disobedience at the outset?" the answer Irenaeus would give is that what God has in store for humankind transcends even such perfection. This *felix culpa* of human disobedience reveals God in such a way that could not otherwise be grasped, and it enables human beings to become what they were intended to be. It is bearing in mind all this that we must understand the statement that, "The Glory of God is a man or woman fully alive". It takes the glory of God in Christ and in the Trinity to make any man or any woman fully alive. The other half of this great statement by Irenaeus is that, "the life of man consists in beholding God". In other words, this quality of aliveness is found, and only found, in beholding God. Beholding him in creation, yes; but more especially beholding him in the face of Jesus Christ (John 14:9; 2 Corinthians 3:12-18). As Augustine put it, the remedy is plain, "For the meantime, let the scriptures be the countenance of God."[14] It is through the lens of Scripture that we behold him, and in beholding him we become fully alive, and in our becoming fully alive, the glory of God is shown.

What kind of message might Irenaeus have today for our contemporary world? In some respects, the modern Western world could not be more different from the Gnostic sects which confronted Irenaeus in the second century. In many ways, those mystical sects were far more religious than the scientific materialism that lies behind much of our present culture in the West. The cosmology of the Gnostics, involving scores of intermediaries (*aeons*) with the created order, is a far cry from the modern scientific understanding of how the universe came into being. Stephen Hawking reflected that, "we are insignificant creatures on a minor planet of a very average star in the outer suburbs of one hundred thousand million galaxies. So, it is difficult to believe in a God who would care about us or even notices our existence."[15] And yet for all his lack of scientific knowledge Irenaeus would say that humanity or an individual human being remains the apex of God's creation, invested with the image and likeness of God: marred and no longer innocent but capable of restoration and repair because of the Incarnation. And the planet we occupy still remains the only planet of colour (blue) in the perceived solar system, even with the aid of the James Webb telescope looking deep into the history of the universe.

Whereas the Gnostics doubted that anything good could come from our flesh, but rather considered it a dead weight on the soul and spirit, and not worthy of resurrection, the present age is so taken up with our flesh that it remains almost the centre of our existence, to the exclusion often of soul and spirit. The need to train the body through diet, exercise and healthy living and to squeeze the last morsel from our sex lives is heralded almost every weekend in our newspaper supplements. Yet what makes humanity fully alive, we are told by Irenaeus, is the glory of God, or to put it the other way round, the glory of God is perceived best in a human being fully alive. And for a man or a woman to shine forth the glory of God, he or she must behold God. In other words, the glory of God is best perceived, not in terms of outstanding personal grooming, a fit, well-exercised body, a well-balanced diet, a fulfilled sex life and strong mental health (good as each of these things may be), but in perceiving, experiencing and *increasingly knowing* the glory of God for ourselves. Beholding his glory results in all the parts of our humanity becoming fully alive: the spirit and the body, the soul and the mind. For that to happen, for a human to become fully alive, it is not a matter of youth, beauty or the physical perfection of a Greek sculpture, but rather consists in the life of a woman or man beholding God. Such beholding will harmonize and fulfil all our deepest gifts. Having the time, the inclination, the desire and the effect of beholding God in Christ is what enables each human to become fully alive, and that is, surely, Irenaeus' message and promise for us today.

Notes

[1] Diskin Clay, *Preface to Meditations by Marcus Aurelius* (Harmondsworth: Penguin Classics, 2006), p. xiv.
[2] Marcus Aurelius, *Meditations*, tr. Martin Hammond, Bk 11.3, p. 106.
[3] *Historia Augusta*, Loeb Classical Library, Vol. 139 (Cambridge, MA: Harvard University Press, 2022), pp. 277-9.
[4] *Historia Augusta*, op. cit., p. 263.
[5] *Historia Augusta*, op. cit., p. 363.
[6] *Historia Augusta*, op. cit., p. 393.
[7] Minns, *Irenaeus*, pp. 140ff.
[8] *AH* II.22.4-5.
[9] See also Calvin's *Institutes* 1.1.
[10] *AH* V.32.2.
[11] *AH* IV.30.7; Augustine, *Confessions* I.i.
[12] *Demonstration of the Apostolic Preaching* §12 and *AH* IV.38.1.
[13] Minns, *Irenaeus*, p. 89.
[14] Augustine, Sermon 22.7.
[15] Stephen Hawking, *A Brief History of Time*.

Timeline

*c.*4 BC	Birth of Jesus Christ in Bethlehem
AD 14	Death of the Emperor Augustus
*c.*30	Crucifixion and resurrection of Jesus Christ
48/9	Council of Jerusalem
64	Martyrdom of Peter and Paul and Great Fire of Rome
68	Death of Nero; end of Julio-Claudians
69	Year of the Four Emperors
70	Emperor Vespasian; age of the Flavians
	Destruction of Jerusalem by Titus and Roman Legions
79	Eruption of Vesuvius; destruction of Pompeii
98–117	Emperor Trajan
*c.*99	Death of the Apostle John in Ephesus (in his nineties?)
117–38	Rule of Hadrian
122	Building of Hadrian's Wall, the limits of Empire
138–61	Rule of Antoninus Pius
*c.*140	Birth of Irenaeus at Smyrna
157	Martyrdom of Polycarp in Smyrna
161–80	Rule of Marcus Aurelius and Lucius Verus (until 169)
160s	Irenaeus moves to Lugdunum via Rome
175–89	Eleutherius, Bishop of Rome
*c.*177	Irenaeus travels to Rome
177/80	Vienne martyrs and persecution in Lugdunum
c.180–5	Writing of *Against Heresies*
181–93	Emperor Commodus
185–90	Writing of *Demonstration of the Apostolic Preaching*
189–99	Victor, Bishop of Rome
193–211	Accession of Septimius Severus, from Leptis Magna in present-day Libya
*c.*200	Death of Irenaeus

Dramatis Personae

Antoninus Pius, Emperor (138–61)   Emperor during Irenaeus' early life. He was the fourth of the "Five Good Emperors". He was an adopted son of Hadrian and married his niece, Faustina. For the most part, his reign was peaceful, save for a campaign in the lowlands of Scotland and the building of the Antonine Wall between the Firth of Clyde and Firth of Forth in 142, taking six years to complete, later abandoned. He concentrated on law reform, good administration and strengthening the treasury. There was even a diplomatic mission to China in 166. He lived into his seventies and was succeeded by Marcus Aurelius.

Eleutherius, Bishop of Rome (174–89)   A Greek-speaking bishop/pope who succeeded Anicetus. Anicetus had actively opposed Gnosticism and Marcionism and was a close associate of Polycarp. It is probable that Irenaeus had contact with them both, and that Irenaeus visited Rome for a second time at the time of the persecution of Christians in Vienne and Lyon.

Ignatius (*c*.50–*c*.108)   One of the great figures of the post-Apostolic period and along with Clement and Polycarp called one of the Apostolic Fathers. He was Bishop or Patriarch of Antioch and the second or third Bishop of Antioch after the Apostle Peter. He was arrested in Antioch for his faith and marched by soldiers to Rome to await trial and death. *En route* he wrote to the churches he passed and to Polycarp, encouraging unity, commitment to the bishop and fortitude.

John, the Apostle, the Beloved Disciple (*c*.8–99)   Author of the Fourth Gospel (*c*.90) and the Epistles of John. He lived in Ephesus until his death in the reign of Trajan and was buried in the Basilica of John. He suffered exile in Patmos, probably in the reign of Domitian, and wrote the Revelation of St John the Divine. He consecrated Polycarp Bishop of Smyrna who himself taught the young Irenaeus in Smyrna (*AH* III.3.4)

Justin Martyr (*c*.100–165)   Born in Nablus, a Gentile Greek interested in Philosophy. Initially he followed Stoic and Pythagorean Philosophers; he soon became a Platonist. Meeting a Syrian Christian, he then devoted himself to the following of the Jewish Prophets and gaining wisdom from Christ. He emigrated to Rome, put on the garb of a philosopher and began teaching there, gathering students in *c*.145. Known for his works *Dialogue with Trypho the Jew* and his *Two Apologies* addressed to the Emperor Antoninus Pius, he sought fair treatment for Christians who, he argued, were no threat to the Empire. His case was heard by the Prefect Junius Rusticus, but he and his companions were beheaded in *c*.165.

Marcion (*c*.85–160)   Originally a shipbuilder from Sinope on the Black Sea, he was a lay theologian with definite Gnostic views who came to Rome with money in his pocket and seeking wider acceptance for his views. He believed that the Old Testament was an account of a separate demiurge or God with tribal connections. He developed ideas of two gods: one a transcendent God revealed in Jesus, the other a demiurge or artisan responsible for a corrupt creation and with belligerent tendencies. This latter god or being was revealed in the Old Testament, while the former was made known through the Apostle Paul's writings and Luke's Gospel especially. For a while he had influence in the churches of Rome with possibly one or two funded by him. But by 150 his influence was waning. Both Irenaeus and Tertullian exposed his false teachings in their writings.

Marcus Aurelius, Emperor (161–80)   The last of the so-called "Five Good Emperors", a term coined by Niccolò Machiavelli in his book *The Discourses of Livy*. He was adopted by his predecessor as emperor, Antoninus Pius in the Nerva-Antonine Dynasty which included Nerva, Trajan and Hadrian. Although persecution of Christians increased during his reign, it was not at his behest, and he was praised by Justin Martyr and Tertullian as a good ruler. A military commander who was almost permanently campaigning against the German tribes, he was, nevertheless, most at home as a Stoic philosopher and known for his *Meditations*. The Antonine Plague broke out in his reign and destroyed 15 per cent of the population, between five and ten million people. Influenced by the Second Sophist Movement, his tutors being Marcus Cornelius Fronto and Herodes Atticus—both renowned orators but with differing convictions—he relished the Greek thinkers and writers. He co-governed with Lucius Verus until 169. Wars against Parthia and German tribes occupied most of his reign leaving little time for philosophy. He had 13 children with his wife Faustina, and was succeeded by the unruly and erratic Commodus, ending the run of the "Five Good Emperors".

Pliny the Younger (61–113)   Being from a Patrician Roman family, his uncle Pliny was a polymath and admiral who died in the eruption of Vesuvius at Pompeii in 79. He was a lawyer and magistrate in Rome and was promoted to Governor of Bithynia and Pontus by Trajan, the Spanish soldier-emperor. His correspondence with Trajan is enlightening especially on the treatment of Christians in the courts. He despised them as being un-Roman while he himself was Stoic in outlook. He was told by Trajan to deal with Christians if they came to court, but not to begin a campaign against them.

Polycarp, Bishop of Smyrna (69–155) Both Irenaeus and Tertullian tell us that he was a disciple of John the Apostle, meaning that since John lived to about 99 in the reign of Trajan, they must have had some twenty years of overlap. John consecrated Polycarp as Bishop of Smyrna. Known mostly for his martyrdom and noble words of witness before his death, it is becoming clearer that he was an authority in the Church both in the East and in Rome. His life appears in *Against Heresies*, *The Epistle to Florinus*, his martyrdom in *The Apostolic Fathers*, in Jerome's work on *Illustrious Men* and in Ignatius' Letters. He, like Irenaeus, visited Rome and taught actively against Gnosticism.

Pothinus, Bishop of Lugdunum (*c*.87–177) He was the first Bishop of Lugdunum before Irenaeus and martyred in the outbreak or persecution in 177. Greek-speaking, and probably sent by Polycarp of Smyrna, he established a flourishing church there from *c*.155, soon after the Apostolic era.

Tertullian (*c*.155–220) Called the Father of Latin Christianity he was a prolific author, lawyer and layman from Carthage in the Province of *Africa Proconsularis*. He was in many ways the father too of African Christianity, projecting a puritan and demanding spirituality, separating Church from society. More or less a contemporary of Irenaeus, he wrote also against contemporary Gnosticism, especially in his exhaustive critique of Marcion. Many of his works were about Christian behaviour, e.g. attitudes to the spectacles or gladiatorial combat, the veiling of women, marriage, penitence and perseverance, and his famous *Apology* which demonstrated the growth of the Church through the blood of the martyrs and its persecution by the Roman authorities. In many ways, he set the theological tempo of the African Church. Tiring of ecclesiastical control, in later life he joined the Montanist Church which valued prophecy, lay leadership and greater prominence being given to spiritually gifted women.

Valentinus (100–180)   One of the chief Gnostic teachers in the second-century Church. He was educated in Alexandria and was a follower of Theudas, and was no doubt influenced by both the Platonism and Jewish studies prevalent in Alexandria since Philo (20 BC–AD 50), and Philo's desire to meld them. Valentinus claimed a secret knowledge communicated through Theudas in which Pauline teaching was placed within a Gnostic system of an unknowable God (Bythos), intermediate *aeons*, a corrupt creation and evil flesh, so that both the Incarnation and the resurrection were brought into doubt, and salvation gained through apprehending a secret knowledge. Valentinus moved to Rome hoping to become bishop, and when disappointed sought to lead his church instead.

Victor, Bishop of Rome (189–99)   Born probably in Leptis Magna and of Berber origin. According to Eusebius in his *Ecclesiastical History*, he was involved in the controversy about the proper date for celebrating Easter. The Eastern Bishops, following the example of John, the Evangelist Philip and his virgin daughters in Ephesus, celebrated Easter on the 14th Day of Nisan, regardless of whether it was a Sunday. Whereas the West, including Irenaeus, kept Easter on the Lord's Day following 14 Nisan. Irenaeus probably consulted with Victor following the publication of *Against Heresies*.

Vienne Martyrs (177)   A spate of persecution occurred in Lugdunum and Vienne in 177, recorded by Eusebius in Bk V.1 during the reign of Marcus Aurelius. The Christians, mainly of Greek descent and Greek-speaking, were first banned from public spaces and then falsely accused of cannibalism and incest. A combination of mob violence and the magistrates' "justice" led to the death of 48 Christians including one woman, Blandina, who was tortured, tied to a stake and eventually gored by a bull. News of these martyrdoms was sent in a letter to churches in Asia Minor. News of this persecution was also taken by Irenaeus to the Bishop of Rome, Eleutherius. The Bishop of Lyon, Pothinus, the predecessor of Irenaeus, was also martyred in this outbreak of persecution.

Glossary of Gnostic terms

It must be stressed that there is no single set of terms common to all Gnostic sects. Rather there is a general approximation of terms, but sects within Gnosticism use different proper names. Gnostic was a later term for the mystical religions of the Roman Empire.

I have divided this list into two categories: the first in relation to creation (cosmology) the second in relation to salvation (soteriology).

Cosmology

Aeons personified emanations from the Godhead associated with life qualities or archetypes e.g. Mind, Word, Life, Forethought, Insight, Living Being (Eve), Messenger of Light, etc. There could be up to 28 *aeons* in some systems.

Archons powers of Darkness in the heavenly spheres.

Barbēlō a senior *aeon* and primal power. Supreme female principle, antecedent of creation.

Bythos the unknowable profound eternal God (similar to the Platonic One).

Demiurge the Craftsmen or creator of the corrupt material world.

Hyle evil matter responsible for evil in the world.

the Ogdoad and Hebdomad respectively kingdoms of eight or seven in the Pleroma which connect with the *aeons*.

Pleroma the full heavenly sphere connected to *aeons*.

Sophia a female principal through whom creation was engineered.

Yaldabaoth a lower, even corrupt, *aeon* or demiurge through whom the fallen and evil word was created.

Soteriology

Apolutrosis a higher form of baptism which enables redemption, greater enlightenment and freedom from material existence.

Eros and Agape Eros is passion that searches for unity and agape is compassion that enables enlightenment.

Gnosis The theory that salvation comes through acquiring secret knowledge and enlightenment from intermediaries.

Jesus a Messenger of light enabling Gnosis.

Seth (Adam and Eve's third child) and **Mary Magdalene** further intermediaries who have received enlightenment.

Stages of Salvation *hylic*, the least enlightened and material in outlook; *psychic*, enlightened but mostly in the intellect: *psychic*, spiritual and truly enlightened and saved.

Bibliography

Primary sources

After the New Testament: A Reader in Early Christianity, ed. Bart. D. Ehrman (Oxford: Oxford University Press, 1999).

The Apostolic Fathers, Vols I & II, ed. and tr. Bart D. Ehrman, Loeb Classical Library, Vols 24 and 25 (Cambridge, MA: Harvard University Press, 2003).

Athanasius, *Contra Gentes and De Incarnatione*, ed. Robert W. Thomson, Oxford Early Texts (Oxford: Oxford University Press, 1971).

Augustine, *City of God*, tr. Henry Bettenson (Harmondsworth: Penguin, 2003).

Dio, Cassius Bks 61–70, Loeb Classical Library, Vol. 176 (Cambridge, MA: Harvard University Press, 2000).

Dio, Cassius, *The History of the Reign of Augustus* (Harmondsworth: Penguin, 1987).

Eusebius, *Letter to the Churches from Lyons and Vienne*, in *Eusebius History of the Church*, tr. G. A. Williamson (Harmondsworth: Penguin, 1989).

Gregory of Nyssa, *Commentary on the Song of Songs.*

Historia Augusta, tr. David Magie, Loeb Classical Library, Vol. 139 (Cambridge, MA: Harvard University Press, 2022).

Irenaeus

Irenaeus, *Against Heresies*, The Ante-Nicene Fathers (TANF), ed., Philip Schaff, and *Demonstration of the Apostolic Preaching* (Grand Rapids, MI: Eerdmans, 1885, 1975, 2001; Aeterna Press Reprint, 2016).

Contres Hérésies (Sources Chrétienne Paris) *Bk IV SC 100, 1965; Bk V SC 152–3, 1969; Bk III SC 210–211, 1974, Bk I SC 263–4, 1979; Bk II SC 293–4, 1982.*
There are also Armenian Fragments of the Greek Text.
Demonstration of the Apostolic Preaching Armenian. 7 Fragments, tr. K Mekerttschian and S. G. Wilson, *Patrologia Orientalis* (Paris 1919).
Demonstration of the Apostolic Preaching, tr. J. A. Robinson (London: SPCK, 1920).
Marcus Aurelius, *Meditations,* tr. Martin Hammond (London: Penguin, 2006).
Nag Hammadi Scriptures, ed. Marvin Meyer (San Francisco, CA: HarperOne, 2007).
Gregory of Nazianzus, *On God and Christ: Five Theological Orations* (Crestwood, NY: St Vladimir's Press, 2002).
Plato, *Timaeus and Critias,* tr. Desmond Lee (Harmondsworth: Penguin, 1977).
Pliny, *Letters of the Younger Pliny,* tr. Betty Radice (Harmondsworth: Penguin, 1963).
Suetonius, tr. Robert Graves, *The Twelve Caesars* (Harmondsworth: Penguin, 2011).
Tertullian, *The Apology,* TANF, Vol. III Eerdmans 1884, reprinted by Cosimo Classics: New York, 2007.
On Shows and Spectacles
Against Marcion
Against The Valentinians
Against Praxeas
On the Resurrection of the Flesh

Secondary sources

Barnes, Timothy, *Tertullian* (Oxford: Oxford University Press, 1985).
Behr, John, *Irenaeus of Lyons: Identifying Christianity* (Oxford: Oxford University Press, 2015).

Bowman, Alan K., Peter Garnsey and Dominic Rathbone (eds), *The Cambridge Ancient History, Vol. XI: The High Empire, A.D. 70–192*, second edition (Cambridge: Cambridge University Press, 2008).

Brakke, David, *The Gnostics: Myth, Ritual and Diversity in Early Christianity* (Cambridge, MA: Harvard University Press, 2012).

Chadwick, Henry, *The Early Church* (Harmondsworth: Penguin, 1993).

Daniélou, Jean, *From Glory to Glory: Texts from Gregory of Nyssa's Mystical Writings*, tr. Herbert Musurillo S.J. (Crestwood, NY: St Vladimir's Press, 1979).

Dunn, James D. G., *Christianity in the Making, Vol. III: Neither Jew nor Greek: A Contested Identity* (Grand Rapids, MI: Eerdmans, 2015).

Foster, Paul and Sara Parvis, *Irenaeus: Life, Scripture, Legacy* (Minneapolis, MN: Fortress Press, 2012).

Gibbon, Edward, *Decline and Fall of the Roman Empire* (Abridged Edition, Wordsworth Classics, 1998).

Goldsworthy, Adrian, *Augustus: From Revolutionary to Emperor* (London: Weidenfeld & Nicholson, 2015).

Gooder, Paula, *Body: Biblical Spirituality for the Whole Person* (London: SPCK, 2016).

Grant, Robert M., *Irenaeus of Lyons* (London: Routledge, 2000).

Griffin, Miriam T., *Nero: The End of a Dynasty* (London: Routledge, 2000).

Hill, Charles E., *From the Lost Teaching of Polycarp* (Tübingen: Mohr Siebeck, 2006).

Holland, Tom, *Dynasty: The Rise and Fall of the House of Caesar* (London: Little, Brown & Co., 2015).

Holland, Tom, *Pax: War and Peace in Rome's Golden Age* (London: Abacus, 2023).

Lampe, Peter, *Christians at Rome in the First Two Centuries: From Paul to Valentinus*, tr. Michael Steinhauser (London: T & T Clark, 2003).

Lane Fox, Robin, *Pagans and Christians* (Harmondsworth: Penguin, 1986).

Lane Fox, Robin, *The Classical World: An Epic History from Homer to Hadrian* (Harmondsworth: Penguin, 2005).

Ludlow, Morwenna, *The Early Church* (London: I.B. Tauris, 2009).

Mansel, Philip, *Levant: Splendour and Catastrophe on the Mediterranean* (London: John Murray, 2010).
Mclynn, Frank, *Marcus Aurelius: Warrior, Philosopher, Emperor* (London: Vintage, 2009).
Metzger, Bruce M., *The Canon of The New Testament: Its Origin, Development and Significance*, second edition (Oxford: Clarendon Press, 1997).
Moorhead, Sam & David Stuttard, *The Romans Who Shaped Britain* (London: Thames & Hudson, 2016).
Morris, Leon, *Revelation* (Cambridge: Tyndale, 1973).
Opper, Thorsten, *The Emperor Hadrian* (London: British Museum Press, 2008).
Parsons, Peter, *City of the Sharp-Nosed Fish* (London: Weidenfeld & Nicholson, 2007).
Roche, Paul (ed.), *Pliny's Praise: The Panegyricus in the Roman World* (Cambridge: Cambridge University Press, 2011).
Russell, Bertrand, *History of Western Philosophy* (London: Routledge, 2004).
Stark, Rodney, *The Rise of Christianity* (San Francisco, CA: HarperOne, 1997).
Stott, John, *What Christ Thinks of the Church* (Nashville, TN: Word Publishing, 1990).
Ware, Bishop Kallistos, *The Orthodox Way* (Crestwood, NY: St Vladimir's Press, 1979).
Whitworth, Patrick John, *Suffering and Glory: The Church from the Apostles to Constantine* (Durham: Sacristy Press, 2018).
Wingren, Gustaf, *Man and the Incarnation: A Study in the Biblical Theology of Irenaeus* (Eugene, OR: Wipf & Stock, 2004).
Wright, Tom, *Paul: A Biography* (London: SPCK, 2020).

Abbreviations

ANF   Ante-Nicene Fathers
CCSL   Corpus Christianorum: Series Latina
FC   Fathers of the Church
HE   Historia Ecclesiastica (Eusebius)
LCL   Loeb Classical Library
PG   Patrologia Graeca
NAPNF   Nicene and Post Nicene Fathers
OECS   Oxford Early Christian Texts
TCAH   The Cambridge Ancient History Series

Index

accommodation, doctrine of 145
Against Heresies 34, 57, 59, 65–9, 72–5, 84, 95, 111–12
   Book I: the nature of false knowledge 121–7
   Book II: refutations of Gnostic theology 127–31
   Book III: on the witness of the Apostles and the Incarnation 151–7
   Book IV: refutation of Gnosticism and the plan for human salvation 157–9
   Book V: the recapitulation of humanity 164, 183
Agricola, General 15
Agrippina (mother of Nero) 5–6, 7
Albina 91
Albinus 57
Alexander the Great 56
Alexandria
   evangelized by Mark 32, 42
   Gnosticism in 121
   Philo's influence in 120–1
Ambrose, St 138
Anacletus of Rome 152
Anicetus of Rome 63, 64, 93
Antioch 18, 32
Antoninus Pius, Emperor 16, 22, 65, 94, 99
Apostolic Age 30, 182
Apostolic Fathers 36–41, 61, 65
Apuleius 25
Aquila of Sinope 58, 149
Aquinas, St Thomas 138
Aristides of Smyrna 24
Aristotle 119
Arius/Arianism 132

Athanasius, *De Incarnatione* 146, 169
Athenagoras 34
Attalus (Christian martyr) 110
Atticus 25
Augustine of Hippo 56, 99, 138, 139, 144–5, 170, 193
   death of mother in Ostia 103
   The City of God 18–19
   Contra Iulanium 17
Augustus Caesar (Octavian), Emperor 3–4, 105
Ausonius 104

Bar Kochba, Simeon 21
Barbeliotes 127
Barnes, Timothy 61
Basilides 74, 126, 127
Bauer, Walter, *Orthodoxy and Heresy in Earliest Christianity* 94
Berlin Gnostic Code 79
Blandina (Christian martyr) 110–11
Bonaventure 138
Borborians 127
Boudicca, Queen of the Iceni 7
Britain
   Boudicca's rebellion 7
   Hadrian's Wall 20–1
   Roman invasion (AD 43) 5
   subjugated by Vespasian 11
Bryennios, Philotheos 38

Caligula, Emperor 5
Cappadocian Fathers 170, 193
   Basil of Caesarea 56, 138, 169
   Gregory Nazianzus 56, 164
   Gregory of Nyssa 133, 138, 169, 170, 193

Caracalla, Emperor 91
Carpocrates 74, 126, 127
Cerdo 94
Cerinthus 126
Chadwick, Henry 75
Christianity, threat to Roman ideals 17, 25
Christians
  expelled from Rome 48
  Jewish persecution of 30, 47–8
  refusal to honour imperial cult 16, 50–1
  scapegoated for the fire in Rome (AD 64) 8–9
Church
  growth of 32–3, 41–5
  main characteristics in the second century 30–1, 35, 41–6
  persecution of 8–9, 16, 30, 47–52
Claudius, Emperor 5–6, 90
birth in Lugdunum (Lyon) 103–4, 105
Clement of Alexandria 58, 94, 108, 150
Clement of Rome 31, 37–8, 93, 150, 152
Codex Alexandrinus 35
Codex Sinaiticus, development of 35
Codex Tachis 79
Codex Vaticanus 35
Columbanus (monk) 34
Commodus, Emperor 22, 111, 189
Constantine, Emperor 51
Constantinople, Council of (AD 381) 132
Corinth 48
Cornelius 89
Cyril of Jerusalem 58

Dacia (Romania) 15, 18
Decius, Emperor 108
Demonstration of the Apostolic Preaching, The 117–18, 131, 140–1, 157, 162
Demosthenes 24
Didache 31, 36, 38–9
Dio Cassius 14
Dio Chrysostom 24
Diocletian, Emperor 108
Diognetus, Epistle to 31, 36, 42–6, 65

Docetism 146, 155, 156
Domitian, Emperor 12, 14–16, 50
Drusus, son of Tiberius 5
Dürer, Albrecht 139

Ebionites 126, 151
Eleutherius, Bishop of Rome 93, 111
Ephesus
  Church in 30, 59
  libraries of 23
  St John's Gospel probably written in 33, 34
  St Paul's preaching in 48–9
Epictetus (philosopher) 15
Erasmus 117
Euodius 152
Eusebius 30, 38, 49, 59, 61, 65, 67, 94, 107, 111

Florinus, Irenaeus's letter to 67–9

Gaius Paulinus, Roman General 7
Galatia 48
Galba, Emperor 9–10
Galen of Pergamum 24, 57
Garrow, Alan 38
Gaul
  Early Church in 106–9
  rebellion (AD 67) 9
  Roman province of 103–6
Germanicus 4–5
Gibbon, Edward 17
Gladiator (film, 2000) 189
Gnostic Gospels 35, 74, 78–83
Gnosticism
  beliefs and characteristics of 72–8, 120, 122–7, 128–31
  in Rome 93–8
Gospels 31–2, 33, 151–2
Goudineau, C. 106
Greek philosophic schools 119–21

Hadrian, Emperor 16, 18, 20–2
Hawking, Stephen 194
Helvidius Priscus 13, 15
Hermogenes of Smyrna 24

INDEX

Hierapolis 62
Hill, Charles 60, 65, 68
Hyginus of Rome 94

Iconium 48
Ignatius of Antioch 16, 31, 36–7, 92, 152
   letters of 61–3
Irenaeus
   birth in Smyrna(c. AD 135) 56
   education and influences 56–9
   influence of Polycarp 60–1, 65–9
   refutation of Gnosticism 84–5
   ministry in Lugdunum 103, 107–8
   appointed Bishop of Lugdunum 111
   on the Trinity 131–4
   on humanity as the image and likeness of God 138–41, 145–7
   on the Fall of humanity 141–7
   on the Incarnation 154–6
   on the recapitulation of humanity 32, 161–5, 192
   on the glory of God 165–73, 192–5
   on the Church and the work of the Spirit 175–82
   on the "Last Things" 182–6
   death 188, 189–90
   legacy 190–5
   surviving texts 117, 184
   Works, see Against Heresies and Demonstration of the Apostolic Preaching, The

James the Apostle 48
Jerome, St 34, 91
Jerusalem
   destruction of the Temple 7, 11, 13
   establishment of the Church in 32
   renamed Aelia Capitolina by Emperor Hadrian 21
   siege of (AD 70) 13
   St Paul arrested in 49
Jewish revolt (AD 127–130) 21
Jewish war (AD 66–70) 7, 11, 30
John Cassian 103
John Chrysostom 56, 138
John the Apostle
   and the Book of Revelation 16, 50
   death (c. AD 98) 30
   Gospel of 32, 33, 34, 42, 59–60, 74, 149, 151–2, 161, 177, 182
   on the Incarnation 74–5
   influence of in Asia Minor 59–60
John the Elder 16, 50, 59
Josephus (chronicler) 11
Judaism and Gnosticism 73
Hadrian's repression of 21–2
Julius Caesar 3
Justin Martyr 34, 45, 98–100, 161
   martyrdom of 188
   Apologies 99–100, 107, 117, 188

Leonides of Alexandria 56
Libanius 56
Licinius, Emperor 51
Linus of Rome 93, 152
Loofs, F. 60
Lucian of Samosata 24
Lucius Verus, Emperor 108
Lugdunum (Lyon)
   amphitheatre extended 18
   Christian persecution in 110–11
   Emperor Claudius's birth at (10 BC) 5
   Emperor Vitellius in 10
   Pliny the Younger's works sold in 23
   provincial capital in Gaul 103–6
   Septimius Severus governor of 90
Luke, St (evangelist) 32, 151
Lystra 48

Manichees 185
Marcella 91
Marcion of Sinope 64–8, 74, 151
   beliefs and teachings of 58, 78, 84, 126–7
   in Rome 96–8
Marcus (Gnostic) 124–5
Marcus Aurelius, Emperor 16, 22, 24, 25, 44, 99, 108–9
Meditations 188–9
Mark, St (evangelist) 31, 32, 151
Martial 25

Massilia (Marseille)   103
Matthew, St (evangelist)   31, 151
Maturus (Christian martyr)   110
Menander   58, 74
Michelangelo   139
Milan, Edict of   50–1
Mithridates, King   10
Moll, Sebastian   60–1
Monica (mother of Augustine)   103
More, Henry   73
Muratori, Ludovico Antonio   34
Muratorian Canon   34

Nag Hammadi, Egypt   78–9
Neoplatonism   25, 121, 193
Nero, Emperor   3, 6–9, 49
Nerva, Emperor   16–17
New Testament
   development of   33–5, 149 *see also* Gospels
Nicaea, First Council of (AD 325)   132
Novatian of Rome   58
numerology   123, 129, 152–3, 191

oikonomia   151, 161, 162
Ophites   127
Origen   39, 56, 149
Ostia, Rome   103
Ostian Way   49
Otho, Emperor   10
Oxyrhynchus Papyri   38, 79

paganism   73, 119
Palmyra, Syria   21
Patmos   16, 50
Paul, St
   Church in Ephesus founded by   30, 59
   epistles (letters)   42, 44, 131–2
   journey from Asia to Rome   88
   Letter to the Corinthians   25
   Letter to the Ephesians   161–2
   Letter to the Romans   89, 90, 92
   First Letter to Timothy   74
   martyrdom of   49
   missionary journeys of   32, 48, 64
   on the perfection of humanity   139
   persecution of   48
Paulinus, Bishop of Nola   104
Pax Romana   45
Peter, St   31–2, 48, 49, 152
Philippian Church   64
Philo (philosopher)   120–1
Philostratus, *The Lives of the Sophists*   24
Pius I, Pope   34
Plato   24, 73, 99
   Timaeus   119–20, 134
Pliny the Elder   14, 57–8, 104
Pliny the Younger   18–19, 23, 25, 51–2, 104
Plotinus   25
Plutarch   24
Polycarp, Bishop of Smyrna   36–7, 158, 188
   life and martyrdom   59–69
Poppaea Sabina (wife of Nero)   6–7
Pothinus, Bishop of Lugdunum   107, 110
Prayer of the Apostle Paul, The   80
Ptolemaeus   24, 95, 122

Revelation, Book of   6, 50, 61, 149, 182, 184
Roman Empire
   second-century culture   23
   Antonine dynasty   16
   consolidated under Vespasian   13
   expansion under Trajan (AD 98–117)   18
   extent of (AD 70)   12
   Flavian dynasty   12–16, 50
   Julio-Claudian Dynasty   3–9
   wars and revolts in   7, 15
   Year of the Four Emperors (AD 69)   9–11
Rome
   building projects under Trajan   18
   Castel Sant'Angelo   22
   Christian persecution in   8–9, 16, 49–50
   civil war (AD 69)   11
   Colosseum   9, 12, 14, 50
   Early Church in   88–93
   false teaching in   92, 93–8

fire of (AD 64)   8, 49, 88-9
Jews and Christians banished from (c.
  AD 49)   90
Pax Romana   24-5
rebuilding under Vespasian   12
social stratification in   23
Rufus   64

Sabellius   132
Sanctus (Christian martyr)   110
Saturninus, rebellion (AD 89)   15
Saturninus of Antioch   126
Scriptures
  central to Christian teaching   30
  development of   33-5
sebomenoi   90
Second Sophist movement   24
Seneca   6, 7
Septimius Severus, Emperor   188, 189-90
Septuagint   34, 58, 149
Sethians   127
Severus, Emperor   108
Severus, General   21-2
Shakespeare, William   137
Shepherd of Hermas   31, 34-5, 36, 39-41, 90
Simon Magus   74, 126
Slusser, Michael   98
Smyrna (Izmir)
  Emperor Nero's death at   3
  history and culture   56-7
Socrates   119
Sophism   24
Sophist School   56-7
Soter of Rome   93
Stephen, St, martyrdom of   48
Stoicism   24
Suetonius   4, 9-10, 14

Tacitus, on the persecution of Christians   8-9, 49
Tatian   127
Tertullian   45, 49-50, 150
  Adversus Marcionem   97
  De Pallio   99

De spectaculis   107-8
On the Flesh of Christ   146
Theodotion of Ephesus   58, 149
Theosis (doctrine)   169
Theudas   94
Tiberius, Emperor   4-5
Titus, Emperor   11, 12, 13-14
Trajan, Emperor   16, 17-20, 51-2, 108
Trinity, Irenaeus's teaching on   131-4

Ussher, Archbishop   190

Valentinus   67, 74, 81, 84
  in Rome   94-6, 98
Vespasian, Emperor   7, 10-11, 12-13
Vesuvius, eruption of (AD 79)   13-14
Victor of Rome   93
Vienne, Christian persecution in   108-11, 182
Vindolanda tablets, Hadrian's Wall   20-1, 24
Vitellius, Emperor   10-11
Vulgate (Latin) Bible   34

women, role of, in second-century Church   45

Xenophanes   57-8
  Apocalypse of John   77
  Gospel of Thomas, The   82-3
  Secret Book of John, The   76, 80, 81-2
  The Gospel of Truth   95
  Treatise on Resurrection   81
  Tripartite Tractate   80-1, 95

Zeno   58
Zenobia, Queen   21
Zosimius   64

In the same series

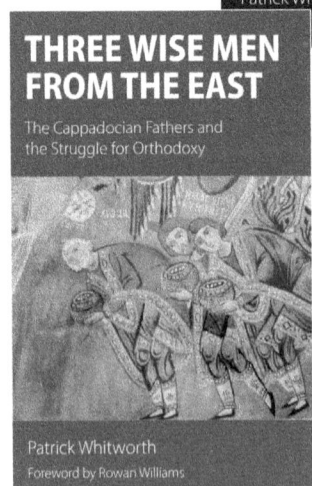

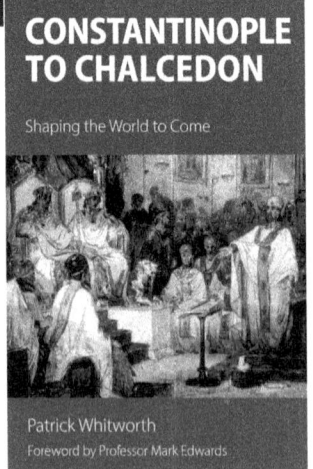

www.sacristy.co.uk

EU GPSR Authorized Representative:

LOGOS EUROPE, 9 rue Nicolas Poussin, 17000 La Rochelle, France

contact@logoseurope.eu

www.ingramcontent.com/pod-product-compliance
Lightning Source LLC
Chambersburg PA
CBHW071437150426
43191CB00008B/1154